ASPECTS OF CONTEMPORARY FRANCE

Aspects of Contemporary France is a study of France from a multidisciplinary perspective. The book highlights aspects distinctive to France in economic, social, political and cultural spheres. It also explains the historical background to controversial issues. The areas covered include: France in the making, the presidency, political parties, defence policy, regions in the market place, higher education, television, women, the Catholic Church, secularism and Islam, linguistic policies, film and French consumers.

The book is divided into two parts: the institutions and policy making which constitute the modern French polity on the one hand, and the controversy and political struggle over the definitions of 'Frenchness' and other forms of socio-cultural identity on the other. Each chapter begins with the present day and then traces the background which will clarify events and provide a context in which they can be evaluated. Each chapter has been written by a specialist in the field and is based on the most up-to-date information and research. A chronology is provided for further guidance, as well as a detailed bibliography and items for recommended further reading.

Aspects of Contemporary France presents an analytical as well as informative approach to French studies. It provides a readily accessible but in-depth understanding for students of France or French civilisation at undergraduate level.

Sheila Perry is Principal Lecturer in French at the University of Northumbria at Newcastle.

ASPECTS OF CONTEMPORARY FRANCE

Edited by
Sheila Perry

London and New York

First published 1997
by Routledge
11 New Fetter Lane, London EC4P 4EE
Simultaneously published in the USA and Canada
by Routledge
29 West 35th Street, New York, NY 10001

Typeset in Times by
Ponting–Green Publishing Services, Chesham,
Buckinghamshire

Printed in Great Britain by
Redwood Books, Trowbridge, Wiltshire

British Library Cataloguing in Publication Data
A catalogue record for this book has been requested

Library of Congress Cataloging in Publication Data
Aspects of contemporary France / edited by Sheila Perry.
Includes bibliographical references and index.
1. France–Civilization–1945–
2. National Characteristics, French.
I. Perry, Sheila, 1952–
DC33.7.A75   1997
944.083–dc20   96–32445
CIP

ISBN 0–415–13179–0 (hbk)
ISBN 0–415–13180–4 (pbk)

CONTENTS

CONTENTS

FIGURES AND TABLES

FIGURES

TABLES

NOTES ON CONTRIBUTORS

Rodney Balcomb teaches French language and politics at the University of Northumbria at Newcastle. He has held a number of posts specialising in foreign and European affairs, including: magazine editor, researcher in the Labour Party's International Department, Assistant General Secretary of the Socialist International (the association of social democratic parties), research associate at the International Institute for Strategic Studies in London and journalist with the BBC External Services. He has also worked as a freelance translator and writer on foreign affairs.

Inès Brulard is Senior Lecturer at the University of Northumbria at Newcastle, where she teaches French language and area studies. She taught applied linguistics and sociolinguistics at the Université Catholique de Louvain, where she completed a Ph.D. in the history of linguistic ideas. Her publications and research interests include contrastive French–English linguistics, French sociolinguistics and French civilisation.

Ann Marie Condron is a Lecturer in French Studies at the University of Northumbria at Newcastle where she teaches on a variety of French language courses. She lectures on French cinema at both undergraduate and postgraduate level and is currently conducting research on the representation of the French under the Occupation in post-war French cinema.

Máire F. Cross is Senior Lecturer in French at the University of Sheffield where she teaches aspects of contemporary French politics at postgraduate and undergraduate level. She has co-authored two books on French feminism, contributes items regularly to the journals *Modern and Contemporary France, European History* and *French Studies*, and is a member of the editorial board of *Modern and Contemporary France*.

Eve Gilliard-Russell is a Senior Lecturer in French Studies at the University of Northumbria at Newcastle. A French national, she lectures on the business and economic environment of France, concentrating on sociodemographics, consumption, the advertising industry, the retail sector and market entry strategies. She gained industrial experience while working as a marketing assistant in France, and translates promotional literature for French companies on a regular basis.

Alison Holland is Senior Lecturer in French Studies at the University of Northumbria at Newcastle. Her research interests include feminism in France and feminist theory. She is currently writing on the fiction of Simone de Beauvoir. Her publications include an article on Virginia Woolf's *Orlando* and translations of the poetry of Seamus Heaney. She has lived and worked in France for eight years.

Richard J. Lund is Senior Lecturer in French Studies at the University of Northumbria at Newcastle. He has lectured extensively on the economic environment of contemporary France at both undergraduate and postgraduate levels and has a particular interest in France's policy of regional development. He has combined this area studies specialism with the teaching of applied modern languages, especially in relation to vocational skills.

Sheila Perry is Principal Lecturer in French and the Modern Languages Department Research Co-ordinator at the University of Northumbria at Newcastle, where she teaches French language and politics at undergraduate and postgraduate level. She specialises in the study of politics and the media in France and has published articles and conference papers on French television and political communication. She is currently researching the development of political programmes on French television since the 1960s.

William Smith is Head of the Division of French Studies at the University of Northumbria at Newcastle. He first researched into aspects of the Catholic novel in France, with particular reference to Henri Queffélec. In recent years the focus of his research has shifted from the literary to the historical, in particular the interaction between the Catholic Church and the Vichy régime and, more recently, the links between Catholic integrist movements and the political extreme right.

Rob Turner is Senior Lecturer at the University of Northumbria at Newcastle where he teaches and researches French politics with a special interest in the presidency and the higher education system. He has forged many links with sister institutions in France, giving him a practical insight into the French university system and its problems.

PREFACE

This book is designed for those who require a readily accessible but in-depth understanding of contemporary France. It consists of a series of discrete chapters each dealing with a different theme. As the title indicates, the book is in no way exhaustive in its coverage of contemporary France, concentrating instead on certain aspects, but an attempt has been made to make the themes wide-ranging and varied, viewed from a multidisciplinary perspective (economic, cultural, political and social). The choice of subjects – always controversial in a book of this nature – has been guided by the desire to break down two potential barriers to understanding. On the one hand, we have sought to highlight those issues which have been contentious in recent years, where polemic and debate may appear confusing to the uninitiated; on the other, we have chosen those aspects which might in some way appear to be characteristically French, either because France does differ from other nations, and so the foreign observer needs guidance, or because the French themselves claim distinctiveness, with what they call *l'exception française*, and examination of the claim is called for. Each chapter seeks to present the main issues of current debate in the given subject and analyse and explain their historical development to the present day. In this way we have sought to combine extensive coverage of aspects of contemporary France with detailed and analytical coverage of the main issues.

Each chapter begins with the present day – in some cases with a specific event which crystallises the issues – as it is this which we seek to explain and make accessible to the reader; the chapter then traces the background which will clarify the events and provide a context in which they can be evaluated. In line with this belief that contextualisation is the key to understanding, an introductory chapter on 'France in the Making' looks at France's less recent past, to set the themes covered by the succeeding chapters in a longer-term perspective, tracing in particular France's road to nationhood through religion, language and territory.

For the fact is that the nation we refer to as France, and the people we call the French, have only existed in their current form for a very brief period of history, and modern-day French identity has been constructed through protracted political struggle. The terms of the struggle may have shifted, but it is by no means over; indeed, recent events in Europe have given it renewed impetus, as the assumptions behind the development of the modern nation-state are currently being challenged. At the same time, the legacy of the old struggles lives on in the new. So, although France has a strong and stable democratic régime in the Fifth Republic, it is facing, from within, accusations of *exclusion* which reveal the limitations of consensus. It is this dual aspect – the institutions and policy making which constitute the modern French polity on the one hand, and the controversy and political struggle over the definitions of 'Frenchness' and other forms of socio-cultural identity on the other – which is the subject of this book. To reflect this duality, the book has been divided into two parts. These different aspects of contemporary France together show that France is a multi-faceted, multicultural society struggling to define what is meant by *l'exception française*, or that which is distinctively French.

We have therefore sought both to explain and to evaluate French distinctiveness and this has guided our choice of subjects to a large degree. For example, many countries have presidential systems, but the rôle of the President of the Republic in France is different, and frequently puzzling to foreign observers, for two reasons. Firstly, because of the executive dyarchy in which power is shared between the prime minister and a president with executive powers; secondly, because the distribution of power varies according to which of the two heads of the executive enjoys the support of the parliamentary majority. The first chapter of Part I therefore analyses and explains the historical factors shaping the constitution of the Fifth Republic, particularly those provisions relating to the presidency, and uses them to explain current presidential practice and the experience of *cohabitation*. The presidency is generally thought to be the corner-stone of France's political régime, and for this reason it is the subject of the first chapter of this section on French institutions and policy making.

Chapter 2 continues with the political theme, this time steering the reader through the multiplicity of French political parties, and explains, in a way that will be accessible to those readers used to the comparatively simple two- or three-party systems of British and American politics, the historical and present-day circumstances which have shaped and moulded their structures and practices. Both these chapters make essential reading for anyone wishing to understand the daily news in France.

France since de Gaulle has pursued a distinctive defence and European policy in keeping with its geographical position and its attitude towards Germany and the USA. Chapter 3 looks therefore at the special relationship France has with NATO, its nuclear defence strategy, its support for increased European integration and its rôle in the establishment of the Franco-German brigade and the Eurocorps, both in a historical perspective and in the light of the New World Order since the fall of the Berlin wall.

To what extent is France able to maximise the opportunities the new European environment offers? Until very recently, one of France's characteristic features has been its centralism, but the reforms of 1982 gave new power to the regions. Much has been written on the political issues surrounding decentralisation, but Chapter 4 looks instead at the regions in the market place, reviewing France's distinctive policy of *aménagement du territoire* through the 1960s and 1970s, the decentralisation period of the 1980s and in the light of the new European context of the 1990s, and asks to what extent France's regions are competitively placed in the business and economic environment.

France is a country which is frequently marked by student unrest, which has sometimes extended beyond the student body, as in May 1968, and more often than not has been effective in influencing government legislation, as in 1986 and the 1990s. Unrest is most frequently initiated in protest at the conditions prevailing in the universities, or to counter proposed reform. Why is it that French students are so quick to take to the streets? Chapter 5 traces the current problems back to the uncontrolled, rapid expansion of the university system and the distinctive contrast between this open-access branch of higher education and the prestigious and élitist *grandes écoles*, which impose strict controls on entry through the system of competitive examination, the *concours*. Finally, the chapter considers attempts to adapt university courses to the demands of the economy and of students who are increasingly aware of the difficulties of the labour market.

The media were described by Honoré de Balzac as 'the fourth power' and Georges Pompidou described television as 'the voice of France', thus justifying the government stranglehold on its political output. Chapter 6 traces the difficult road to freedom for French television and examines the question, if television is *'la voix de la France'*, as Pompidou claimed, whose voice is it? In the new era of commercial television, domestic production is threatened by cheap American imports but the attempts to protect it are rendered problematic by the legacy of French television's highly politicised past: since television was once an arm of government, how is the state to intervene to protect French production while at the same time leaving television channels free from government interference?

Part II begins with the question of women. Is the condition of women in France specific to that nation? How do French women's rights compare with those of other Western democracies? Very favourably, reply many French commentators, men and women alike, who share a certain consensus that the distinctive characteristic of France in this domain is precisely the absence of a problem: French women now enjoy the same legal rights as men and can therefore avoid the 'excesses' of feminism they perceive in Anglo-Saxon countries. Chapter 7 examines this definition of *l'exception française* from a critical perspective, matching it against the realities of legislation and women's everyday lives in contemporary France.

Is the Catholic Church still a significant factor in contemporary French social and political life? Chapter 8 examines the shift over fifty years from mainstream religious observance and intellectual and spiritual vibrancy to apparent apathy and dissension. It traces the movement towards accessibility and reform within the Church and the concomitant reactionary movement with its links to the xenophobic political extreme right wing. Behind the statistics, this chapter looks at the significant personalities – such as the telegenic Monseigneur Gaillot and his altercations with the church hierarchy – and their impact on the Church in modern French society.

As a counterpoint to the theme of the Catholic Church, the next chapter looks at the notion of *laïcité* or the secular state, and the presence of Islam in France. Foreign observers might be hard pressed to understand why it is, for example, that in France the question of whether girls should be allowed to wear the Islamic veil has been the source of much public debate and controversy (whereas, in comparison, British schools solved the 'problem' by simply requiring girls to wear the veil in the school colours!). This chapter will clarify this debate through an analysis of the tradition of *laïcité* in French schools and public life, perceptions of Islam within French society and the challenge which *laïcité* represents for Muslims living in France.

An important aspect of French identity, enshrined in the constitution, is the French language. Nevertheless, observers were just a little surprised to witness an attempt by the Minister of Culture, Jacques Toubon, to legislate on the use of foreign (primarily American) words and phrases in the French language (for which he was dubbed Mr Allgood by a rebellious press!). Chapter 9 looks at the questions of state interventionism as it relates to language, national and regional cultural identity through language, and the processes whereby languages change and develop. The chapter attempts both to explain and to reassess these events in modern France.

Allied to its desire to protect the French language are the attempts by France to protect French culture in general: in the latest round of GATT talks, the French negotiators succeeded in imposing the notion of *exception culturelle* on cinema distribution and the audiovisual media. Chapter 5 looks at French cinema from the New Wave period to *cinéma beur*, examining its reputation as one of the most influential and innovative aspects of contemporary French and European culture, its fight to retain a special place on the world stage and directors' attempts to resist or learn lessons from American domination.

The final chapter takes an unusual look at the French population from the perspective of consumption patterns and behaviour and examines the question of whether there is a specifically French consumer who can be targeted by specialists in marketing. It shows how the development of the retail trade has affected consumer behaviour or, inversely, how developments in the trade have sought to meet changing demand. French behaviour is consistently set in the context of the European average or the varying trends in other European countries.

As this rapid overview shows, while covering a range of disciplines and subject areas, we have opted for specificity rather than breadth of coverage within the individual domains. As far as the media are concerned, for example, we have not covered telecommunications, the press or radio (except very briefly as they impinge on television); nor have we dealt with other forms of cultural output, except the cinema; in education we have concentrated on the higher education system and *laïcité*, rather than giving an overview of the education system as a whole; we have not covered immigration in general but only as it relates specifically to the notion of national identity and the link between this and religion, and so on. We believe these choices can be justified for the reasons of distinctiveness outlined above, but this inevitably means that some appetites will not be satisfied. Nor would we claim to have covered all of those aspects of contemporary France which could be categorised as distinctive: for example, France's foreign policy other than that relating specifically to defence would merit attention, and in particular its relationship with former colonies, not to mention the very special position of the DOM-TOM (*Départements* and *Territoires d'outre-mer*). If these have not been covered, it is simply due to lack of space. In spite of these inevitable limitations, we hope that the reader's understanding of contemporary France will be greatly enhanced in a wide range of fields. Many of the chapters, though complete in themselves, are interlinked and reading of several chapters in conjunction with each other is recommended: cross-referencing has been made where relevant to help with this. As the chapters concentrate by and large on thematic issues and do not always follow a strict chrono-logical development, a chronology is provided as further guidance at the end of each one. Details are given for all works on the subject to which reference has been made in the chapter, plus some items for further reading. Those books which are particularly recommended are marked by an asterisk. In each case, quotations have been translated from the French by the author of the chapter concerned.

ACKNOWLEDGEMENTS

Our thanks go to the following: the University of Northumbria for financial support which has enabled the team to devote time to this project; our subject librarian, Graham Shields, for his expertise and infinite patience; Florence Potot and Sue Hart for their invaluable secretarial assistance; our technicians, Seph Nesbit, Dave Marshall and Dave Crook for their excellent help and support, and many friends and colleagues for their advice and encouragement. The authors are, of course, solely responsible for the final text.

ABBREVIATIONS

ACCT   Agence de coopération culturelle et technique
AFC   Associations familiales catholiques
AGULF   Association générale des usagers de la langue française
APE   Allocation parentale d'éducation
BTS   Brevet de technicien supérieur
CCA   Centre de communication avancé [sic]
CDS   Centre des démocrates sociaux
CES   Comité économique et social
CFE   Conventional Armed Forces in Europe
CGP   Commissariat général du Plan
CIR   Convention des institutions républicaines
CIREEL   Centre d'information et de recherche pour
            l'enseignement et l'emploi des langues
CNAL   Comité national d'action laïque
CNC   Centre national de la cinématographie
CNCL   Commission nationale de la communication et des
            libertés
CNRS   Centre national de la recherche scientifique
CODER   Commission de développement économique régional
COFREMCA   Compagnie française d'études de marchés et de
            conjonctures appliquées
CPGE   Classes préparatoires des grandes écoles
CRITT   Centre régional d'innovation et de transfert de
            technologie
CSA   Conseil supérieur de l'audiovisuel
CSP   Catégorie socioprofessionnelle
DATAR   Délégation à l'aménagement du territoire et à l'action
            régionale
DEA   Diplôme d'études approfondies
DESS   Diplôme d'études supérieures spécialisées
DEUG   Diplôme d'études universitaires générales

DEUST	Diplôme d'études universitaires scientifiques et technologiques
DNTS	Diplôme national de technologie spécialisée
DOM-TOM	Départements d'outre-mer-Territoires d'outre-mer
DUEL	Diplôme universitaire d'études littéraires
DUES	Diplôme universitaire d'études scientifiques
DUT	Diplôme universitaire de technologie
ECO (Fonds)	Fonds (d'aide à la production cinématographique des pays) d'Europe centrale et orientale
ECSC	European Coal and Steel Community
EDC	European Defence Community
EEC	European Economic Community
ENA	Ecole nationale d'administration
EU	European Union
Euromarfor	European Maritime Force
FAF	Fraternité algérienne en France
FLN	Front de libération nationale
FN	Front national
FRG	Federal Republic of Germany
GATT	General Agreement on Tariffs and Trade
GDP	Gross Domestic Product
INA	Institut national de l'audiovisuel
INSEE	Institut national de la statistique et des études économiques
IUP	Institut universitaire professionnalisé
IUT	Institut universitaire de technologie
JOC	Jeunesse ouvrière chrétienne (members usually called *jocistes*)
LICRA	Ligue internationale contre le racisme et l'antisémitisme
LVF	Légion des volontaires français
MBFR talks	Mutual Balanced Force Reduction talks
MLF	Mouvement de Libération des Femmes
MRAP	Mouvement contre le racisme et pour l'amitié entre les peuples
MRG	Mouvement des radicaux de Gauche
MRP	Mouvement républicain populaire
NATO	North Atlantic Treaty Organisation
ORTF	Office de la radiodiffusion-télévision française
OSCE	Organisation for Security and Cooperation in Europe
OTAN	Organisation du Traité de l'Atlantique Nord
PAPIN	Programme d'action prioritaire d'initiative nationale
PAPIR	Programme d'action prioritaire d'initiative régionale
PCF	Parti communiste français
PDG	Président-directeur général
PRDE	Plan régional de développement économique
PS	Parti socialiste
PSU	Parti socialiste unifié

PR	Parti républicain
RI	Républicains indépendants
RPF	Rassemblement du peuple français
RPR	Rassemblement pour la République
RTF	Radiodiffusion-télévision française
SDR	Société de développement régional
SEPT	Société d'édition de programmes de télévision
SFIO	Section française de l'internationale ouvrière
SFP	Société française de production
SLII	Service des liaisons interministérielles pour l'information
SOFICA	Société de financement des industries cinématographiques et audiovisuelles
STO	Service du travail obligatoire
STS	Sections de techniciens supérieurs
TDF	Télédiffusion de France
UDF	Union pour la démocratie française
UDR	Union pour la défense de la République (1968–71) / Union des démocrates pour la République (1971–6)
UN	United Nations
UNR	Union pour la nouvelle République
UPF	Union pour la France
VIS	Vatican Information Service
WEU	Western European Union

INTRODUCTION
France in the making
William Smith

For the birth and consolidation of the modern nation-state over the centuries, three conditions have had to be fulfilled: it required recognisable and defensible natural frontiers, a single language and religious consensus. Examples abound of countries where this has not been the case and which have experienced difficulties in existing at ease with themselves and their neighbours: the former Yugoslavia fulfilled none of these conditions, Belgium is still divided by linguistic disputes and Ireland illustrates the problems posed by a lack of religious consensus. Canada, with what is claimed to be the longest undefended frontier in the world (merely a line on the map), has problems in establishing a distinctive natural identity and avoiding falling under the cultural and economic hegemony of the USA. It is also still beset by linguistic arguments. Switzerland – or more properly The Swiss Confederation – seems at first sight to invalidate this proposition with its four languages (German, French, Italian and Romansch), and with both Catholicism and the reformed religion existing side by side. In fact, the powers of the Confederal government are weak and real power, especially with regard to everyday life, is wielded by the cantons into which the country is divided and where these conditions are fulfilled.

What of France? The French nation-state has been built on this premise. It has gradually expanded over the last millenium to occupy the whole of the land-mass within its natural defensible frontiers, often referred to as the *hexagone*: Channel, Atlantic Ocean, Pyrenees, Mediterranean, Alps, Jura, Rhine – only the north-east frontier (with Belgium) is geographically indeterminate. The use of French followed this expansion. Over the centuries, the state made strenuous efforts to eradicate regional languages, the use of which was deemed to be harmful to national unity. Only since the beginning of the 1980s, with the implementation of a limited devolution of power to the provinces, have regional languages gained more official tolerance and recognition. Catholicism in France, which survived the Reformation, was one of the unifying elements in the state until the Revolution. The bitter conflict between secularism and the Church which followed during the next 200 years

1

had calmed into an uneasy armistice by the late 1960s and now has to meet the challenge of the presence in France of several million Muslims.

The creation of stable nationhood is not an ineluctable process. Struggle, failure, accident, war (the great catalyst of history), apparently insignificant events – all contribute to a movement that only with hindsight seems to have been irresistible. The history of the land-mass which we call 'France', over the last 2,000 years and before, illustrates this dynamic which is an ongoing, never-ending process.

'*Nos ancêtres les Gaulois*,' as children following the common French curriculum from Dunkirk through Africa to Indo-China used to be taught, were a sophisticated Celtic people who occupied what is now France and Belgium from the sixth century BC. They survive in the consciousness of contemporary French people in the cartoon figure of Astérix, whose success tells us more about how the French see themselves in the twentieth century – indomitable, ingenious, cocking a snook at authority – than about the historical reality of the Celts. Their final defeat under their chief Vercingétorix in 51 BC by Julius Caesar at Alésia marked the beginning of the Gallo-Roman period which was to last until the end of the fourth century. As well as bringing the Latin language, the Romans divided the area into four tightly organised provinces where security and peace were guaranteed by powerful standing armies. The northern frontier was secured by the Roman conquest of England, the eastern frontier (which was the Rhine) cut Gaul off from the Celtic and Germanic populations of Central Europe and this allowed the development of a new civilisation in Roman Gaul.

When the Roman Empire broke up at the end of the fourth century, Gaul was conquered by Germanic tribes who divided the country into separate kingdoms. During the fifth, sixth and seventh centuries, northern Gaul was occupied by the Franks, whose name would become that of the country. Clovis founded the Frankish monarchy and, in 496,[1] he converted to Christianity along with his family and followers. Christianity had been progressing in Gaul for more than a century by then and was the majority religion of the Gallo-Roman population. By his conversion, Clovis cemented the unity of the Franks and the Gallo-Romans because intermarriage could now take place at all levels of society. Frankish chiefs governed in concert with local bishops and, very significantly for the future, Paris was selected as the capital.

Over the next two centuries the two populations became one and Christianity held this society together. Charlemagne became King in 768. By conquest he extended his territory to include most of present-day Germany and Italy and in 800 he was crowned Emperor of the West. Charlemagne's empire was a theocratic state, he saw himself recreating the Roman Empire with himself as its consecrated Christian leader. However, his empire was short-lived and after his death in 814 a series of quarrels between his sons resulted in the Treaty of Verdun (843) when the empire was divided up between Charles the Bald who governed most of France west of Lyon, Louis the German who had the territories east of the Rhine, and Lothair who ruled the area in between (known as Lotharingia which would become Lorraine, an area neither entirely French nor entirely German, which would continue to be a source of conflict between modern France and Germany until the mid-twentieth century) and Italy. The present-day linguistic frontier was therefore in place, German to the east of the Rhine, and to the west dialects developed from Latin.

The Norman invasion of the ninth century devastated a country where royal authority had become weak. Churches and villages were sacked and burnt, commerce and cultural life came to a standstill, Paris was besieged in 885. Out of this weakness and the need for political coherence and self-defence emerged the feudal system which was to regulate the social and political life of France and of much of Europe until the end of the fifteenth century. Local lords governing provinces such as Burgundy, Poitou or Champagne were virtually autonomous. They had their own courts, exacted their own justice, raised their own armies, coined their own money. Their lands were divided into a number of hereditary fiefdoms, each governed on behalf of the lord by vassals who owed him homage and fidelity, assisting him when he went to war and paying him a portion of their income. The system was essentially pyramidal and at the base the serf existed in conditions of virtual slavery. At the apex of the pyramid was the king, the first of whom was Hugues Capet, elected in 987, the founder of the Capetian dynasty, who personally governed only the area around Paris known as the Ile de France and whose power outside his own lands was virtually non-existent. The system was humanised by the elaboration of a philosophy of Christian chivalry which urged a code of conduct based on bravery, justice and help for the oppressed.

Even though skirmishes between rival lords continued, the country was now stable enough to begin to evolve into a nation-state. The Normans had settled down in the area now known as Normandy and were to slake their thirst for territorial expansion by invading England in 1066. Towns were expanding and trade developing. The Church, with its bishops as the counterparts of the local lords, was a powerful partner in government. Throughout the Middle Ages, churches and cathedrals were built all over France, first in the Romanesque style (called 'Norman' in England) then in the Gothic style. It was a dynamic, theocratic society which found an outlet for its energies in the eleventh century in the crusades which were to take French and Norman Lords and their armies across Europe and Eastern Asia to Jerusalem in an attempt to reconquer the holy places.

The twelfth and thirteenth centuries were in many ways the apogee of French medieval civilisation. The power and influence of the French monarchy were massively strengthened and extended. In 987 Hugues Capet had only ruled over the Ile de France. By 1328, at the moment of the accession to the throne of the first Valois King, Philip VI, conquest or annexation had extended his direct rule to the whole of northern France with the exception of the duchies of Brittany and Burgundy, the Comté of Blois, and Aquitaine which was ruled by the English. The Church was all powerful within this society: universities were founded, the Dominican and Franciscan religious orders wielded huge influence and heresy was ruthlessly rooted out. The Manichean heresy[2] which had many adherents in south-west France was eradicated with considerable cruelty and bloodshed in the Albigensian Crusade (1207–1223). France was even the seat of the papacy for a period in the fourteenth century when, after a disputed election, the Pope and his court fled to Avignon in 1303.

This glittering civilisation was placed in considerable jeopardy by the wars against the English which dominated the fourteenth and fifteenth centuries. The so-called 'Hundred Years War' initially went England's way with the Kings of France obliged to retreat over the years to the area south of the Loire. Things changed with the arrival on the scene of the emblematic figure of Jeanne d'Arc who, at the head of the French armies, freed Orléans and Reims in 1429 before being burnt at the stake by the English at Rouen in 1431.[3] By 1452 the tide had turned totally against the English who lost all their territories in France except Calais. The French monarchs then turned their attention to Burgundy, the most powerful remaining threat to them, which was conquered by Louis XI after twenty years of war in 1483.

Whilst the virtually continuous wars of the fourteenth centuries had left the French monarchy more powerful than ever before (the French Kings now governed three-quarters of modern-day France and were becoming increasingly the symbol and focus of national unity), social conditions were appalling. To the deaths and mutilation brought about by the wars were added the ravages of the Black Death. The orderly fabric of the feudal system had almost totally broken down and social unrest and even anarchy were rife. Nevertheless, the recovery during the first fifty years of the sixteenth century under the leadership of Louis XII, François I and Henri II was to be astonishing. A new social class based on money and commerce, the bourgeoisie, was emerging as a powerful force in society. This merchant class was far removed from the chivalric ideals which had been the ideology of the nobility during the Middle Ages. Their aim was to make money and they were so successful that the economic fabric of France was transformed. This newfound wealth coincided with the discovery or rediscovery of the cultures of Ancient Greece and Rome (the Renaissance) and allowed the building of prestigious palaces such as Fontainebleau or the Louvre and the castles of the Loire valley as well as the development of literature and of the arts.

The last forty years of the sixteenth century were disfigured by the horrors of the Wars of Religion. France was not alone in this loss of religious consensus. In Spain, Philip II had ruthlessly exterminated both Muslim converts to Christianity and Protestants. England had witnessed the institution of the Anglican Church and the German states had divided between

Protestantism and Catholicism on the principle (which prevailed through the rest of Europe) of *cuius regio, eius religio,* in other words, each state adopted the religion of its monarch. The Catholic Church was undergoing its own reformation or counter-reformation. The Council of Trent (1545) retained all the dogmas to which the Protestants objected, reaffirmed the authority of the Pope and established a normative form of the mass (known as the Tridentine mass).[4] The Company of Jesus (Jesuits) was set up in 1540 and organised on quasi-military lines to be the Pope's 'shock troops' under his direct authority in the re-evangelisation of Europe.

The events of the French Wars of Religion, which may be said to have run from 1559 until 1610, are characterised by implacable enmities between rich families, deepening economic crisis and religious fanaticism on both sides. Effective political power was exercised for much of the period by Catherine de Medici as *de facto* or *de jure* regent as her three sons François II (who reigned from 1559–60), Charles IX (1560–74) and Henri III (1574–89) either died prematurely or were assassinated. Her daughter Marguerite de Valois ('La Reine Margot')[5] married the Protestant Henri de Bourbon, King of Navarre, in August 1572. The event was attended by the fine flower of the Protestant nobility and the presence in Paris of so many Protestants inflamed Catholic opinion. What started out as a policing operation culminated in the St Bartholomew's Day Massacre (24 August 1572) which was replicated during the following days and weeks in other French cities and cost up to 20,000 Protestant lives. The savagery of this religious conflict was such (and the St Bartholomew's Day Massacre is but one example) that by 1588 Henri III controlled only the towns of the Loire and Normandy, Bordeaux and the Dauphiné. The Wars of Religion had ruined the country economically and religious fanaticism was making it ungovernable as well as laying it open to Spanish aggression. The only solution open to Henri III was an alliance with the Protestant Henri de Bourbon, King of Navarre, his brother-in-law and next in line of succession to the French throne. The latter appealed for reconciliation around the person of the legitimate King and promised freedom of practice to Catholics within his territories. The two Kings met and joined their armies to march on Paris but on the 1 August 1589 Henri III was stabbed to death by a fanatical monk, Jacques Clément. The Protestant Henri de Navarre was now Henri IV, King of France and Navarre.

Catholic intransigence fomented by the Jesuits and the Spanish and the overwhelmingly Catholic character of Paris, the seat of real power, made it imperative that Henri IV convert to Catholicism: 'Paris is worth a mass', as he is supposed to have said. He did so in June 1593 and was able to enter his capital in March of the following year. The twelve years of his reign (cut short in 1610 when he was assassinated) are remembered as a time of peace and reconciliation, of economic reconstruction and of great progress in agriculture. The first of the Bourbon monarchs had healed the religious divisions of his country to the extent that it was possible to do so and had

5

brought Navarre into the *hexagone*. Only the far north-east and east of the country were now not under the rule of the French King.

He had secured the religious peace at Nantes in April–May 1598 and the outcome of these negotiations with Protestant leaders was the famous Edict of Nantes which granted to them the right of freedom of conscience, equality of rights and freedom of worship in designated places. The Protestants were allowed to retain their powerful political and military organisation together with 151 strongholds or 'safe havens' whose governors and garrisons were paid by the King himself. For the Catholics, this went too far; for the Protestants, it did not go far enough – but the compromise was enough to ensure at least relative religious peace over the next decades. The notion of tolerance was unknown at this time and it was felt that allowing two religions to coexist somehow disfigured the state because France was the only country in Europe which had gone counter to the *cuius regio, eius religio* principle, but this *exception française* was only to last until the Edict was revoked in 1685, to the virtually unanimous approval of the non-Protestant population.

The assassination of Henri IV in 1610 removed a strong and effective ruler. Under the regency of his second wife, Marie de Medici, and the reign of his son Louis XIII (1610–43), rivalry between different factions once more took France to the edge of anarchy, which was only brought to an end between 1625 and 1642 when the chief ministers of the crown, the Cardinals Richelieu and Mazarin, restored effective central leadership. This was achieved first of all when Richelieu finally crushed Protestantism as a military force, thus bringing the Wars of Religion to an end, and then put down a rebellion known as the *Fronde* (1648–52) which had been provoked by massive tax increases imposed by the central government and by the nobility which was jealous of the power and resentful of the methods and policies of the two cardinals.

For most people, the seventeenth century in France is seen as the century of Louis XIV (1643–1715), the Sun King, whose dazzling court at Versailles was an early triumph of image-making. When he reached his majority and assumed personal control of the government in 1661, Louis XIV's first priority was to complete the process of internal pacification started by his predecessors. This was followed by territorial expansion towards the east and north-east, filling out the natural fronters of the *hexagone*. This alarmed the rest of Europe and ensured that much of his reign would be disfigured by wars. Virtually permanent mobilisation kept much of the nobility in the army and a complex system of patronage both there and at Versailles allowed the King to buy their loyalty. The sumptuous palace at Versailles served as a focal-point for royal power and for an aristocratic civilisation where literature, music and the arts flourished. The great dramatists and musicians of the time – Corneille, Racine, Molière, Lully – were, in reality, court entertainers, as dependent upon the King's bounty as all the other courtiers.

The political system established, or at least strongly consolidated, by Louis XIV was firmly centralist with a clear social hierarchy and convoluted etiquette. The national bureaucracy reflected this pyramidal structure with *intendants* (the precursors of the *préfets*) ensuring that the will of the central government was enacted in the provinces.

The dazzling image which we still have today of the seventeeth century in France – the arts, the architecture, even the language which was codified during this period and given its modern form – masks the realities of the last fifteen years of the Sun King's reign. There was considerable social unrest brought about by heavy taxation and crop failures. Repeated military disasters had taken a heavy toll of both human and financial resources. Louis XIV was succeeded by his 5-year-old great-grandson Louis XV who was to reign for sixty years (1715–74) during which time France initially recovered administratively and economically because the country was, for twenty-five years, not involved in foreign wars. From 1741–83, a series of wars (the War of the Austrian Succession 1741–8, the Seven Years War 1756–63 and the American War of Independance 1777–83) bankrupted a state which was totally incapable of reforming itself financially. Colonies were lost – Québec (1759), Pondichéry in India (1761), the West Indies (1763), and the régime was undermined internally by the *philosophes* – Voltaire, Diderot, Rousseau, Montesquieu – who attacked intolerance, obscurantism and unenlightened absolutism. The task which faced the 20-year-old Louis XVI (1774–92) and his young Queen Marie-Antoinette was one which even a wise and experienced statesman would have found daunting. In the event, it became evident that he was not up to the job. Although well-intentioned and high-principled, he was weak. His fits of enthusiasm and energy in following through policy were followed by periods of vacillation and weakness. His wife was of little help to him. Although initially very popular with the French people, she quickly became very unpopular because of her pride and futile wastefulness. The conspicuous and frivolous consumption of the royal court stood in stark contrast with the catastrophic state of the national finances which a series of royal ministers had been unable to reform.

Thus, the essential problem in the 1780s was not revolution but the impending bankruptcy of the state, which could only be warded off by taxing the wealth of the better-off, but this had proved to be impossible without resorting to force since the time of Louis XIV. For more and more Frenchmen of the time, the inability of the government to share the burden of taxation equitably between the social classes was a symptom of a whole range of abuses which needed reform. It was on the privileged nobility that anger focused and when, in 1788, the government finally accepted that conflict with the privileged was inevitable, rather than take an executive decision, it vacillated and instead summoned the Estates General, a body representing nobility, clergy and commoners which had not met since 1614 (there was, of course, no parliament). It was hoped that this body would have sufficient moral authority to persuade the rich to pay higher taxes. This complex political crisis was coming to a head against a background of other strains:

7

an increasing population had outstripped the growth in food production, rents had been increased, an economic recession was affecting the textile industry. The effect of all of this was that elections to the Estates General in 1789 took place in an atmosphere which was embittered, over-excited and filled with unrealistic expectations about what might be achieved. No-one sought revolution. It was assumed that once the King (who was at that time trusted by his people) had been informed of their needs and desires he would immediately act to ensure that they were fulfilled. The Revolution occurred, not quite by accident but certainly not in a premeditated way, because of a combination of governmental ineptitude and powerlessness, social injustice, economic crisis and reforming ambitions born of the Enlightenment and the example of the American Revolution which had only recently taken place.

In the summer of 1789 the Estates General met, bringing with them their *cahiers de doléances*.[6] Four days after their first meeting, on 27 June, the three estates joined together to represent, against the monarch, *la nation assemblée*, and this *Assemblée nationale* now claimed sovereignty as the representatives of the entire nation. It was able to take this step because of the increasing anarchy now spreading throughout the country: revolts in the countryside and riots in Paris (including the storming of the Bastille prison) had cowed monarch, ministers and those in the National Assembly who were opposed to such a change. There was now quite a clear division in the National Assembly between those who were in favour of revolution and those who were against it. The former sat on the left and the latter on the right. This fortuitous seating arrangement was to give the entire world a new conceptual political vocabulary – the Left and the Right.[7]

Between 1789 and 1791 the National Assembly radically reformed the institutions of France: church property was nationalised, centralised representative government was instituted, the provinces and feudal divisions of France were abolished to be replaced by the *départements* which still exist to this day. Sovereignty was deemed to be vested in the people rather than in the monarch, equality before the law was proclaimed and a Declaration of the Rights of Man published.

The Revolution did not attract the unanimous support of the French in 1789 and, 200 years later, it is still the subject of controversy, with an irreconcilable Right attempting to undo its provisions. Louis XVI had initially enjoyed the goodwill of his people. By 1791 he was suspected as an antirevolutionary and when he attempted to flee to Germany in June of that year to seek foreign support to put down the Revolution (only to be ignominiously apprehended at Varennes and brought back to Paris), support for him evaporated. In the summer of 1792 an insurrection in Paris overthrew the monarchy and led to the summoning of a new assembly (called the *Convention*) to draw up a new, republican constitution. The Convention was the effective French government until 1796 and it achieved the survival and consolidation of the Revolution which was beset by wars against Austria and

Prussia, by the continuing economic crisis and by civil wars largely brought about by the treatment which the Revolution had meted out to the Church. For the first time since the conversion of Clovis, the Church became an opponent of the régime rather than a supporter and Church–State relations were to be a contentious issue for many decades to come.

The Convention voted for the execution of Louis XVI and his Queen in January 1793 as a measure to mark the beginning of a new democratic age and as a punishment for what were seen as his treasonable and anti-revolutionary activities in trying to win foreign support for his restoration. The English were deeply shocked by this regicide (forgetting that they had treated Charles I in the same way in 1649) and declared war, although a more plausible motive may have been that they feared the strategic and commercial consequences of the success of the Revolutionary armies against the Austrians in the Netherlands.

To ensure the survival of the Revolution and to win the ideological struggle in the country, the Convention attempted by intimidation to cow its opponents. This period is known as the Terror and its symbol was the guillotine. It is estimated that some 40,000 people died during this time, a minority on the guillotine, most of them in the uprisings, particularly in the Vendée and in Brittany, where the population deeply resented the persecution of Catholicism and its substitution by a nebulous Cult of the Supreme Being. The Terror came to an end in 1794 when its originators, including Robespierre, went in their turn to the scaffold.

The new republican constitution, devised by the Convention, was known as the Directory – a group of five men wielding executive power with two legislative assemblies. It came into operation in 1796 by which time the Revolution was firmly established, although the émigré royalists were still seeking allies to overthrow it and, within the country, the old disparities of wealth still existed. Universal conscription had produced enthusiastic armies, no longer inhibited by the old, aristocratic class distinctions. As well as expelling foreign invaders, the French attacked in their turn, annexing Belgium, Savoy and Nice to secure France's 'natural' frontiers. Army officers who owed their promotion to the revolutionary idea of the 'career open to talent' extended French power beyond those frontiers into Italy, Switzerland and Holland, exporting the revolution to sister republics where the experience of revolutionary institutions was to have a lasting effect.

One of the most outstanding of these young generals was Napoleon Bonaparte who led a campaign in Italy before carrying the revolution to Malta and Egypt. When he returned to France, he discovered a country where the corruption of the Directory and the exhaustion of the population had brought about economic crisis and political discontent. On the 9 November 1799 (or in the revolutionary calendar, 18 Brumaire year VIII[8]), Napoleon seized power, styling himself First Consul of the new régime before becoming the first Emperor of France in 1804.

This was in no sense a restoration of the old monarchy. The foundation of the empire was approved by popular vote, sovereignty was still vested in the people. All the reforms of 1790s were left intact, including the sales of land and the confiscation of Church property which guaranteed the loyalty of bourgeois and peasants to the régime. This was the consolidation of the Revolution, not its destruction.

In twelve years, from his coronation by the Pope in 1804 until his final defeat in 1815 at Waterloo, the Napoleonic legend was created. It was fostered at the time by his stunning military successes which, for a while, gave him control either directly or indirectly of the whole of Western Europe with the exception of Great Britain. It was pictured in the larger-than-life paintings of David showing the Emperor in heroic poses. It was sustained throughout the nineteenth century by those who were nostalgic for lost glories and has been maintained in the twentieth century by film-makers such as Abel Gance. The lasting seduction of the Napoleonic myth – grandeur, nationalism, progress, glory, freedom, revolution to overthrow tyrants – is present even today in monuments such as the Arc de Triomphe at the top of the Champs Elysées.

And yet the dream of imposing a new social and political order in a Europe under French hegemony was extinguished in 1815 with his final defeat at Waterloo and France was pushed back from the natural frontiers – in Belgium, Nice and Savoy – which he had secured. His lasting legacy lies rather in the fact that he laid the legislative, administrative, financial, judicial and religious foundations of France. During his reign, the Revolution became an integral part of the established order.

The civil code (known as the *Code Napoléon* after 1806) acknowledged the principles of civil liberties, guaranteed equality before the law (for men, that is), affirmed the secular character of the state and the right to own property and destroyed the aristocratic principle of primogeniture (inheritance by the eldest male child) by requiring equal division of inheritance. The administration of justice (the court system) was centrally organised and its basic provisions still remain in force. The division of the country into *départements* established by the Constituent Assembly was consolidated and reinforced by subdivisions into *arrondissements* and *cantons*. The *département* was headed by a prefect, the direct representative of the central government, whose function it was to ensure that the policy of the government was carried out in his area. Unifying centralism was the underlying principle which would only be modified by a measure of decentralisation during the first Mitterrand presidency in the 1980s.

Religious peace was achieved with the Concordat of 1801 which revised and regulated relations between France and the Vatican. This put an end to the Catholic insurrections in the west and effectively, to revolutionary secular cults such as that of the Supreme Being. The Church accepted the loss of its properties, the map of dioceses was redrawn to coincide with the *départe-*

10

ments and it was agreed that the head of state would nominate bishops who would be confirmed by the Pope. Salaries of priests and bishops would be paid by the state. These provisions still apply today in Alsace and Lorraine.

The education system (known as *l'université*) was revised and reformed on the centralist model. Its structure was essentially pyramidal, with primary schools at the bottom, then the *lycées* and finally *grandes écoles*.[9] The system was uniform. The same syllabus was taught everywhere (to avoid the danger of anything subversive to the régime being disseminated) and its goals were strictly utilitarian – to provide administrators, soldiers and teachers who would carry out the will of the state. In essence, this centralized structure has remained in place and has only been liberalized very slowly.

A new aristocracy was created, men who had given outstanding service to the empire, but these titles would not survive for long. What did survive was the *Légion d'honneur*, still a coveted decoration in French society today.

The Napoleonic era, characterised by fierce nationalism, revolutionary zeal and the rejection of the dynastic regimes which had lasted in Europe since medieval times, officially came to an end in 1815 when representatives of the victorious powers met in Vienna to undo its achievements. Whether these conservative statesmen thought that it was possible simply to turn the clock back and act as though the French Revolution had never occurred, is open to question. What is certain is that the issues raised by the Revolutionary and Napoleonic years – nationalism, democracy, liberalism, human rights – were not going to go away and would make the events of the following sixty years extremely turbulent, not just in France but in the rest of Europe also.

The restoration of Louis XVIII, finally achieved in 1815 after the hiatus of Napoleon's return from exile in Elba and the Hundred Days, was inevitably marked by reprisals and vengeance. The nobility returning from exile demanded the restoration of their privileges and the return of their property which had been confiscated by the Revolution. The White Terror harrassed or assassinated these new property owners and Protestants. Bonapartist generals and the administration were purged and a number of men, including General Ney, were executed by firing squads. There then followed a period of moderate and peaceful government which came to an end in 1824 when Charles X succeeded his brother as King. His reign (brought to an end by insurrection in 1830) was one of the most incompetent and partisan which the French have ever endured. His ministers gerrymandered electoral procedures to exclude the middle classes, muzzled the press, gave financial compensation to those members of the aristocracy who had gone into exile during the Revolution and dissolved parliament at their whim. When the barricades went up in Paris, Charles X abdicated and a prince of the Orléans branch of the royal family, Louis-Philippe, hijacked what had started as a republican insurrection to proclaim himself 'King of the French' waving a tricolour flag.[10]

The July Monarchy (as it is known because the *coup d'état* took place on

31 July 1830) was also the Bourgeois Monarchy. Louis-Philippe fostered the middle class and encouraged thrift and the consolidation of wealth. He extended the franchise by reducing the property qualification to vote but did nothing for the working classes, who were treated with contempt. Napoleonic nostalgia was still a potent force at this time. The news of the death of the Emperor's son in 1832 left the way clear for his nephew Louis-Napoléon (the next in line of succession) to attempt armed uprisings in 1836 and 1840 to restore the empire. Both ended in disaster. In an attempt to harness this nostalgia for his own aggrandisement, Louis-Philippe had the body of the Emperor (who had died in exile on St Helena in 1821) brought back to Paris and buried in great pomp in Les Invalides in 1840.

France, in common with Great Britain, was developing at this time an extensive colonial empire in Africa and the Far East. The conquest of Algeria went on for much of Louis-Philippe's reign and was completed in 1848, the year of his downfall. This particular colonial episode was to have very far-reaching consequences which still bedevil French society at the end of the twentieth century for, unlike all the other colonies, Algeria was incorporated into France as an integral part of French territory, on the same footing as Normandy and Brittany or as Savoy and Nice would be in 1860. This annexation breached all three of the conditions mentioned at the beginning of this chapter for the successful existence of a nation-state: Algeria was on the other side of the Mediterranean and therefore outside the recognisable and defensible natural frontiers of the country; the country had many different ethnic groupings often speaking different languages and nine-tenths of the population were Muslims with whom religious consensus would never be achieved.[11] The French presence in Algeria was to cost thousands of lives before the country became independent in 1962 and problems of immigration, discrimination and political terrorism are still poisoning French social life today.

The July Monarchy instituted free primary education. Under a law enacted by Guizot, each commune was required to maintain a primary school and teacher training colleges were set up to staff them. Jules Ferry would complete this work later in the century. Although the country was still essentially agricultural with little real industry, the first stirrings of the industrial revolution were beginning in transport, where canals and railways were being developed and which would make possible subsequent economic development.

In 1848 a wave of revolutions spread across Europe from which France was not exempt, and once again a republican revolution would be hijacked by the Right. This revolutionary spirit was fostered by disastrous harvests throughout the continent in 1846 which had led in Ireland to mass emigration to the United States. In France, hunger, unemployment and bankruptcies provoked lawlessness and demonstrations, particularly in Paris. Louis-Philippe abdicated on 24 February 1848 and the Second Republic was proclaimed. The provisional régime was coloured very strongly by utopian socialism and included among its leaders a symbolic worker known only as *l'ouvrier Albert*. It decreed freedom of the press and of assembly, the abolition of slavery in the colonies, universal male suffrage at the age of 21 (thus increasing the electorate from 0.25 million to 10 million) and the institution of national workshops to mop up unemployment. All of this awakened the fears of the middle classes who were quick to react to the threat of what they saw as 'the red peril' and who organised themselves in alliance with the Church to ensure that they held a majority in the new Assembly.

The new constitution established the office of President of the Republic and in the elections of December 1848, Louis-Napoléon Bonaparte was elected overwhelmingly as the champion of order and the defender of property, family and religion. To eliminate the 'reds', some provocation was required which would allow the new government to crush these potential dissidents. Freedom of the press and of assembly were curtailed and the national workshops were closed. These measures inevitably provoked riots which were savagely put down by the army – 7,000 were killed and 5,000 were compulsorily deported to Algeria. Louis-Napoleon's mandate as president was due to end in 1852 with no possibility of re-election under the constitution. He pre-empted events on 1 December 1851 when the army occupied strategic areas of Paris and arrested possible opponents. Violent riots were once more put down with considerable savagery and a further 10,000 possible dissidents were deported to Algeria. By the end of 1852 Louis-Napoleon had devised yet another constitution which gave him extensive powers, and after a plebiscite where potential opposition had been purged from the electorate, he was proclaimed Emperor with the title of Napoleon III. The Second Empire had begun.

The twenty years of the Second Empire are graphically recounted in Emile Zola's twenty-novel saga about the Rougon-Macquart family. Zola was, of course, an opponent of the régime and he loses no opportunity to detail its cruelties and venalities through his characters drawn from every social class. It has to be said, however, that the lasting legacy of the Second Empire for France was economic prosperity. Extensive railway building brought the country together as never before and made possible real administrative centralism. The French industrial revolution, which had lagged behind developments in Great Britain, got underway: coal and metallurgical industries replaced textiles as the major economic muscle of the country. Agriculture, still the major employer, was gradually becoming more mechanised, thus releasing more people to work in the new factories. These were the beginnings of the rural exodus which was to continue at an accelerating rate until the late twentieth century. The great French banks were established which would provide credit and investment funds for the new industries. Retailing began to assume its modern form with the introduction and proliferation of department stores[12] and massive public works – sewage and

13

water systems, covered markets and the creation of vast new boulevards in Paris, designed by Baron Haussmann, not only gave the city its modern appearance but also made it more difficult to set up barricades and mount insurrections.

The French Church, which had gone through some torrid times since the 1789 Revolution, experienced a dramatic revival. Numbers of religious vocations, encouraged by the régime, soared and the number of new female religious congregations, attracting tens of thousands of women, is almost impossible to calculate. The new moneyed bourgeois were among its most enthusiastic adherents, seeing the Catholic Church as a bulwark against anarchy and a guarantor of social order.

Education virtually fell under the control of the Church too with the *loi Falloux* of 1850. From being a state monopoly, the education system now encouraged the establishment of schools – *écoles libres* – outside the state system but subsidised by the state, staffed by priests or nuns. The favour in which the Church was held under the Second Empire and the many material advantages granted to it, provoked resentment among liberals and republicans and their anti-clericalism was to be a potent factor in French political life for many decades to come.

As has been so often the case in French political life, war would prove to be the undoing of the régime. The first two wars in which Napoleon III participated had relatively successful outcomes. His intervention in the Crimea alongside the British against the Russians left him with a victory but 100,000 Frenchman had died in Sebastopol and their only lasting memorial is a Parisian boulevard named after that city. His intervention in Italy in support of Italian unity brought Nice and Savoy into France in 1860. The country had once more expanded to fill its natural frontiers. His intervention in Mexico in support of the Austrian Archduke Maximilian, who was to be Emperor of a Catholic Latin America, ended in total military defeat and ridicule when the unfortunate Maximilian was shot by his Mexican subjects in 1867. Three years later, in 1870, in order to neutralise any French threat to German unification, Bismark, the prime minister of Prussia, manipulated Napoleon III into declaring war. The French armies, which were badly organised and led, were routed within six weeks by Prussian forces with twice as many men and much superior equipment. The Emperor was captured and sent into exile in England. Parisian rioters invaded the National Assembly, a provisional government was formed and a Republic proclaimed on 4 September.

The new provisional government attempted to continue the war but by January 1871 the situation had become desperate. Bismark (based in Versailles) demanded the surrender of Paris, the disarmament of a substantial part of the French army and a payment of 250 million f. in gold as the price for a three-week armistice during which the provisional government would hold elections to determine whether to continue the war or not. Those in

14

favour of peace (mostly royalists) won a large majority and had to submit to a humiliating peace treaty: 5 billion f. were to be paid in reparations, the Prussian army was to occupy part of the country for three years and Alsace (except the territory of Belfort) and northern Lorraine were annexed to Germany. Once again France had lost her territorial integrity within her natural frontiers. Thousands of francophones from these provinces left all their possessions behind and emigrated to Algeria, and the will to recover these provinces – *la revanche* – would be a powerful motivation in French political life until 1914. The King of Prussia was proclamed Kaiser Wilhelm I, Emperor of Germany, at Versailles on 18 January 1871 and Germany replaced France as the dominant land power in Europe.

The last tragic act of the Franco-Prussian War was still to be played between March and May 1871. The people of Paris believed that they had been betrayed by the defeatist government and by the middle classes and set up their own government or *commune* made up of democrats, utopian socialists, anarchists and revolutionaries of every variety. Amid scenes of bloody chaos (the Archbishop of Paris and two generals were shot by the *communards*) and starvation in the besieged city (even the animals in the zoo were eaten), the new government counter-attacked to restore its authority in the capital. Buildings were burnt and thousands of people were killed. In the purges which followed, thousands more were deported to Guyana.

These horrific events, with all the repression which followed, should have killed off the revolutionary myth in France. In fact, the Right continually used them to terrify the population, evoking the dangers always ready to engulf society, and for the Left, there was an example of martyrdom and heroism to add to the revolutionary mythology. Socialism, by which was meant economic and social egalitarianism, was not going to go away easily and its most extreme proponents, who believed that 'property is theft', would be known as 'communists'.

It is one of the great paradoxes of French history that the Third Republic, so far the most durable political régime that France has experienced since the Revolution (it lasted 80 years), was proclaimed by an assembly with an overwhelming royalist majority. The presidential term of office was established as seven years (the longest term in any democracy and a provision still in force today) to allow the first incumbent to prepare the way for the return of the monarchy. There was no agreement about which royal pretender should be invited to assume the throne and by 1876, when the republicans won a majority in the National Assembly, the new régime had taken root.

The Church was vigorously opposed to the new régime which realised that if it was to educate the population in Republican values, it would have to reclaim control of the education system which had been dominated by the Church since 1850. In the 1880s Jules Ferry extended the public education system which was to be free, compulsory and secular, with absolute respect for freedom of conscience and no religious teaching. Each department had its own *Ecole Normale* for the training of primary school teachers and in each village the *instituteur* was the intellectual and ideological counterweight to the priest. The wrongful condemnation of Alfred Dreyfus,[13] whose accusers were virtually all anti-republican, further polarised Church–State relations and the clerical–anti-clerical conflict became even more venomous. By 1902 the anti-clericals, under the new prime minister Emile Combes, turned the screw on the religious congregations by forbidding them to teach. Relations with the Vatican were broken off in 1905 and complete separation of Church and state declared. All Church property was taken over by the state, a provision which caused riots in the more Catholic areas of the country. The Catholic schools issue is one which still inflames passions today and the secular nature of the French education system came close to provoking a constitutional crisis during the second Mitterrand presidency when Muslim girls were refused permission to wear the Islamic veil at school.[14]

Discussion of the causes of the First World War goes well beyond the scope of this chapter but, in so far as France was concerned, the conflict with Germany was greeted initially with enthusiasm, as an opportunity for *la revanche*, to recover the lost provinces of Alsace and Lorraine. *L'union sacrée* was proclaimed and bitter religious and political disputes were put aside. Priests (still wearing cassocks), although non-combatants, served as stretcher-bearers bringing wounded men to safety in the trenches. The war was fought largely on French soil with about one-tenth of the country under German occupation behind the line of trenches which cut off the north-east of the country. The economic cost was immense: to sustain the war effort, France took out large loans from the United States and the value of the franc collapsed. The human cost was almost unimaginable: a million and a half French people died and a further three million were wounded, and even today one of the most poignant sights in any French village or town is the war memorial where the names of the dead are listed, often entire families. Victory came in 1918 along with the return of Alsace and Lorraine and massive economic, political and social problems. Extensive areas of rich agricultural land had been devastated. Factories had been destroyed. The work-force had been seriously weakened. The instability of the parliamentary régime left it unable to confront problems in a consistent way, especially since the National Assembly contained all the extremes of the political spectrum: a monarchist, anti-Semitic right wing which would lurch towards fascism during the 1930s and a powerful Communist Party.

Perhaps the most significant government of the inter-war years was the Popular Front, elected in 1936, which included communists, socialists and radicals. It was led by Léon Blum, a Jew who attracted all the hatreds of the anti-Semitic Right, and who did more than had ever been done in France previously to improve social conditions: the working week was reduced from forty-eight to forty hours (for the same pay) and workers were given two weeks of paid holiday. However, these were years of economic and demographic decline as France paid the price for the huge sacrifice of the First World War.

French military strategy reflected these conditions. It was passive and defensive, relying on the allegedly impregnable Maginot line to ward off any German invasion. Unfortunately, the Maginot line stopped at the Belgium border and when Hitler's tanks invaded France in 1940, they simply went around it and cut off the French armies in the north-east from the rest of the country. There followed a complete military collapse and the government, now in the hands of Marshal Philippe Pétain, signed an armistice with Germany and Italy in June 1940. The north of the country was occupied, Alsace and Lorraine were incorporated into Germany, Savoy and the area around Nice were under Italian occupation. The rest of the country remained a *zone libre* governed by Vichy. Full powers were voted by the French parliament to Philippe Pétain who became Head of the French state, and *Travail, Famille, Patrie* replaced *Liberté, Egalité, Fraternité* as the motto of the new state. The Third Republic was over, swept aside by war.

Pétain was adulated by the French people before being reviled four years later when Charles de Gaulle, who had proclaimed himself head of *la France libre*, returned in triumph with the allied armies in 1944. The Vichy régime was collaborationist, adopting many of the policies of national socialism. It encouraged 'family values', forbade divorce, protected organised religion, suppressed freemasonry and persecuted Jews who were arrested by the French police. It participated in the anti-Bolshevik crusade against the Soviet Union and had its own Gestapo, known as the *Milice*.[15]

Resistance, initially insignificant, grew over the years when the tide of war turned against the Germans and de Gaulle established himself from London, and in France's colonial empire, as the head of Free France. His apotheosis, as he walked down the Champs Elysées at the head of a huge procession in August 1944 should not disguise the fact that, six months previously, the same population had been cheering Philippe Pétain.

The provisional government (1944–6), headed by de Gaulle, set about designing a new constitution and governing France. Women were given the vote for the first time and key industries nationalised. The right wing, discredited by its activities during the war, was not part of the political process which gave France a Fourth Republic under which all power was vested in a National Assembly elected by proportional representation. De Gaulle had resigned, impatient with the intrigues of the political parties, sardonically announcing that he had not saved France in order to get involved with '*le prix des macaronis*' ('the price of pasta'). His recall to power, which he had probably thought would be imminent, would have to wait for twelve years until 1958.

The period of the Fourth Republic (1946–58) was one of chronic political instability as governments (all coalitions) fell as soon as they had to take a difficult decision because one of the coalition partners deserted it. It was a period of reconstruction, of political and social unrest during which the Communist Party, in the depths of the cold war, regularly won 25 per cent of the vote. It foundered because of the Algerian War.

The Algerian War of Independence started on 1 November 1954. It was never referred to in France as a 'war' because Algeria was part of France and 'operations for the maintenance of order' were the responsibility of the Minister of the Interior, François Mitterrand among others. Deputies elected by the million French people living in Algeria (or *pieds noirs* as they were called) systematically blocked even the most timid attempts to grant some measure of autonomy to France's North African province. The war was conducted on both sides with pitiless cruelty. This culminated in the French army torturing *Front de libération nationale* (FLN) suspects in order to win the Battle of Algiers. Rumours that a peace process might be under way provoked the army in Algeria into setting up a Committee of Public Safety in May 1958 at a time when there was no government in power in Paris and an appeal to de Gaulle was launched. Faced with a crisis which could have degenerated into civil war, the National Assembly capitulated and invested de Gaulle as the last prime minister of the Fourth Republic with authority to revise the constitution.

The constitution of the Fifth Republic was approved overwhelmingly in a referendum held in September 1958 and de Gaulle became its first president in January 1959. The essential differences between the Fourth and the Fifth Republics lie in the powers of the presidency (considerably strengthened under the Fifth Republic) and the abandonment of proportional representation in favour of the election of a single representative from each constituency under a two-round voting system, designed to produce coherent majorities.[16] De Gaulle was intensely nationalistic, sceptical about Europe and anti-American but, before he could set about reshaping France, he had to get rid of the Algerian problem. At first idolised by the European population of Algeria, he rapidly became their arch enemy when, with a mixture of subtlety, guile and dishonesty and with the military operations in Algeria won, he moved towards self-determination and independence. Four generals and a number of colonels attempted a military *putsch* and there were numerous attempts on de Gaulle's life. Algeria became independent in March 1962 and the entire European population, more than a million people, fled to France, abandoning all their possessions and becoming intractable opponents of de Gaulle and the bedrock of the support for the *Front national* in the 1980s and 1990s.

The Fifth Republic successfully pursued the policies of economic re-generation begun under the Fourth. It largely defused the Catholic school problem in 1962 with the *Loi Debré* which paid the salaries of teachers but gave the state control over standards. De Gaulle was re-elected in 1965 (this time by universal suffrage) but his rather paternalistic and even autocratic style of government were beginning to irritate some sections of the population. Student agitation, which began at the University of Nanterre in May 1968, quickly spread to other campuses and strikes paralysed the economic life of the country. The violence and chaos of the demonstrations, as well as the utopian idealism of many of the participants, was reminiscent of 1848 and the Commune of 1871. Although May 1968 achieved little in itself beyond a round of wage increases and a reduction in the working week, the ideas and attitudes generated at that time challenged virtually every aspect of French political, social and even religious life, and their effects are still visible today.

De Gaulle's authority rested on his direct appeal to the people, often by referendum rather than through a political party, and in 1969, in order to restore this authority which had been tarnished by the events of the previous year, he called a referendum on reform of the Senate and regionalisation, which he lost. He resigned the same night and totally withdrew from public life until his death in November 1970. His successors, Georges Pompidou (1969–74), Valéry Giscard d'Estaing (1974–81), François Mitterrand (1981–8, 1988–95), and Jacques Chirac (1995–to date) have all found the presidential system bequeathed to them by de Gaulle to be to their liking. Even François Mitterrand, who attacked it when he was in opposition, used it with some relish once he gained power.

The Fifth Republic has given France constitutional provisions flexible enough to accommodate both the monarchical or presidential side of the French character and the parliamentary side. There is the built-in corrective of *cohabitation* when a president who may have lost the confidence of the people finds himself having to share power with the leader of a majority party in the National Assembly of a different political persuasion. This is probably a happy accident rather than the result of the prescience of Michel Debré who was the architect of the constitution in 1958.[17]

The conflicts between Church and state which erupted regularly over 200 years have calmed down, although the *école libre* question can still bring hundreds of thousands of demonstrators on to the streets, either for or against church schools. There is currently a different challenge to the secular state: that of Islam. Islamic immigration is a potent factor in French social life and the state is having problems in coping with the demands of several million people of Maghrebin origin that their religious culture should be afforded special privileges. Their demand is for *'le droit à la différence'* (that girls be allowed to wear the Islamic veil when they go to school, for example) rather than that they be constrained (as Catholics and Jews are) to *'le droit à l'indifférence'* under which everyone is treated equally and no overt religious identity may be fostered in any state organisation, particularly in education. Consideration and resolution of the problems posed by the Islamic phenomenon in France are however poisoned and made even more intractable by the still bitter memories of the Algerian War.[18]

The extension of the use of the French language followed the country's political expansion into its natural frontiers, progressively eliminating the perceived threat to national unity from regional languages such as Provençal, Breton, Alsatian and Basque. This was a matter of deliberate policy: state education required the exclusive use of French and children were punished for using regional languages at school. Compulsory military service consolidated this process by sending young men as far away from their home area as possible and deliberately combining men from different areas in the same units. By the 1980s, after 200 years of centralism, the state had become sufficiently confident in its unitary identity to allow limited public use of these regional languages as part of the process of political devolution. The only real outstanding problems are those of Corsica and the Basque provinces, which straddle the Pyrenees and where the defence of a still-powerful cultural and political identity continues to provoke violence.[19]

The perceived threat from Germany (three invasions in seventy years) which dominated French thinking for nearly a century, has now all but disappeared, subsumed into the process of European integration which has been the policy of all the Fifth Republic's presidents since de Gaulle.[20]

The most significant reform of the Mitterrand presidencies will probably be seen in future years to have been the devolution of power to the regions.[21] This reform is an acknowledgement of the fact that France, like most modern medium-sized nation-states, is too big to look after the small things efficiently using centralised structures. At the same time, it is too small to handle the big things on its own. Global economic and military forces are so immense that countries such as France can only play a role within a larger grouping of like-minded states. France's dilemma (shared by the other European nations) is to find a way to preserve a painfully forged national identity while holding the ring between the supra-national confederal powers of Europe and the increasingly autonomous regions within its frontiers.

NOTES

1 The date is probably inaccurate. Modern scholars have situated the event in different years between 496 and 509. Its location in 496 was made arbitrarily in school textbooks at the beginning of the Third Republic to mark one of the founding dates of French nationhood which had been wounded by the loss of Alsace and Lorraine in 1871. The powerful symbol of baptism and hence of consecration of the nation to Christianity were being appropriated and exploited during 1996 (the supposed 1,500th anniversary year) by the *Front national* and integrist Catholic groups (see Chapter 8).
2 Manicheists believed that the world was governed by two coexisting principles, good and evil, God and Satan.
3 Jeanne d'Arc has since served as a national symbol of resistance against foreign (particularly English) oppression and was used extensively in propaganda in the Second World War by the Vichy régime. The *Front national* currently exploits her as a symbol of French nationalism in the face of 'hostile' (by which they mean *maghrébin*) invasions.

4 See Chapter 8.
5 Used as a title for a film by Chérau (1994): see Chapter 11.
6 The *cahiers de doléances* were documents in which members of the three assemblies which made up the Estates General – Nobility, Clergy, Third Estate – noted their complaints which the assembled Estates General were supposed to rectify.
7 See Chapter 2.
8 The republican calendar, intended to mark the beginning of a new age, was instituted by the Convention. The year began at the autumn equinox (22 September) and was divided into twelve months, each of thirty days. The remaining five or six days were devoted to republican holidays. These months were given the following names: autumn – *Vendémiaire, Brumaire, Frimaire*; winter – *Nivôse, Pluviôse, Ventôse*; spring – *Germinal, Floréal, Prairial*; summer – *Messidor, Thermidor, Fructidor.* Each month was divided into *décades* or ten-day weeks.
9 See Chapter 5.
10 Until the Revolution (which instituted the tricolour), the emblem of the royal house and hence of the state, had been the white flag bearing a *fleur-de-lys*. The Restoration had reinstated the *fleur-de-lys*.
11 See Chapter 9 for a discussion of the possible integration of Islam into French society.
12 See Chapter 12.
13 Captain Dreyfus was accused in 1894 of having communicated secret documents to the German military attaché in Paris. He was condemned to life imprisonment in Guyana. Anti-semitism (Dreyfus was a Jew) among high-ranking army officers ensured that the real culprit, Commandant Esterhazy, was acquitted by the *Conseil de Guerre*. Emile Zola then published in the newspaper *L'Aurore* an open letter to the President of the Republic entitled '*J'accuse*' which gave full details of the lies and cover-up. The *affaire Dreyfus* was to drag on until 1906 when the *Cour de Cassation* finally overturned the original judgment and rehabilitated Dreyfus.
14 See Chapter 9.
15 See Chapter 8 for further details on the legacy of Vichy.
16 See Chapters 1 and 2.
17 See Chapter 1.
18 See Chapter 9.
19 See Chapter 10.
20 See Chapter 3.
21 See Chapter 4.

RECOMMENDED READING

Goubert, P. (1994) *Initiation à l'histoire de la France*, Paris: Fayard.
A comprehensive history of France from pre-Roman times to the present day. Most detailed on the sixteenth and seventeenth centuries. Also available in an English translation.
Price, R. (1993) *A Concise History of France*, Cambridge: CUP.
A lucid, compact account of the history of France.

Part I

FRENCH INSTITUTIONS AND POLICY MAKING

1

THE PRESIDENCY

Rob Turner

The presidency is the corner-stone of the French state, the *'clé de voûte'* of the régime, to borrow the expression first used by Michel Debré in presenting the constitution of the Fifth Republic to the *Conseil d'Etat*. It is also in many ways quite unique to France. This unique nature was amply illustrated in the 1995 presidential election campaign. The major event in the preliminary stages of the campaign was the announcement by Jacques Delors that he would not be standing, despite his substantial lead in the polls over all other major candidates. He gave as his main reason the fact that he would be unable to implement his political programme in the event of his election:

> the absence of a majority to support such a policy, whatever measures might be taken after the election, would not allow me to put my solutions into effect. . . . I would not wish, once elected, to cohabit with a government that did not share my options.
>
> *(Sept sur sept* (TF1) 11 December 1994)

By contrast, Jacques Chirac, the eventual victor, was hailed as potentially the most powerful president of the Fifth Republic, controlling virtually all aspects of political life.

What marks out the French Presidency is not only the nature and extent of the power and influence wielded by the president of the Republic but also the degree to which this power and influence wax and wane according to the political circumstances, a phenomenon far exceeding, for example, the vicissitudes experienced by Bill Clinton as a hostile Senate curtailed his freedom of action. The fluid nature of the régime has in the course of the history of the Fifth Republic given rise to many debates – over the intentions of the authors of the constitution, over the true nature of the régime – whether parliamentary or presidential, over the concept of the *domaine réservé* which implies presidential supremacy in defence and foreign affairs and over the lack of accountability of the president despite his executive rôle. Although these debates continue and indeed have given rise to many proposals for reform of the presidency, the unfolding history of the Fifth Republic has clarified some of these issues and made it possible to arrive at an understanding of the complex and changing rôle played by the President of the Republic.

DE GAULLE AND THE CONSTITUTION

The dominant influence in shaping the Fifth Republic and particularly the institution of the presidency was that of Charles de Gaulle. De Gaulle's views on constitutional reform were rooted in his own experience of the Third Republic and of the Second World War. He had expressed these views as early as 16 June 1946 in a speech at Bayeux, and the subsequent experience of the Fourth Republic and the Algerian conflict only served to confirm his analysis. De Gaulle believed that the Third and Fourth Republics had been weakened by party rivalry and quarrels, what he termed in the Bayeux speech 'our longstanding gallic propensity for divisions and quarrels', which he felt was often detrimental to the interests of France: 'party rivalry often takes on a fundamental character in France constantly throwing everything into question and taking precedence over the higher interests of the country' (in Quermonne 1980: Annexe II,1).

Certainly, the Third and Fourth Republics had been characterised by chronic governmental instability – the Fourth Republic had seventeen prime ministers between 1946 and 1958 – and this was due to the weakness of multiparty governmental coalitions which tended to collapse when faced with controversial issues, the Algerian conflict which finally led to the fall of the Fourth Republic being a case in point.

De Gaulle felt that France's institutions should be designed to compensate for the nation's 'constant political upheavals' and proposed that 'over and above the contingencies of political life there should be established a form of national arbitration to favour continuity amongst the shifting alliances' (in Quermonne 1980: Annexe II,1). This rôle was to be entrusted to the head of state who would appoint governments to reflect the political orientation of the parliament but also to serve the national interest, who would act as an arbiter standing apart from party rivalries and who, in addition to ensuring continuity of government, would safeguard France's independence. In de Gaulle's thinking the president was clearly to have a key rôle in ensuring that France no longer suffered the constant breakdown of government that characterised the Third and Fourth Republics and also in providing the leadership in times of emergency that France had lacked at the time of the Second World War and the Algerian crisis. This strengthening of the president's rôle should not be taken, however, to indicate an intention to institute a full-blown presidential system.

The final act of Fourth Republic parliamentarians before handing over power to de Gaulle to draw up a new constitution was to vote a framework law for the new constitution which attempted to ensure that the basic principles of republican and parliamentary democracy would be observed.

26

These included governmental accountability to parliament, giving parliament the power to force governments to resign through the vote of a motion of no confidence – a central characteristic of parliamentary systems. François Luchaire recounts that when a first draft of the new constitution gave the president explicit policy-making powers, Guy Mollet pointed out to the General in the interministerial committee considering the draft that such powers were not compatible with parliamentary democracy (*Le Monde* 5 September 1988: 2).[1] If de Gaulle drew back from a presidential system it was perhaps also, as Michel Debré, whom de Gaulle charged with drafting the constitution, explained to the *Conseil d'Etat*, that in addition to being contrary to French republican traditions, such a system, which would necessarily involve the election of the president by popular vote, could offer a convenient route to power to the still influential French Communist Party of 1958 (Michel Debré, in Maus 1982: 3). However, we shall see that the issue of presidential involvement in governmental policy making was far from resolved.

The definitive text of the constitution of the Fifth Republic which was given overwhelming support by the electorate in the referendum of 28 September 1958 demonstrated the increased significance of the presidency by placing the articles dealing with it before those dealing with either government or parliament. The first of these articles, Article 5, provides a general definition of the president's rôle, very much in line with the ideas previously put forward by de Gaulle in his Bayeux speech. The president's responsibilities fall into two main categories: he ensures the proper functioning and continuity of state institutions through his interventions as an 'arbiter' and he is the guarantor of France's independence, territorial integrity and treaty obligations.

These twin responsibilities may be best understood in the light of France's recent history and de Gaulle's personal experience. The president as 'arbiter' would act to avoid the breakdowns of government, the power vacuums and the constant shifts of policy in key areas which characterised the Third and Fourth Republics as a result of the instability of governmental coalitions. The president would also intervene in times of emergency to protect France's independence and territory in a way that had not been possible on the outbreak of the Second World War. The remaining articles dealing with the presidency, other than those dealing with the ceremonial aspects of his rôle as head of state, can be seen as providing the president with the necessary powers to fulfill this dual rôle. In order to play his rôle as guarantor of France's independence in times of grave emergency the president under Article 16 can take full executive powers. Although the circumstances under which this may happen are clearly defined – there must be a grave threat and government must be unable to function – it is left wholly to the president's discretion to determine whether these circumstances apply. This provision of the constitution amounts to an attempt to institutionalise de Gaulle's rôle in the

Second World War. Although it has only been invoked once for a brief period at the time of an attempted *putsch* during the Algerian crisis, it is clearly of vast potential significance both in the unlimited scope of the executive powers that it can enable the president to take and in the lack of constraints on the president in deciding to implement Article 16. In both these respects it goes well beyond the powers granted to the head of state by any other comparable Western democracy. In addition to Article 16, Article 15 makes the president commander-in-chief of the armed forces and chairman of the defence councils and committees. At a later date the president was also to take charge of France's nuclear deterrent. Article 52 states that the president negotiates and ratifies the treaties which Article 5 requires him to uphold. These powers relating to defence and foreign affairs, while no different, apart from control of the nuclear deterrent, to those attributed to the presidents of the Third and Fourth Republics, were to be interpreted so as to involve the president in areas of defence and foreign affairs that had previously been the preserve of government, and we shall see that they were to be the source of much debate.

The other major aspect of the president's dual rôle is that of 'arbiter', intervening to ensure the proper functioning of the institutions of the state and to ensure continuity of government. To enable the president to carry out this rôle the constitution gives him the power to appoint the prime minister, to chair the Council of Ministers, to call a referendum, to ask parliament to reconsider proposed legislation and to dissolve the National Assembly, powers which are all reserved to the president alone and which he exercises without the need for the agreement of the prime minister. Once again these measures may be best understood in the light of France's recent history. The president can henceforth resolve the kind of governmental crises that occurred under the Fourth and Fifth Republics by calling referenda to resolve controversial issues, by asking parliament to reconsider controversial legislation, by appointing a new government with parliamentary support or, in the event of a situation deadlocked by parliamentary antagonisms, by calling an election. It should be noted, however, that this is a facilitating rather than an executive rôle and that it implies that the president must be impartial in relation to party politics with the priority of ensuring effective government from whatever part of the political spectrum is best placed to provide it. De Gaulle himself made this quite clear to the Comité consultatif constitutionnel:

> the head of state ... is impartial and ... does not and should not involve himself in politics. .... He is an arbiter, he has no call to involve himself with political circumstances and that is the reason why, among others, the prime minister and the government are not accountable to him..
>
> (De Gaulle, in Luchaire 1987: 300)

28

Articles 20 and 21 of the constitution make it quite clear that it is indeed the government, headed by the prime minister, which governs, stating unambiguously: 'The government decides and implements the policy of the nation. The prime minister directs the action of the government.' Even this restricted interpretation of the constitution is not without problems. The president must choose how and when to intervene and these choices are necessarily political, if not party political. Raymond Janot, who advised de Gaulle on the drafting of the constitution, made it clear that the president's rôle would be an active one and that he would wield substantial reserved powers not subject to prime ministerial countersignature:

> Of course an arbiter is not a party political figure. But neither is he a spectator. An arbiter is a person who takes a decision in certain particularly serious cases and who in consequence has his own powers to decide in these serious cases.
>
> (Raymond Janot, in Luchaire 1987: 257)

Although de Gaulle makes frequent reference to the president's rôle in safeguarding the higher interests of the nation, it is difficult to conceive of this notion as truly apolitical. As Véronique Alibert-Fabre explains (1990: 701), de Gaulle distinguishes 'the general interest which comes before the fixed attitudes and the claims of particular sections of society' from sectarian interests, but many political movements would claim to have an all-embracing political philosophy which rises above purely sectarian interests yet which would differ radically from de Gaulle's. In the first years of the Fifth Republic, however, this debate was to be rapidly superseded by developments of yet greater consequence.

THE EVOLUTION OF THE PRESIDENT'S ROLE IN PRACTICE

In September 1959, less than a year after taking office as the first president of the Fifth Republic, de Gaulle moved to resolve the Algerian crisis by initiating the policy of Algerian self-determination and, in so doing, shattered the restricted interpretation of the president's rôle given above. This policy was personally launched by de Gaulle and he took personal responsibility for it. Furthermore, it was imposed on a government some of whose members, including the prime minister, Debré himself, had had severe misgivings concerning the prospect of Algerian independence. In acting this way de Gaulle was clearly exercising power directly and determining government policy. Moreover, by proposing a highly controversial solution to the burning issue of Algeria he was no longer acting with the political impartiality required by an arbitral rôle. However, it might have been argued that it was implicit in the circumstances in which de Gaulle came to power that he had been entrusted with the twofold mission of reforming the régime and

29

resolving the Algerian crisis. Such indeed was the belief of de Gaulle's first prime minister, Michel Debré, who charitably assumed that de Gaulle would limit his interventions in the sphere of government to the Algerian issue. However, as Jacques Fauvet acerbically commented:

> Michel Debré opposed de Gaulle's conception with great respect but great firmness: he considered that with the end of the Algerian drama the government should recover its functions and exercise them to the full. De Gaulle on the other hand considered that it was enough to change his prime minister.
>
> (Fauvet, *Le Monde*, 8 June 1976)

(This interpretation remains debatable since the reasons for de Gaulle's dismissal of Debré have never been satisfactorily elucidated, not least because of Debré's continuing loyalty to the General: see Institut de Gaulle, 1990). Be that as it may, the balance of power between president and prime minister had clearly swung in favour of the president.

De Gaulle not only resisted pressure to return to a restricted arbitral rôle but sought to legitimise his expanded rôle through a change in the method of election of the president. The 1958 constitution had made provision for the president to be elected by indirect universal suffrage by a restricted electoral college made up of parlementarians and local councillors. De Gaulle proposed a change to election by direct universal suffrage as is the norm for an executive president who has responsibility for government. When the parliament resisted this proposal he put the issue to a referendum and it was carried by a substantial majority.

This change meant that de Gaulle could now claim to exercise national sovereignty as an elected representative of the people, as Article 3 of the constitution demanded. This change not only strengthened the democratic status of the presidency, it also politicised it. A presidential candidate would have to campaign on the basis of a political programme, thus invalidating the concept of the president as an impartial arbiter. De Gaulle exploited his newly acquired democratic legitimacy to the full, claiming in a television broadcast of 31 January 1964 that the presidency was now the source of all executive power: 'It should be clearly understood that the indivisible authority of the state is wholly entrusted to the president by the people who elected him and that there is no other whether ministerial, civil or judicial.' Whatever had been intended by the authors of the constitution in 1958, France was now a long way from the British model of parliamentary democracy with a titular head of state.

1962 also saw a second, equally significant, change. Following the deputies' resistance to his reform, de Gaulle exercised his right to dissolve the rebellious parliament. In the subsequent parliamentary election campaign he openly expressed support for the gaullist UNR (Union pour la nouvelle République) candidates. This was not only a further indication of the politicisation of his rôle but was to have far-reaching implications for relations between the president and government. The president was now the *de facto* leader of a political movement. What is more, in the elections this movement went on to win a virtual majority of seats in the National Assembly. The president now had enhanced democratic status equivalent to that of executive presidents in full-blown presidential systems.

With hindsight, it can be seen that the rôle of the impartial president-arbiter had been an almost impossibly impractical concept and that presidential interventions, even those which remained within the spirit of the constitution and were intended to ensure continuity and effective government, were bound to take on a political tinge. More importantly, the overlapping rôles assigned by the constitution to president and government in defence and foreign affairs inevitably posed the question of who wielded executive authority in these vital areas. Given de Gaulle's autocratic nature, it was not surprising that he bid to shape policy. As he wrote in *Le Fil de l'épée*:

> Faced with events the man of character relies on himself. His impulse is to make his mark, to take over and to make events his business. And far from sheltering behind the hierarchy or the letter of the law he draws himself up, takes up his position and faces up to events. . . . he embraces action with masterful pride.
>
> (de Gaulle 1990: 54)

Or, as he put it rather more succinctly, he did not intend his rôle to be simply to '*inaugurer les chrysanthèmes*', that is, to 'lay wreaths' (*Le Monde Dossiers et Documents* no. 144, May 1987: 1). Indeed, de Gaulle later let it be understood that if the 1958 constitution was the best compromise he could obtain, given the political constraints of the time and most notably the pressure from political parties to retain a parliamentary system, he had never intended to let himself be shackled by the constitution once he had acceded to the presidency.

The Gaullist movement naturally supported a maximalist interpretation of presidential powers, and as early as 1959 Jacques Chaban-Delmas, speaking at the UNR conference in Bordeaux on 15 November, distinguished a 'presidential sector' from the 'governmental sector': 'In the first sector the government implements policy, in the second it makes policy.' The presidential sector included defence, foreign affairs and the French community of former colonies and became known as the *domaine réservé*. This concept, as Marie-Anne Cohendet points out (1993: 217–18), was rejected on all sides, by the Left because the presidential powers on which the theory was founded were not reserved powers exclusive to the president but powers subject to prime ministerial countersignature, and by de Gaulle and his successors in the presidency because they viewed this interpretation as far too restrictive in that it implicitly excluded presidential intervention in areas outside the *domaine réservé*. Indeed, having replaced the constitutionally minded Michel Debré by Georges Pompidou and in his turn the independent Pompidou by the more compliant Maurice Couve de Murville, de Gaulle began to extend his domination of policy making to other areas. A notable example came with the post-1968 policy of 'participation' which aimed to involve workers in consultation with management and profit-sharing schemes.

Following de Gaulle's departure from the presidency, political comment-ators speculated that his successor, Georges Pompidou, who possessed neither de Gaulle's historical legitimacy nor his personal charisma, might not dominate policy making in the same fashion, but in fact Pompidou, who had been de Gaulle's prime minister, in effect retained this rôle along with his new presidential powers, dealing with both the formulation and the execution of policy in every sphere of government, consolidating presidential influence over the economy and financial issues which de Gaulle had largely chosen to ignore. Clearly, the legitimacy conferred by Pompidou's electoral victory in the presidential elections and the political clout provided by the support of the parliamentary majority for the new president were sufficient to maintain presidential domination of the executive.

After Pompidou's death in office political circumstances changed with the succession of Valéry Giscard d'Estaing. Giscard had been elected on a reformist platform and was determined to supervise the implementation of his policies personally. However, he was backed by the minority partner of the parliamentary majority, the UDF (*Union pour la démocratie française*) and did not enjoy the unquestioning support of the Gaullist movement, whose own candidate, Chaban-Delmas, he had defeated in the first round of the presidential elections. He found, nevertheless, that when the Gaullist group in parliament jibbed at his reformist measures it was sufficient to threaten recourse to his power of dissolution of parliament to bring them into line, particularly given the rising electoral power of the Left.

François Mitterrand, who defeated Giscard in the 1981 presidential elec-tions, had been one of the régime's harshest critics, describing it in a parliamentary debate on 24 April 1964 as 'an authoritarian régime without accountability' and most famously in the same year as *'un coup d'état permanent'* in his leaflet with that title. However, once in power, he announced: 'I shall exercise fully the powers that the constitution confers on me' and he went on to shape and oversee government policy as thoroughly as his predecessors.

These sustained presidential incursions by successive presidents into policy making were carried out at the expense of government and particularly of the prime minister, to whom, as we have seen, the constitution formally attributes the rôle of head of the executive. De Gaulle made the subordination of the prime minister and government explicit in a television broadcast on 20 September 1962:

> It goes without saying that these attributions taken as a whole lead the president to inspire, give direction to and organise the nation's action.

It may happen that he has to take direct charge. Of course the prime minister and his colleagues have on this basis to determine policy as appropriate and run the administration.

(de Gaulle, *Conférence de presse*, 20 September 1962)

Not only did prime ministers and governments lose their policy-making prerogatives, but their continuation in office became dependent on presidential support. The constitution gives the president the power to appoint prime ministers but not to dismiss them. However, as we have seen, in reality de Gaulle dismissed Michel Debré, although the constitutional formalities were observed in so far as Debré then formally offered his resignation, and this pattern was to be repeated many times, with Pompidou, for example, dismissing Chaban-Delmas when he appeared to be constructing an independent power base and Edith Cresson being replaced by Mitterrand to revitalise a faltering government. All had in common that they were removed for reasons of political expediency and not on the only constitutionally valid ground that they had lost the confidence of the National Assembly.

Institutionally, presidential usurpation of governmental powers was expressed in the creation of a presidential infrastructure which took over the executive rôle from government. Although the prime minister's working parties, known as *comités restreints*, continued to do the donkey work in preparing dossiers it was the president's *comités restreints* which took the decisions, and it became clear that in some cases the president's personal advisers wielded more influence than their ministerial counterparts. The president's 'kitchen Cabinet' in effect became what Viansson Ponté, then editor of *Le Monde*, termed a 'parallel government' or 'superexecutive'. The most extreme examples of the marginalisation of the prime minister came on occasions when the president chose to act on a significant issue without troubling to inform his prime minister. The best known example is de Gaulle's flight to Baden-Baden to consult the French army of the Rhine in May 1968, leaving Pompidou not only uncertain of his intentions but ignorant of his whereabouts. A more recent example came when François Mitterrand failed to inform Laurent Fabius that he had invited the controversial Polish premier, General Jaruzelski, to talks at the Elysée.

Clearly, some Fifth Republic prime ministers such as Chaban-Delmas, Chirac in 1974 or Mauroy in 1981 were heavyweight political figures in their own right, and it is not easy to envisage such figures readily accepting their subordination to the president, given the powers accorded them by Article 20. Maurice Duverger in his illuminating work '*La Monarchie républicaine*' explains the mechanism permitting presidential domination:

The prime minister cannot exercise the immense powers that the constitution gives him without retaining the confidence of the National Assembly and the nature of this confidence determines the way in which he exercises these powers. . . . In France the parliamentary majority considers the president to be their leader and not the prime minister. In such a situation the latter can do nothing other than to stick closely to the president, follow him like his shadow and obey all his orders because that is the will of the parliamentary majority.

(Duverger 1974: 157)

As Giscard d'Estaing demonstrated, should the majority waver in its support for the president it can be brought into line most effectively by the threat of an early dissolution of parliament.

Duverger also deals convincingly with the question of whether this extension of presidential powers is unconstitutional:

In this way the president exercises considerable powers which obviously go beyond what the constitution gives him. But the constitution is not violated since everything depends on the docility of the prime minister which reflects the docility of the parliamentary majority.

(ibid.: 193)

But if the letter of the constitution, if not its spirit, is respected, these developments do none the less raise a fundamental issue of accountability. The prime minister and his government are, as in any parliamentary democracy, accountable to parliament and can be forced to resign by the vote of a motion of censure. The president, on the other hand, once elected, only becomes accountable to the electorate at the end of his term of office should he wish to stand for re-election. Essentially, though, the difficulty does not lie in the lack of accountability of the head of state, which is a standard premise of constitutional law, but in the betrayal of the principle of executive responsibility which means that the prime minister is held accountable for executive acts of which he is not in reality the author, so emptying the concept of accountability of all meaning.

The presidentialisation of the régime which we have noted, consisting of a maximalist interpretation of presidential powers provided by the constitution, the *de facto* acquisition of new powers such as that of dismissal of the prime minister and, most importantly, encroachment into government's sphere of action have been the subject of much criticism from Duverger's *La Monarchie républicaine* (1974) to *La Cinquième République: un démonarchie* of Jacques Georgel (1990), both of which consider that the Fifth Republic amounts to a democratically sanctioned monarchy. Much of the problem lies in the unique hybrid nature which the régime acquired, as de Gaulle put it in 1961 (*Conférence de presse*, 11 April 1961): 'Let's say, if you like, that our constitution is both parliamentary and presidential.' Georges Pompidou and Jean Gicquel put it less flatteringly, referring to a 'mongrel régime' or a *pot pourri* respectively. Certainly, the addition of governmental powers to the president's arbitral powers makes the president both referee and player, enjoying the sacrosanct status of head of state and

34

able to influence the course of political life to his own advantage in determining the timing of parliamentary elections and the composition of governments, and in having recourse to referenda but also in determining government policy and legislation. It is worth noting in this respect that the 1958 constitution had greatly strengthened government's power in relation to parliament, particularly government's power to promote legislation, but the ultimate beneficiary of Debré's rationalised parliamentarism was in fact to be the president. This accumulation of power in which the president has the status of head of state, the *de facto* powers of an executive president and, albeit at second hand via a subordinate prime minister, control over the legislative process, which goes well beyond that of American presidents (Kramer 1995: 31), and even British prime ministers, does indeed amount to an institution unique among Western democracies.

The extension of presidential powers into the field of governmental policy making has in this analysis been attributed essentially to a favourable conjunction of political circumstances. However, successive presidents eager to consolidate these developments and to render them permanent sought a constitutional foundation. We have seen that presidential responsibilities in defence and foreign affairs had been used to justify a policy-making rôle in these areas, although that had never been the case in the Third and Fourth Republics. De Gaulle had argued in 1964 that the introduction of direct elections to the presidency endowed the president with supreme power which was his to wield himself or to delegate, if he so chose, through his power of appointment. Claims were also made that the rôle of the president as defined in Article 5 implied that he had at his disposal any power necessary to carry it out, over and above those specified in the remainder of the constitution.

These arguments were tenuous at best and political scientists struggling to find a schema which would incorporate both the text of the constitution and the increasingly divergent practice resorted, as Cohendet catalogues (1993: 61–7), to references to the presidentialist 'spirit' of the constitution which is considered to spring from its historical origins, to the legitimation of presidentialisation by custom and practice and to the existence of differing 'interpretations' of the constitution. However, set against the unchanging text of the constitution, these approaches were only valid in the limited number of instances where there existed genuine ambiguity or imprecision in the text. Seen in this light, the comprehensive presidentialisation of the régime which occurred appears to demonstrate a wilful disregard of the constitution, which was only to change in 1986.

COHABITATION

It had long been recognised that the election of a parliamentary majority hostile to the incumbent president would clarify many of the issues relating to the division of powers between president and government. Above all, it would reveal which of his powers the president held by virtue of the constitution and which of his powers he exercised only by reason of favourable political circumstances. This long-anticipated event finally came about when in the parliamentary elections of March 1986 the socialists, who had been in power since 1981, lost their majority. The new majority was composed of an alliance between the centre-Right UDF coalition and Jacques Chirac's gaullist RPR (Rassemblement pour la République). François Mitterrand, however, still had two years of his seven-year presidential term to run. Chirac and Mitterrand were in agreement on the basic elements of the situation. The president, for his part, had to accept the electorate's verdict: 'The president will have to accept the parliamentary majority elected by the country, that's all there is to it' (Mitterrand, in Claisse 1980: 41). On the other hand, the new majority had to accept that the president would remain in office and retain his constitutional powers: 'Nothing in the constitution forces the president to leave office on the pretext that there is a new majority in the National Assembly' Jacques Chirac had stated in 1986 (in Duverger 1986: 9). He added: 'The powers and prerogatives of the president as they are defined in the constitution are inviolable' (in Gicquel: 70).

Indeed, there was agreement that this co-existence or '*cohabitation*', as it came to be called, should be based strictly on the constitution: 'The constitution, nothing but the constitution, the whole of the constitution', as François Mitterrand expressed it in his message to parliament on 8 April 1986. Seen in this light, it rapidly became clear that France was to experience for the first time the strict implementation of the 1958 constitution without the extension of presidential powers that had been imposed by de Gaulle and his successors. The president retained his vast but almost unused emergency powers under Article 16 and his control over France's nuclear strike force. He also retained his reserved arbitral powers to dissolve parliament, to appoint the prime minister, to chair the Cabinet, and to determine whether referenda should be held but, just as political circumstances in the past had allowed presidents to extend these powers, now circumstances conspired to limit their effectiveness.

Constitutionally, the president could not dissolve parliament within twelve months of the preceding dissolution and, even after that period had elapsed, to anticipate the next elections which were due in only another twelve months would probably be electorally unwise and amount to inviting the electorate to repeat its verdict. (In fact, Mitterrand allowed events to run their course and only after his successful presidential re-election campaign did he dissolve parliament and regain the support of a new socialist majority in the National Assembly.) Whilst the president in theory still had a free choice of prime minister, his nominee needed the support of the National Asembly to function. Again Mitterrand accepted the logic of events and appointed Jacques Chirac, the leader of the largest party in the new majority. (He probably also made the political calculation that two years would not be sufficient to allow Chirac to make the hoped-for impact before the presidential elections.) As far as chairing the Council of Ministers was concerned, this now in effect became a purely titular rôle with the decisions being made in advance at Matignon by the prime minister and his ministerial colleagues. Lastly, while the president had the final say over whether a referendum should be called, the initiative had to come from the prime minister, which left the president with no more than the power of veto. In this deadlocked situation it is not surprising that in the event no referenda were called.

The president disposes of a similar power of veto over the ministerial nominations put forward to him by the prime minister. There were strong rumours to the effect that in the so-called *domaine réservé* Mitterrand made use of his veto to turn down Chirac's initial suggestions of François Léotard for the Defence Ministry and Jean Lecanuet for the Foreign Ministry, as these were heavyweight political figures with their own power base and political agenda who would have fought to impose their own views. However, this deadlock had to be broken and Mitterrand and Chirac reached a compromise on the appointment of two civil service 'technocrats', Jean-Bernard Raimond and André Giraud for foreign affairs and defence respectively. Mitterrand accepted without demur Chirac's nominations in other areas where he had less claim to presidential influence including the socialists' *'bête noire'* Charles Pasqua as Minister of the Interior.

A similar situation obtained with regard to the nomination of ambassadors, prefects and some other state officials, although in this case the power of nomination lay with the president but was subject to prime ministerial veto by virtue of the requirement for prime ministerial countersignature. Once again, however, the potential political damage of a lasting deadlock was such as to ensure that a compromise was eventually reached, with Mitterrand only delaying fresh appointments to ensure that his ousted protégés were moved to equally prestigious posts.

On the face of it, a potentially more significant power resided in the requirement for presidential signature of the governmental decrees known as *ordonnances* which were used to implement legislation following the passage of an enabling bill. Since Chirac had only two years to make an impact before the next presidential elections, he was heavily dependent on the use of enabling bills to rush through key legislation in complex areas such as privatisation which could have easily become bogged down if subject to lengthy parliamentary scrutiny. Invoking his rôle as defined by Article 5 of the constitution, Mitterrand refused to sign decrees on privatisation, on changes to the electoral boundaries system and a decree relating to changes to legislation on working hours.

There was considerable technical debate amongst political scientists and constitutional jurists over this issue with some observers, notably Duverger (1974: 79–109), maintaining as always that all presidential powers subject to prime ministerial countersignature were shared powers, with each protagonist being entitled to give or withhold their consent as they saw fit. Others argued that constitutional jurisprudence dictated that presidential signature was a formality which could only be withheld if the proposed measure was unconstitutional (Cohendet 1993: 101). This was clearly not Mitterrand's position, since he justified his decision in the case of privatisations and working practices by arguing the proposed changes reversed the progress achieved in these fields – clearly a political judgement. In the event, however, Mitterrand's stand had little practical impact since Chirac responded by making these issues a matter of confidence through the use of the infamous Article 49.3, and the legislation was only delayed by a matter of hours. A similar and – to political scientists at least – equally controversial refusal of the presidential signature occurred when Mitterrand refused the government's request for an extraordinary session of parliament to push through the privatisation of the Régie Renault, again delaying the government's legislative timetable.

Although Mitterrand exploited to the full, in highly debatable fashion, such loopholes as the constitution offered, this minimal delaying power was to represent the limit of the president's power to intervene in domestic issues, and it was significant that Chirac barely bothered to protest. Otherwise the president could only express disapproval of government policy and align himself as he did with groups of striking workers or students, but his power to make or directly influence policy had gone. *Cohabitation* had demonstrated once and for all that there was no solid constitutional basis for presidential domination of policy making in the domestic field – it was solely dependent on the parliamentary majority giving the president their support.

The area of foreign and defence policy, which was an area of special presidential interest, was to prove to be a different case altogether. There was no doubt that in times of national emergency the president could take all necessary powers under Article 16 to guarantee national independence and protect the integrity of French territory as his rôle under Article 5 required, and these dispositions had been buttressed by the decree giving the president control over the nuclear deterrent. However, as we have seen, the claim that in normal times foreign and defence policy constituted a presidential *domaine réservé* had a much shakier basis. His powers of nomination of ambassadors and signature of treaties were subject to prime ministerial countersignature and, according to normal constitutional practice and Third and Fourth Republic precedent, were no more than the formal endorsement of prime ministerial decisions. His position as commander-in-chief of French forces was again, according to precedent, a purely titular rôle and chairmanship of defence committees did not, *per se*, as had been demonstrated at an even higher level in relation to presidential chairing of the Council of Ministers, imply any decision-making powers.

This interpretation was further strengthened by Articles 20 and 21 which explicitly assigned policy-making powers to the government and responsibility for defence to the prime minister. Given these circumstances, many observers expected that cohabitation would destroy the 'myth' of the *domaine réservé*. However, the constitution comprises more than the text alone, and presidential dominance in these areas dated back to the birth of the Republic and had gathered considerable force of precedence. The Fifth Republic had been created as much to enable de Gaulle to resolve the Algerian crisis as to reform state institutions and twenty-eight years of presidential domination of foreign and defence policy had embedded this practice in the public consciousness. The political circumstances obtaining in 1986 also weighed heavily on the issue. Chirac had only a wafer-thin majority in parliament and many Gaullist deputies were imbued, as one might expect, with a presidentialist approach to French institutions. Chirac himself, given his presidential ambitions, would not want to weaken the presidency in any permanent manner, but above all knew that he would probably face a challenge in the forthcoming presidential elections from Raymond Barre, who was predicting that cohabitation would lead to a dangerous weakening and possible breakdown of French institutions. In these circumstances Chirac was concerned that *cohabitation* should be seen to run smoothly. Finally, opinion polls indicated that the electorate wanted *cohabitation* to succeed and would probably severely sanction either a president or a prime minister who was perceived to have sabotaged it.

In the field of foreign affairs it rapidly became established policy that at international summit meetings France would be represented by a 'tandem' of both president and prime minister who pursued a bipartisan policy. 'France must speak with a single voice with regard to foreign affairs', stated Mitterrand (in Favier 1991: 533), although with his well-practised ambiguity he left it unclear whether France's voice would be that of the president or that of president and prime minister speaking in unison. The reality was, however, given the well-established and long-standing consensus on foreign policy and the desire on both sides to avoid provoking conflict which would be seen as putting French interests at risk, that common policy was arrived at relatively easily with post-summit communiqués being jointly signed. The diplomat François Bujon de l'Estang who worked for the prime minister's office stated: '90 per cent of France's diplomatic activities were jointly managed in a flexible and problem-free manner' over these months and his counterpart Jean Musitelli from the presidential staff at the Elysée concurred: 'The necessary consensus over 90% of foreign policy meant that conflicts mainly surfaced over issues of protocol and over the fine print' (both in Favier 1991: 547). So it was that although there were behind-the-scenes squabbles over the number of government delegates to summits, over the flow of information between the Quai d'Orsay and the Elysée and over the replacement of ambassadors, little disagreement emerged over policy issues. Foreign policy had become, to quote Samy Cohen (in Cohendet 1993: 226), 'a sector of compulsory joint management'.

The same was not entirely true of defence policy, where there was not the same pressure to appear united to the outside world. Chirac's Defence Minister, André Giraud, although not a heavyweight politician, proved to have strong views of his own and Chirac himself set out to make use of the prerogatives which the constitution afforded him. The first disagreements came over modernisation of France's nuclear deterrent, with Mitterrand favouring improvements to France's nuclear submarine-borne strike force while Giraud and Chirac favoured mobile land-borne missiles. After the initial clashes, however, Chirac, mindful perhaps of the effect of an open row on public opinion and the ammunition it would give the Barristes, gave way. A subsequent quarrel over France's strategy for the use of short-range nuclear missiles again ended in victory for Mitterrand, who ironically supported the traditional Gaullist concept of their use as a final warning before all-out nuclear retaliation against Chirac's advocacy of NATO's flexible response strategy.[2]

With presidential influence prevailing in this manner it seemed that the theory of the *domaine réservé* had been vindicated, but the second period of *cohabitation* from 1993 to 1995, under the premiership of Edouard Balladur, took place against a very different political backdrop. The Right enjoyed a massive parliamentary majority and dominated every sphere of political life. Mitterrand, on the other hand, was perceived by many to be politically and personally discredited and this was borne out by the collapse of his opinion poll ratings. If it was still politically impossible to exclude the president from the policy-making process in the foreign and defence field, it seemed that it might no longer be possible for him to impose his views in the case of disagreement. The first indication that this might be the case came with the appointment without any resistance from the Elysée of two leading right-wing politicians to the Foreign and Defence Ministries: Alain Juppé of the RPR and François Léotard of the UDF, respectively. Such established politicians with their own power bases would be harder to override than their counterparts of the first period of *cohabitation*. However, the government still had to take account of the public's belief in presidential supremacy in this area and, as Balladur began to prepare his own bid for the presidency, of the public opprobrium that would attach to the protagonist perceived as responsible for any breakdown of *cohabitation*. Since the 'institutionalisation' of cohabitation structures described by Jean-Claude Zarka (1994b) which led to regular meetings between the president and his advisers and the prime minister and the foreign and defence ministers resulted in a joint formulation of policy and, as intended, muffled any policy disagreements, it is difficult to establish with any exactitude the respective influence of the Elysée and Matignon, particularly since both protagonists quite naturally stressed their own part in the decision-making process. Mitterrand's decision to continue the suspension of French nuclear testing, against Balladur's advice, seemed to indicate that Balladur was accepting that Mitterrand should have the final say: 'We do not agree but in the event it is the president who decides', as Mitterrand put it (in Bigaut 1995: 15), and Bigaut argues that the president generally prevailed in cases of disagreement. However, when in February 1995 Mitterrand, in one of the few tactical mistakes of his long career, suggested without prior consultation with either French or Algerian governments that a European conference should be called to discuss the conflict between Muslim fundamentalists and the Algerian military government, Alain Juppé and the Quai d'Orsay dissociated themselves from the proposal in the face of the Algerian government's hostility, leaving Mitterrand to twist in the wind. Clearly, with Mitterrand's prestige at its lowest ebb following a succession of scandals and with his presidency in its final 'lame duck' phase, it could no longer be assumed that where the president led in the *domaine réservé* the government would follow. There is some irony in the fact that just as the Algerian crisis in the late 1950s and early 1960s gave de Gaulle the opportunity to make foreign and defence matters his own preserve, so a new Algerian crisis thirty years later should finally reveal the limitations of the theory of the *domaine réservé* which, like other aspects of the presidential rôle, is finally subject to the prevailing political circumstances.

COHABITATION AND THE CONSTITUTION

The final question raised by *cohabitation* was whether, given the new-found importance attributed to the strict interpretation of the constitution, *cohabitation* finally represented the implementation of the constitution as presented by its authors in 1958. Was Maurice Duverger right in stating (1986: 7): 'The cohabitation of a left-wing president and a right-wing parliamentary majority will finally make it possible to implement the constitution of the Fifth Republic'? The answer in terms of the distribution of power is a qualified 'yes' – in economic and home affairs the government governs and in foreign and defence affairs it plays its part in the formulation of policy. However, the President of the Republic, although he wields the powers of the president arbiter, uses them for political purposes rather than in the impartial manner originally envisaged. He becomes the *de facto* leader of the opposition just as in normal times he is the *de facto* leader of the majority and it is this perspective that conditions his use of his powers.

As Jacques Chirac took over the presidency in 1995, holding in his grasp every lever of power, he cut a very different figure from the lonely president in internal exile that was François Mitterrand in his last days in office. But Chirac of all people knows that the political tide which swept him to power can ebb just as rapidly, taking with it much of his power and influence.

THE PRESIDENCY: CHRONOLOGY

1958 (May) Fall of Pflimlin government.
(June) Investiture of de Gaulle as last prime minister of Fourth Republic.
(September) Fifth Republic constitution approved by referendum.
(December) De Gaulle elected president by restricted electoral college.
1961 (April–September) De Gaulle takes emergency powers under
Article 16.
1962 (October) Referendum approves direct election of the president; Pompidou
government loses confidence of the National Assembly.
(November) Gaullist virtual majority elected to National Assembly.
1965 (December) De Gaulle elected president by universal suffrage.
1968 (May) Student revolt and general strike: de Gaulle dissolves National
Assembly.
1969 (April) De Gaulle resigns following 'no' vote in referendum on
regional reform.
(June) Pompidou elected president.
1974 (April) Death in office of Pompidou.
(May) Giscard elected president.
1976 (August) Chirac resigns as prime minister.
1981 (May) Mitterrand elected president.
(June) Mitterrand dissolves National Assembly.
1988 (March) Beginning of '*cohabitation*': Chirac appointed
prime minister.
(May) Mitterrand re-elected president.
1993 (March) Second period of *cohabitation*: Balladur appointed prime minister.
1995 (May) Chirac elected president.

NOTES

1 For the text of the constitutional draft, see Luchaire 1987: 251
2 See Chapter 3.

REFERENCES AND RECOMMENDED READING

Alibert-Fabre, V. (1990) 'La Pensée du Général de Gaulle à l'épreuve des cir-
constances', *Revue française de science politique*, 40, 5: 699–713.
Bigaut, C. (1995) 'Les Cohabitations institutionnelles', *Regards sur l'Actualité*,
211: 3–30.
Claisse, G. (1980) *François Mitterrand, Ici et maintenant (conversations avec G.
Claisse)*, Paris: Fayard.
* Cohendet, M-A. (1993) *La Cohabitation, leçons d'une expérience*, Paris: PUF.
A detailed analysis of cohabitation in theory and practice.
* Colliard, J-C. (1995) 'Qui gouverne la France?' *Pouvoirs 68*, Paris: Seuil.
A lucid analysis of presidential/prime ministerial relations.
de Gaulle, C. (1990) *Le Fil de l'épée*, Paris: Plon.
Duverger, M. (1974) *La Monarchie républicaine: comment les démocraties se donnent
des rois*, Paris: Laffont.
—— (1986) *Bréviaire de la cohabitation*, Paris: PUF.
Favier, P. (1991) *La Décennie Mitterrand* (Vol. 2), Paris: Seuil.

Georgel, J. (1990) *La Cinquième République: un démonarchie*, Paris: Librairie Générale de Droit et Jurisprudence.

Gicquel, J. (1989) 'De la cohabitation', *Pouvoirs. La Ve Republique: 30 ans*: 69–79.

Institut de Gaulle (1990) *De Gaulle et ses premiers ministres*, Paris: Plon.

Kramer, S. (1995) 'Interview', *Le Point*, 179.

Luchaire, F. (1987) *Documents pour servir à l'élaboration de la constitution de la Ve République* (Vol. 1), Paris: La Documentation française.

Maus, D. (1982) *Textes et documents sur la pratique institutionnelle de la Ve République*, Paris: La Documentation française.

Quermonne, J-L. (1980) *Le Gouvernement de la France sous la Ve République*, Paris: Dalloz.

* Zarka, J-C. (1994a) *Le Président de la Ve République*, Paris: Ellipses.

A concise, probing and up to date study of the presidency.

—— (1994b) 'Le Domaine réservé à l'épreuve de la deuxième cohabitation', *Revue politique et parlementaire* 969: 40–4.

Zorgibe, C. (1993) *De Gaulle, Mitterrand et l'esprit de la constitution*, Paris: Hachette.

2

PARTY POLITICS

Máire F. Cross

Parties are a product of long-term historical developments. Contemporary events are usually loaded with historical significance: on 7 May 1995, Jacques Chirac regained possession of the presidency for the Gaullist party, once the largest right-wing movement France has ever seen, after an absence of twenty-one years (Georges Pompidou was the last Gaullist to hold this office from 1969 until his death in April 1974). The public sector strikes in December 1995 and the death of François Mitterrand on 8 January 1996 rekindled memories of past glories and polemics of left-wing politics in France.

Historical legacy does not go the whole way to explaining the structure of the party system in France, however. New developments are also constantly shifting the political scene. In recent elections in France the mainstream parties were challenged by breakaway movements from within and by new organisations. The *Front national* which has captured an increasing number of votes since 1974, is the most notorious threat to the egalitarian principles of the Republic. The ecologists have made several incursions into the democratic process. The system in which the political parties have evolved in France over the past 200 years is highly centralised, characterised by frequent institutional changes in the formal process of democracy, a multitude of different kinds of electoral consultations and a propensity for spontaneous, informal short-term action on the part of the citizens the parties wish to represent, rather than an enduring tradition of party involvement. While there seems to be constant change, nevertheless there is some historical consistency of party structure.

HISTORY OF PARTY STRUCTURE AND IDEOLOGY

The decisive moment in the creation of modern French politics is usually considered to be 1789, but it was not until the foundation of the Third Republic in the 1870s that a regularly elected parliamentary system began to emerge and with it a party system. Since then strident and often rigid ideological differences have existed alongside a loose and almost chaotic party structure.

Left-inspired politicians who all accepted the tenets of the 1789 Revolution created the first organised parties with official titles, electoral programmes and organisations structured from elected executive officers at national level down to local bases. The *Parti radical* is one of the oldest parliamentary parties, dating from the beginning of the twentieth century. Its hegemony of the Left was challenged by the SFIO (*Section française de l'internationale ouvrière*), in turn challenged by the *Parti communiste français* (PCF) after the party congress in Tours in 1922. The *Parti radical* was a party of *notables* or local powerful personalities with no interest in building up a mass movement. It relied on local personalities to drum up support and votes. It was adamantly anti-clerical, promoting a lay egalitarian centralised education system as the essence of modern republicanism. When challenged on social issues by the new socialist movement it defended farmers, shopkeepers and employers against an interfering state and it defended the principles of liberal capitalism against an interventionist collectivist workers' movement championed by the SFIO and the PCF. The three parties were often at loggerheads in the Chamber although they also entered into successful electoral alliances against the Right, such as in 1924 and 1932. When the alliance finally succeeded in forming the *Front populaire* government of 1936 the ideological differences were such that the period of reform brought very limited results. Nevertheless, it was an historic alliance of these three parties into a broad Left movement and it fully involved the communists in the electoral process as a party like any other democratic organisation, fully accepting the legitimacy of parliamentary democracy it had previously condemned as bourgeois. While the *Parti radical* was a party of lower-middle-class and petty-bourgeois *notables*, after 1922 the two socialist parties were more interested in competing with each other for workers' and peasant support and for ideological supremacy, the main bone of contention being whether to follow the example set down by the successful Bolshevik Revolution in Russia, as the PCF wished, by insisting on the importance of the class struggle, or to continue along social democratic lines favoured by the SFIO, tempted to seek electoral support from sections of enlightened lower-middle- and middle-class as well as working-class voters.

The peak of PCF popularity was as a result of heroic acts of its members during the German occupation of France after military defeat in 1940. The PCF, already outlawed by Third Republic politicians in 1939 after the Hitler–Stalin pact, proved a formidable resistance movement, encouraging women to join its ranks, and won its highest electoral score in the legislative elections immediately after the war as one of the three most popular parties. In spite of having the most active recruitment policy of any political party in France, it has been in steady decline ever since due mainly to failure to renew leadership or policy, to the disappearance of the traditional voters in the blue-collar industries, and to the position as junior partner with the successful *Parti socialiste* in electoral alliances of the 1970s and 1980s. This period saw a swing to the centre of policies advocated by the socialist government.

For the Left the tradition of a strong ideological inheritance based on revolutionary principles of class equality and abolition of privilege through a programme of massive state intervention to regulate the economy on collectivist principles was a luxury of opposition, far removed from the reality of what could be achieved within the constraints of office. This lesson in government occurred relatively late for France, in 1981, compared to the experience of the British Labour party in the 1960s and 1970s. The ambition of holding office has altered the original priorities of the socialist party; the Fabius government (1984–6) heralded the end of attempts to alter the *status quo* by interventionist means. The socialist party became the party of compromise with the presidential régime and with the capitalist economy, with Mitterrand becoming more Gaullien than de Gaulle, distancing himself from the socialist party as he ran the 1988 election campaign on his presidential merits. Efforts by socialists at grassroots level to enter into dialogue with and take on board new pressure groups of feminists, ecologists or immigrants cannot disguise this shift to the right by the leadership.

While the Left derived its inspiration from the need for social reform through state intervention and collective organisation of the economy and is associated with the constant need to reaffirm an identity with the egalitarian principles of the revolutionary past, the Right has a greater problem of ideological identification. The inherent contradiction of the Right in France is that it is economically divided between interventionists and liberals and, until de Gaulle's exercise of power, its experiences were associated with failed régimes: monarchy (1815–48) and empire (1852–70) in the nineteenth century and the *Etat Français* led by Pétain (1940–4) in the twentieth. Formal party structures were anathema to the Right before the creation of the *Rassemblement du peuple français* (RPF) in 1947, and even then the Gaullists strenuously avoided using the term '*parti*'. The Right has traditionally preferred the terms '*mouvement*', '*rassemblement*', '*union*', or '*groupe*'. The many factions composed of historical leftovers of monarchism, Bonapartism and retrograde Catholicism refused to combine into an organised movement but presented themselves as moderate republicans or independent candidates during elections. The Pétain collaborationist régime discredited the Right in the first elected chamber after the war, but its chance for revival came when de Gaulle, in an attempt to shake off the *régime des partis* formed the new political group, the RPF, to promote a vision of France in his name. The Gaullists denounced the communists but were equally in favour of state intervention for national prestige, were socially conservative and appealed largely to the Catholic and rural vote. Many women who voted for the first time in 1945 favoured the Gaullists. Parties have often been divided in name only: the Fourth Republic was blighted from the start when the PCF and the RPF refused to fully endorse its constitution for different reasons. The

Gaullists wanted a stronger executive, the communists wanted a single chamber to represent the nation, and an abolition of the Senate.

The immediate post-war period also saw the transformation of another resistance group into a briefly successful centrist Catholic force, the *Mouvement républicain populaire* (MRP), which also assiduously avoided the term *'parti'*. It upheld social reforms proposed by the Left and favoured French involvement in the construction of the European Community, but was unrepentant in allegiance to Catholicism and its demand for state aid for Catholic schools. Although it gained as many votes initially as the SFIO and PCF, it did not last beyond the Fourth Republic, which collapsed in 1958 during and as a result of the Algerian War of Independence.

BIRTH OF THE FIFTH REPUBLIC AND THE PRESIDENTIAL SYSTEM

The Fifth Republic came into being because of a disastrous lack of co-operation between political parties on the working of the régime under the Fourth Republic. In spite of a wide consensus on social and economic recovery through modernisation, politicians of the Fourth Republic could agree on little else. Governments were accountable to the majority vote in the National Assembly. The fact that no political party had an overall majority meant ministries lasted weeks, even days, before being forced to resign from lack of support for their decisions. This was supposedly the nightmare scenario never to be repeated once de Gaulle's model constitution of the Fifth Republic was in place.

After a period out of office (1946–58), known as the *traversée du désert* (crossing the desert), the hero of the Liberation, General Charles de Gaulle returned to the presidency, the pinnacle of political power, by-passing political party structures, but having ensured the creation of a movement, the RPF, which this time would sustain him in the position he had lost in 1946. There was now to be a much stronger executive in charge of the legislature (the National Assembly), thereby reducing the traditional power base of electoral parties. As a result of this reorganisation, the Centre disappeared, the Left went into decline. The decline was engineered at least in part through the electoral systems. The communists had deputies in the ten most-populated constituencies created in 1958 and the Gaullists had deputies in the ten least-populated constituencies. The non-Gaullist Right was over-shadowed by the populist all-embracing movement which went through several changes of name (*Rassemblement du peuple français* (RPF) in 1947, *Union pour la nouvelle République* (UNR) in 1958, *Union pour la défense de la République* (UDR) in 1968, *Union des démocrates pour la République* (UDR) in 1971, *Rassemblement pour la République* (RPR) in 1976) but rigidly stuck to the notion of loyalty to the General and the authoritarian constitution put directly to the French.

De Gaulle had introduced the use of the referendum in his new style of constitution in 1958 and used this process to appeal directly to the French for a decision about the first direct election of the president by universal suffrage, thus further weakening the authority of the parliamentary process by proposing in this referendum to introduce a two-round ballot with the two best-placed candidates going through to the second round. In a perverse way, the process has strengthened the *régime des partis*, giving the French citizens the luxury of stating their preference among several candidates (see Table 2.1) in the first round before having to choose between two in the second. As far as legislative elections were concerned, it was not long before multiple lists reappeared, bearing a strong resemblance to Third and Fourth Republic parties, with several small right-wing parties – the *Républicains indépendants* (RI) (becoming the *Parti républicain* (PR) after 1974), the *Centre des démocrates sociaux* (CDS) (the rump of the MRP) and the right-wing split of the old *Parti radical*. This non-Gaullist Right made a comeback in 1974 when Valéry Giscard d'Estaing made a successful bid for the presidency against François Mitterrand after the death of de Gaulle's successor, Georges Pompidou. The smaller groups soon created a new umbrella organisation, the *Union pour la démocratie française* (UDF) in 1977, to combat the *Rassemblement pour la République*. This move epitomised the specificity of the French political party system: small groups clinging to their separate identity in a loosely structured movement created around a personality in power, this time Valéry Giscard d'Estaing. The changes in the electoral system and new rules of parliamentary procedures ensured greater discipline and defined party politics more clearly into two camps: the government side, *la majorité*, or the opposing side, *l'opposition*.

Table 2.1 Votes for candidates in the presidential elections, May 1995

Candidate	% Vote
Round 1	
Lionel Jospin, Parti socialiste (PS)	23.31
Jacques Chirac, Rassemblement pour la République (RPR)	20.73
Edouard Balladur, Rassemblement pour la République (RPR)	18.54
Jean-Marie Le Pen, Front national (FN)	15.07
Robert Hue, Parti communiste français (PCF)	8.69
Arlette Laguillier, Lutte ouvrière (Extrême gauche)	5.32
Dominique Voynet, Les Verts (Ecologiste)	3.32
Phillipe de Villiers, Mouvement pour la France (Extrême droite)	4.75
Jacques Cheminade, Parti ouvrier européen (Extrême droite)	0.27
Participation Rate	78.3
Round 2	
Jacques Chirac, RPR	52.59
Lionel Jospin, PS	47.41

Source: Portelli 1995: 3–14

It was this process in the legislative and presidential elections of an initial eliminatory round and a two-candidate second round which forced parties of the Left and the Right to reorganise into a larger movement if they were to rule France. This reinforced what traditionally had already occurred frequently in some areas, whereby electoral pacts would be formed among allies of the Left or Right to vote for the most strongly placed candidate to prevent the opposition gaining a seat. Although the legislative elections in particular had already established a tradition of what is known as republican discipline since the earliest Third Republic elections, under the Fifth Republic this process was more significant for the stronger executive. The success of the presidential campaigns depends on the candidate's ability to override animosity among the various camps and ensure mutual recognition of the need for closer partnership in government, not always forthcoming between socialists and communists, nor between the UDF and RPR outside electoral campaigns. The trajectory followed by François Mitterrand will illustrate this. After a few false starts, notably in 1965 and 1968, Mitterrand, an outsider to the SFIO (whose electoral fortunes were by now at their lowest ebb), reorganised the Left, giving it a new party name, the *Parti socialiste*, created in 1971, and engaged in fresh dialogue with the other left-wing political parties, chiefly the PCF under Georges Marchais, with whom the *Programme commun de gouvernement* was signed in 1972. During the 1974 campaign the old *Parti radical* split into two camps – Mitterrand and Giscardian supporters. The leader of the *Parti socialiste unifié* (PSU), a breakaway party of 1958, Michel Rocard, joined the PS after the close defeat of François Mitterrand in 1974, further strengthening the chances of a left-wing victory, which eventually occurred in 1981. Thus the strong ideological division which de Gaulle was so anxious to eliminate was momentarily reinforced by his introduction of a presidential election by direct universal suffrage.

In the meantime, the Centre parties withered very quickly. By the 1970s the bipolarisation of the French electorate seemed to be rigidly in place. Within each of the two ideological camps appeared two major groups with almost equal electoral weight: on the Left the PS and the PCF, on the Right the RPR and the newly formed UDF. As long as the Left was condemned to permanent opposition it was hardly an equal balance of power. This 'equilibrium' of a *quadrille bipolaire* (UDF–RPR and PS–PCF) was not to last. At this stage citizen participation in elections was at a peak and the smallest percentage of votes went to parties outside these four.

1981: THE LEFT IN POWER AND THE RIGHT IN OPPOSITION

The decline of traditional ideological differences among the mainstream parties truly became apparent after 1981 with new movements coming on stream. A new era had begun for party politics from 1981 onwards when there began a more equitable experience of majority and opposition for the Left and Right, with the *Parti socialiste* winning the presidency and an unprecedented absolute majority of seats in the National Assembly in 1981. This victory changed the balance of power among parties. The PCF was now a minor partner. Its voters had followed the logic of republican tactics and voted for Mitterrand's government in 1981. The PCF was rewarded with four ministries in Prime Minister Mauroy's team, but the party became quickly disillusioned by the U-turns in policy and left the government in July 1984. Communists became more critical thereafter and were less loyal to the socialists in 1986, and to the Mitterrand candidate for the presidency in 1988. This time many centrist votes went to securing Mitterrand's second term in office as the Right in opposition floundered and lost its ability to form the cohesive electoral force necessary to oust the socialists from power.

From 1981 onwards the RPR changed tack under the leadership of Jacques Chirac and moved away from being a neo-Bonapartist populist movement to become a right-wing party of liberal economic policies proposing privatisation to counter the effect of socialist interventionist measures. As the socialists had already made their own economic adjustment to the right by 1983, the differences between the mainstream parties were to decline. The experience of cohabitation of a left-wing president and right-wing government in two periods – 1986 to 1988 and 1993 to 1995 – further eroded the benchmarks of Right and Left. While the decline of the Communist Party did not provoke any alarm, especially among the mainstream parties, new developments did (Bayle 1995): first the rise of the *Front national* (FN), a threat to the Right, and second the rise of an ecology movement which was a potential threat to the Left. While the mainstream parties, the RPR, UDF and PS, have elected representatives at all levels (European, national, regional and municipal), the smaller outside or minor parties can field candidates at certain levels only, that is, in the first round in the presidential elections, European, regional and municipal elections – with considerably more success at the regional elections of 1994 and the municipal elections in June 1995 than the mainstream parties would care to admit.

THE MULTI-PARTY SYSTEM

The French electorate has never voted so often as it has done in the past sixteen years. At the same time, the highest ever number of parties in the Fifth Republic (see Table 2.2) is in stark contrast to the lowest ever level of party membership. Yet, as we have seen, there has been a historical fragmentation of political groups in France. We have seen that the electoral system goes a long way to imposing discipline on the multiparty system.

The bodies to which the French elect party representatives are the various local councils (*municipal, cantonal, régional*), the National Assembly and the Senate, the European Parliament, and the presidency. The main parties

Table 2.2 Affiliations of candidates at the municipal elections, June 1995

AC A Cuncolta (Corsican Nationalists)
AD Association des démocrates
ADS Alternative pour la démocratie et le socialisme (ex-Parti communiste)
Alternatifs
AREV Alternative rouge et verte
Autonomistes
CNI Centre national des indépendants
Divers inclassables
Divers droite
Divers gauche
Extrême gauche
Extrême droite
FN Front national
GE Génération écologie
Indépendantistes
LCR Ligue communiste révolutionnaire
LO Lutte ouvrière
MD Mouvement des démocrates
MDC Mouvement des citoyens
MDR Mouvement des réformateurs
MEI Mouvement des écologistes indépendants
Nationalistes
PC Parti communiste
PCG Parti communiste de Guadeloupe
PCM Parti communiste martiniquais
PCR Parti communiste réunionnais
PH Parti humaniste
PPDG Parti progressiste démocratique guadeloupéen
PPM Parti progressiste martiniquais
PS Parti socialiste
PT Parti des travailleurs
Régionalistes
RPR Rassemblement pour la République
SEGA Solidarité écologie gauche alternative
UDF Union pour la démocratie française
UDF – CDS Centre des démocrates sociaux
UDF – P. et R. Clubs perspectives et réalités
UDF – PR Parti républicain
UDF – PSD Parti social–démocrate
Un.d listes d'union de la droite
Un.g listes d'union de la gauche
UPC Union du peuple corse

Source: *Le Monde* 20 June 1995: 20

capable of obtaining enough electoral strength to have formed the national governments of the past fifteen years are the Gaullist movement, now known as the RPR, ruling jointly with the Centre-Right broad alliance, the UDF and the left-wing Social Democratic Party modernised by Mitterrand in 1971, the PS. Parties which have been junior partners in government and electoral alliances with the PS are the PCF, the PSU and the *Mouvement des radicaux de Gauche* (MRG). Marginal parties with little hope of obtaining a place in national government but which have been increasingly successful at local and European elections since the mid-1980s are the ecologists, now split into the *Mouvement des écologistes*, *Génération Ecologie*, and *Les Verts* and the extreme right-wing party the *Front national*.

Parties with populist appeal such as the *Front national* have the same values as the new group *Mouvement pour la France*, created by Philippe de Villiers, a presidential candidate in April 1995; both are anti-European and anti-immigrant but use different tactics. The PCF shares an anti-European ticket with the *Front national* and appeals to the masses in its grassroots approach, whereas the PS has become a well-oiled party machine with a declining popular base after its recent experience of government and rapid downfall in the 1993 parliamentary elections. Similarly, the RPR likes to portray itself as a movement of ordinary French people, and the more élitist UDF approach relies on a small number of activists to lead the country. Populist/élitist, mainstream/marginal, these categories are particular to both sides of the other great divide in French politics, the Left and Right.

Table 2.3 Results of legislative elections, March 1993

Political affiliation	Votes	Votes (%)	Seats in National Assembly (577)
Abstentions	—	31.1	—
PCF	2,331,399	9.2	24
PS and allies	4,874,978	19.2	67
Ecologists	2,716,313	10.7	—
UPF (= RPR and UDF)	10,074,796	39.7	449
Other Right	1,118,032	4.4	36
FN	3,152,543	12.4	—
Non-party	—	4.4	1

Source: Hall, Hayward and Machin 1994: 302

Whom do parties represent? In 1981 over 90 per cent of votes cast at parliamentary elections went to the candidates of the four parties in two blocks, Left and Right; in 1993 only 68 per cent of the votes went to the same four main parties. In 1993, 82 per cent of the elected members in the National Assembly belonged to a group which only scored 41 per cent of votes cast in the first round. Thirty-three per cent of the electorate were not represented in parliament (see Table 2.3). This is a distortion between reality and legality, between what is termed the *pays réel* and the *pays légal*.

The Left is still coming to terms with its fall from government in 1993, when it found itself back in opposition with fewer than 100 of the 577 seats. This result was an unmitigated disaster for the Left but the election was equally significant for the mainstream right-wing parties forced into a pre-electoral alliance called *Union pour la France* (UPF, created in 1990) which resulted in a return to parliament of the new right-wing coalition of RPR and UDF with a massive overall majority of seats. The new hegemony was further reinforced on 6 May 1995 when Jacques Chirac, leader of the RPR since 1976, won the most prestigious political prize of the Fifth Republic, elected president with 52.7 per cent of the votes cast. His seven-year mandate in the Elysée Palace means the Right is now in control of the legislature with a UDF–RPR partnership holding an absolute majority in the National Assembly and the Senate. Together with the majority of seats in the 22 regional councils, the local councils, and in the European Parliament, the right-wing parties hold considerable power at all levels of democracy in France. There have been few occasions in French politics when power has been so concentrated in the hands of one movement and even more significantly with a reduced opposition of minuscule proportions.[1] Nonetheless, the most significant recent change since 1981 was that for the first time in the history of the Fifth Republic there has been a change of parties in power, *alternance* of left- and right-wing governments, an essential requirement for any parliamentary democracy.

Constitutional changes of rules have not been the only factor to alter the face of party politics; the social and economic backdrop has also changed. The rapid growth of the industrial and service sectors after the war, the modernisation of the agricultural sector and ensuing rural exodus, the development of long-term unemployment since the 1970s and ensuing poverty of a deprived urban population have had repercussions on voting patterns and political affiliations. One explanation for the growth of marginal parties is the expression of protest and insecurity as the voters seek a scapegoat to blame for the disappearance of their old way of life, such as European bureaucrats or immigrant workers. Comfortably-off citizens in a rural setting, voting for ecology movements, in reaction to the modern discomforts of pollution, waste and unemployment, are also protesting at the lack of relevance of old ideological divisions to their daily lives. Yet, of the recent developments in party politics in France there has been no strong ideological challenge to the institutional *status quo* of the Republic on any party agenda during elections (Ehrmann and Schain 1992: 71). Social and political dissent exist, provoking massive street demonstrations against policies or single issues, particularly since the Right returned to power in 1993. The 1993 Bayroux law intended to increase funding to private schools provoked massive demonstrations in favour of public education and was withdrawn just as the socialist government's Savary laws of 1984, intended to reduce private schools' autonomy, had to be withdrawn in the face of public outcry. The Balladur government also withdrew plans for changes to a nationalised company after the prolonged strikes in Air France in 1993. In 1995, the Juppé government's proposals to reduce public spending deficits by altering pension schemes and the national health system met with fierce hostility and strike action in which millions of public sector workers participated.

However rife social discontent may be, political parties in France have rarely benefited from an upsurge in membership; the majority of French citizens traditionally do not channel their frustrations into planned involvement in political parties. Although figures for membership are notoriously difficult to obtain and extremely unreliable as there is no official or accurate record of membership kept by any party (Hall, Hayward and Machin 1994: 46), at present all parties reluctantly acknowledge a crisis of membership which began in the early 1980s.

ELECTORAL PROCESSES

The growth of new parties coincided in France with the period when democracy was considerably extended during the 1980s. As part of their reform programme, the Mauroy and Fabius socialist governments introduced new electoral consultation procedures. The European and regional assemblies were established with universal suffrage. Proportional representation has been introduced using a national single-party list system alongside the well-established practice of the single-member constituency two-round poll. The Communist Party was rescued from oblivion in 1986 by the socialists' introduction of single-ballot proportional representation, which gave them thirty-five seats in the National Assembly. But with the same system, intended as a damage limitation exercise for the socialists' electoral chances, the *Front national* gained an equal number of seats in the 1986 elections, thereby gaining a new level of legitimacy, and weakening the mainstream right-wing parties, to the benefit of the Left. In the legislative elections of 1988 and 1993 run under the old single-member constituency system with two ballots, the FN gained as many votes as the PCF nationally, but they have no seats in parliament. In France, electoral rules are not defined in the constitution, which renders it possible for parties in power to manipulate results. It was a fear of electoral defeat that drove the socialists to alter the electoral system in 1986, and the same disquiet inspired the RPR to reverse this decision.

These latest alterations fit into a method that has been used frequently for strategic purposes over the past 200 years. The extension of voting rights had also been a gradual process over the same period. All men were first granted the vote in the Second Republic of 1848, although many were disenfranchised by residential qualifications introduced by Louis Napoléon. Women have voted since 1945. Valéry Giscard d'Estaing extended the vote to all eighteen-year-olds when he was elected president in 1974. One issue which has yet to reach the statute books is the question of immigrants' franchise. Mitterrand's suggestion for immigrants to have a vote at the municipal elections came to nothing as did the attempt to have parity of men and women on candidates' lists. This latter proposal was blocked by the *Conseil constitutionnel*.

The extension of the suffrage and the creation of bodies newly elected by universal suffrage – presidency, regional councils and European deputies – has further increased the uneven involvement of political parties in the democratic process, as only those candidates with well-organised election teams can succeed in winning seats. On the other hand, the increasing cost of electioneering has placed pressure on party funds, which would explain the numerous scandals of financial corruption in all parties. Until 1988 there was no system in place to control party finances nor to subsidise funding.

So far it has been established that the numerous parties in France have been affected by presidentialisation and electoral changes. Recent changes are also due to the decline of traditional ideological differences between the mainstream parties and the fragmented nature of any ideological renewal within the marginal parties.

TRADITIONAL IDEOLOGY IN DECLINE

To win the presidency candidates must appeal to a broad spectrum of voters in order to obtain over 50 per cent of the electorate's support; as a result the programmes of mainstream party candidates have become secondary; ideological differences have altered. Historic differences among parties have become blurred in the centre; in both left- and right-wing parties new movements appear around ambitious personalities, anxious to obtain support from the waverers in the opposite camp. Chirac's electoral promises of building a France to eliminate social exclusion, traditionally a theme of the Left, appealed to the electorate; his failure to keep his promises is now being challenged (Kahn 1995: 8).

The definition of Right and Left is critical not only to define party politics in France but also in our assessment of French specificity. The question which concerns political activists and commentators alike in France is whether the apparent recent decline of the traditional ideological Right–Left divide since 1981, which has been inherent in France since 1789, is really a positive development for the party system. There are reasons for disquiet about the disappearance of distinctive traits among the mainstream parties, mainly the following: the fear of massive abstention and withdrawal of the citizen from the political process, thereby rendering the democratic process meaningless; the lack of renewal or replacement of a new ideological motivation which would give identity and purpose to new movements and engage the voters in political participation at party level; the inability of existing mainstream parties to retain the majority of voters in their camp, and the haemorrhaging of votes to extreme parties of the Left or the Right. Paradoxically, according to surveys, more people than ever before accept the labels Right and Left while the floating-voter phenomenon is increasing. While the numerous opinion polls carried out in the months running up to the election found that voters were deciding at the very last minute which way to vote, the two rounds of the presidential election of April and May 1995 revealed that the electorate is more faithful to the Left and Right than was anticipated (Mayer 1995: 36). Electorally there has never been such a broad consensus on the workings of the French system than there is today, a factor essential for its survival. This in itself is no reassurance; votes for both Louis Napoléon and for de Gaulle were high just before their respective downfalls. The fears arise when the present situation is seen in a long-term view as a revival of constitutional instability.

Passivity of citizens as obedient voters as an outward sign of political stability has been deceptive in the past. Chirac has been successfully elected to power but the discontent of the citizens who did not vote at all or whose candidate did not succeed, is a constant worry; 15 per cent of the vote went to Jean-Marie Le Pen, who proposed simplistic solutions to complex problems with which many voters identify as relevant to their own anxieties. The gap between the *pays légal* and the *pays réel* means that the democratic process is once more under duress in France, the country traditionally reputed as liable to revolution by spontaneous rioting. Alongside the bipolar divide, institutional instability, considered to be one of the inherent characteristics of French politics, is a great hang-up from the past. As a consequence of unpredictable and uncontrollable political participation, the French historical experience of revolution and upheaval produced relatively volatile changes of régime.

STRENGTHS AND WEAKNESSES OF THE SYSTEM

On the one hand the French proudly vaunt their rich revolutionary past as a contributing factor to their unique political system, a sophisticated parliamentary and presidential régime with frequent electoral consultations and, on the other, they realise there is an undercurrent of potential protest which could spring to the surface unexpectedly. For this reason they worry about the abstention rates in elections. To a much lesser extent they note the lack of openness or transparency in the life of political parties either at grassroots or national level. Some ecologists have attempted to construct a more open, decentralised democratic process as part of their critique of traditional politics. However, sources on internal party structures or on party finances and membership are rare. Instead of expressing any disquiet, leaders and commentators assert that this is a further characteristic of French politics. This lack of citizen participation has a debilitating effect on the structure of political parties. It is one thing to vote, it is another to leave national politics to a small number of party activists who jealously guard their privileges. Women find it extremely hard to penetrate the inner sanctum of party leadership. While political parties now tend to be run by élites who are very secretive about party membership, this does not reduce the cost of running elections. Poor membership levels provide little in the way of party revenue. Parties are not only quashed by a domineering presidency, they also suffer financially from lack of support from a buoyant party membership.

Lack of party membership does not imply a lack of interest in party politics. There is a constant observation of changing party strengths through the media. The interplay between perceptions of party popularity and citizen behaviour is subject to permanent scrutiny by radio and television comment-ators appealing directly to citizens to provide information about their opinions without encouraging them to take an active part in the political process through political affiliation. Opinion pollsters predict results and political scientists analyse them; the parties are stranded in between.

As a consequence of the primordial rôle of television and opinion polls in information-gathering exercises, the traditional rôle of parties as sole pro-viders of political information has diminished. On the other hand, parties play an essential rôle in the politics of communication. Television channels and radio programmes provide a particularly vital platform for personalities seeking power as individuals and as representatives of political parties. Of course, the mundane running of a political party is not interesting to the media unless there is a crisis. There is a morbid interest in the details of the dramatic downfall of political leaders implicated in financial corruption. Media attention has a fixation for the malfunctioning of parties from an individual perspective and not from an ideological or tactical dimension. Indeed, it is no coincidence that financial political scandals have come to the fore in France in the 1980s and 1990s. For political parties coping with the soaring financial costs of frequent, costly electoral consultations, the temptation to seek funding from the business world in an unorthodox manner was rife, on the Left and on the Right. It was not until the late 1980s that attempts were made by governments to wipe the slate clean by declaring an amnesty for past misdemeanours and providing legislation for party funding by subsidising election costs according to the percentage of votes gained, putting a ceiling on party spending and establishing accountability by public transparency. The existence of political financial scandals also has historic precedents in French politics such as the Panama scandal and the Stavisky affair of the Third Republic.

All of the above indicates how the traditional rôle of political parties has altered in recent years. Internal party structure is the least-discussed aspect of party politics. Little is known beyond the outward structure of executive, national and regional committees, *assises nationales*, the party conferences, usually held every two years, summer schools and think-tanks. The PCF is the most highly structured party; in its revived form the *Parti socialiste* created a structure which enabled *courants* (tendencies) to exist and to be allocated places on its executive according to popularity within the party, but any real ideological differences between the different *courants* deteriorated into personality differences during the 1980s. In internal politics contemporary thorny issues are the power of the central committee to override decisions taken at grassroots level, the underrepresentation of women at the top level, resistance of party hacks once in power to attempts by younger generations to renew policy or remove ageing leaders from the head of the movements. This aspect of party politics has not changed.

Because party politics have rarely functioned with mass movements in France, considerable attention is given to election performance rather than to membership or activities around party structure other than changes of leadership. Changes of leadership in the PS are now seen as a prolongation of the presidential campaign. The person who controls the party has a fair chance of becoming presidential candidate.

The French political party landscape is just as fragmented as it was in the past but for different reasons. Yet the institutional structure ensures that the division between *majorité* and *opposition* conceals the fragmentation of parties, full of contradictions which, more often than not, are apparent around personalities rather than policy. This diversity of parties, which for a long time dominated local politics, is now manifest in the national contests such as in the presidential elections with no single party candidate able to command beyond 24 per cent of the first choice of the voters. By dint of the presidential system the mainstream parties command the stage without acquiring the majority of the citizens' votes. However, this also gives encouragement to the smaller parties such as the *Centre des démocrates sociaux*, the *Parti républicain*, or the *Front national*, or the ecologists, to use their success in local, regional and European elections as a springboard to achieve power nationally. While this is the traditional route to party expansion, the new parties are a long way from achieving this position.

CONCLUSION

In this chapter we have looked at the overall developments of French political party structure. The tradition of the distinctive cleavage of Right and Left is as strong as ever, because it is electorally useful if not ideologically relevant. The equally important tradition of fragmentation along strategic lines remains. Television, presidentialisation, economic changes of a post-industrial society and new urban problems have also had an effect on party politics but have not eradicated French specificity. There is a hierarchy of importance of parties with a hierarchy of importance of elections. The ecologist movement has succeeded in putting forward concerns on to the political stage but has been particularly prone to personality clashes and fragmentation. Immigrant issues have been absorbed into a new form of extreme-Right nationalism. Jean-Marie Le Pen's *Front national* can command a regular show of strength in presidential and local elections without ever hoping to win power under the present electoral system. Political parties have reverted to their Third and Fourth Republic rôles of stages for potential national leaders to launch their political career. The *partis des notables* have returned. Small wonder that the ecologists cannot create a powerful structure to hold together, women cannot penetrate the ranks of power, many voters are no longer faithful and Le Pen calls them all gangsters.

Any anxieties about the malfunctioning of the French party system stem from an inability or unwillingness to remove the constraints of a weighty historical legacy of weak party structure. However, the fact that the present party system continues to function within a régime which has survived now for nearly forty years is evidence that there is a new kind of consensus: there are increasingly fewer ideological or policy differences between the mainstream parties which have been in government, the RPR–UDF (now the UPF) from the Right and the PS from the Left, and it is for that same reason that the new and old fringe or peripheral parties – the PCF, the FN and the ecologists – have attracted an increasing percentage of votes over the past fifteen years. Beyond this, these alternative protest parties have yet to prove their ability to change the historical tradition whereby all successful parties in France function as small organisations tightly controlled by élites capable of sustaining frequent electoral campaigns and attracting votes but frequently split and divided over tactics and issues and now, with presidentialisation, more often over personality clashes driven by individual ambitions for office.

PARTY POLITICS: CHRONOLOGY

1901   Founding of *Parti radical.*
1905   Unity of socialist movement to form SFIO (*Section française de l'internationale ouvrière*).
1922   *Congrès de Tours*, split of the Left, creation of Communist Party.
1944   Creation of Christian Democratic party, MRP *Mouvement républicain populaire.*
1958   RPF changes name to UNR – *Union pour la nouvelle République.*
1960   Breakaway socialist group founded, PSU, *Parti socialiste unifié*, led by Michel Rocard.
1966   MRP changes to *Centre démocrate.*
        Liberal conservatives form RI, *Républicains indépendants.*
1968   UNR changes name to UDR, *Union des démocrates pour la République*
1971   *Congrès d'Epinay*, SFIO changes name to PS, *Parti socialiste*, led by François Mitterrand, CIR, *Convention des Institutions républicaines.*
1972   Joint Programme of Government signed between PCF and PS.
1974   Jean-Marie Le Pen candidate in first round of presidential elections.
        Parti radical splits, one group the MRG, *Mouvement des radicaux de Gauche* supporting the Mitterrand candidacy, and the other, the *Parti radical*, supporting the Giscard camp.
        Giscard d'Estaing, RI, narrowly wins presidency against François Mitterrand. Michel Rocard joins PS.

1976 UDR changes name to RPR *Rassemblement pour la République*, with Jacques
      Chirac as leader.
      Two centrist groups merge to become CDS, *Centre des démocrates sociaux*.
1977 Giscard's Party changes name to PR, *Parti républicain*.
1978 Creation of UDF, *Union pour la démocratie française*, (union of PR, CDS
      and *Parti radical*)
1981 Election of first socialist to presidency.
      Four communist ministers appointed to Mauroy government.
1984 *Front national* scores over 10 per cent of votes in European elections.
1986 Victory of RPR–UDF at legislative elections.
      First *cohabitation* period.
      Front national has 32 deputies in National Assembly under the PR voting
      system; *Parti communiste* has 35.
1988 Re-election of François Mitterrand to the presidency.
      PS has a relative majority in National Assembly.
      Prime Minister Rocard invites the Ecologist, Brice Lalonde, and the Centrists
      to join his government.
1993 Combined Right UDF–RPR to form UPF, *Union pour la France*; gains
      absolute majority in National Assembly.
      Second period of *cohabitation*.
1995 Split Ecologists succeed in fielding one candidate in first round of presidential
      elections.
      Election of Jacques Chirac to presidency.
      Jean-Marie Le Pen scores 15.07 per cent in first round of presidential
      elections; *Front national* makes further gains, taking control of towns of
      Orange, Toulon and Marignane in June municipal elections.

NOTES

1 Other notable occasions were in 1815 in the *Chambre introuvable*, in the 1860s
   at the end of the Second Empire, in 1919 in the *Chambre bleu horizon*, in June
   1968 after the student unrest and in 1981 when the PS was in the happy position
   of having an absolute majority for the first time ever, although they did not hold
   the balance of power at all levels, as does the Right at the time of writing.

PARTY POLITICS: REFERENCES AND
RECOMMENDED READING

Bayle, M. (1995) *Ça n'arrive pas qu'aux autres*, Toulon: Plein Sud.
Ehrmann, H.W. and Schain, M.A. (1992) *Politics in France*, New York: HarperCollins.
Hall, P., Hayward, J. and Machin, H. (1994) *Developments in French Politics*,
      Basingstoke and London: Macmillan.
Kahn, J-F. (1995) 'Chirac, pourquoi sa capitulation conduit au désastre', *L'Evénement
      du jeudi*, 2–8 November: 8–12.
Mayer, N. (1995) 'Elections and the Left–Right Division in France' *French Politics
      and Society*, 13,1, Winter: 36–44.
Plenel, E. and Rollet A. (eds) (1992) *La République menacée: dix ans d'effet Le Pen*,
      Paris: Le Monde éditions.
Portelli, H. (1995) 'L'Élection présidentielle d'avril–mai 1995', *Regards sur
      l'actualité*, 212, June: 3–14.

* Safran, W. (1991) *The French Polity* (3rd edn), New York and London: Longman.
  Contains chapters on recent economic and social contexts, parties and elections, interest groups, the executive and administration.
Stevens, A. (1992) *The Government and Politics of France*, Basingstoke and London: Macmillan.
* Wright, V. (1989) *The Government and Politics of France* (3rd edn), London: Unwin Hyman.
  Contains chapters on the growth of presidentialism and the government of France, presidential coalition building within the Left and the Right, and local influences on the centralised state.
* Ysmal, C. (1989) *Les Partis politiques sous la Ve République*, Paris: Montchrestien.
  A theoretical and historical discussion of the rôle of the parties and their strengths in the late 1980s.

3

DEFENCE POLICY

Rodney Balcomb

French foreign and defence policy has long been characterised by a concern for status and prestige, and on many occasions France has played, or attempted to play, a leading rôle in international, and especially European, affairs. Often original and creative, French policy has at times been successful and led to significant progress in, for example, Western European integration. At other times it has seemed to go against the grain of history and has failed or left France with policies which have been inconsistent and contradictory. Nowhere is the phrase *l'exception française* more appropriate than in the field of international affairs.

Since the Second World War, the main long-term preoccupations of French foreign and defence policy have been relations with the United States and the countries of the former Soviet bloc, and relations with France's European neighbours, in particular the Federal Republic of Germany.

Relations with both the United States and the former Soviet Union have been cool or cordial at different times in the post-war period. Today co-operation with the United States is much improved compared with the low point reached during the presidency of Charles de Gaulle and France is concerned to ensure that Russia, in its transition from communism, should receive support from the West. One consequence of President de Gaulle's efforts to distance France from the United States at a time when he wanted to develop closer relations with the Soviet bloc was France's withdrawal from NATO's integrated command structure (although not from the Atlantic Alliance as such), a situation which has persisted until the present day.

With regard to European policy, France in the 1980s and early 1990s has played a central rôle in promoting closer integration within the European Community, later to become the European Union. In this, France has tended to work in tandem with the Federal Republic of Germany, and the Franco-German axis is widely regarded as the main driving force within the Community.

Where defence is concerned, France is a major military power. In 1994 it had the largest armed forces in Western Europe,[1] and a range of air-, sea- and ground-launched nuclear weapons. The French armed forces have the duty of defending not only metropolitan France but also a number of far-flung overseas *départements* and territories. They took part in the Gulf War of 1991 and have in recent years participated in an increasing number of peacekeeping and humanitarian operations in places as far apart as Bosnia, Somalia, Rwanda and Cambodia. French troops are also stationed in several former African colonies with which France has signed defence treaties.

In addition to its membership of the Atlantic Alliance, France also belongs to Europe's two other security-related bodies, the Western European Union and the Organisation for Security and Cooperation in Europe (OSCE). France has long called for greater European influence within NATO. French governments under Presidents Mitterrand and Chirac have also pressed strongly for development of a 'European defence identity'. Such pressures have led to reactivation of the Western European Union and creation of the European Corps, discussed below.

Final determination of foreign and defence policy during the Fifth Republic has traditionally been regarded as the *domaine réservé* (preserve) of the president. The constitution of the Republic is ambiguous as to the rôles of the president and prime minister in the definition of policy in this area, but a number of factors have combined to create a situation in which, in practice, it is the president who has supreme authority over foreign policy and defence. This is particularly true of periods when the president and parliamentary majority – and hence the prime minister – are of the same political persuasion, but it is also generally true of periods of *cohabitation* (when president and parliamentary majority are politically opposed). During the *cohabitation* of 1986–8, it was President Mitterrand, not Prime Minister Chirac, who had the final say on major elements of foreign and defence policy such as East–West relations and European affairs, although there is evidence that the government effectively took over direction of some areas of external relations with a strong domestic aspect – foreign trade and matters relating to terrorism, for example (Howorth 1992: 45).[2]

Since the fall of the Berlin Wall in 1989 and collapse of communist régimes in Central and Eastern Europe and the former Soviet Union, the strategic landscape has changed profoundly. For forty years, defence policies of East and West, and the foreign policy positions which they reflected, were based on a bipolar international system, on the confrontation of two blocs, one led by the United States, the other by the Soviet Union. For member countries of NATO, the overriding concern was defence against the possibility of a massive attack with conventional and/or nuclear forces by Moscow and its Warsaw Pact allies. In the 1990s, this situation no longer exists. The former Soviet republics have gone their separate ways, the Warsaw Pact has been dissolved and Russia is not regarded as a potential enemy.

Though the risk of major international conflict has disappeared for the foreseeable future, the political changes in Eastern and Central Europe and the former Soviet Union have engendered new dangers. With the demise of communism there has been an emergence of long-suppressed nationalistic feelings and ethnic disputes which have led to situations of actual or potential conflict.

The end of the Cold War has also brought about another important change in international affairs. For decades, the United Nations Organisation often found itself deadlocked by East–West rivalry. Now that this has gone, the world body is able to play a more active rôle, and this has led to an expansion of international peacekeeping, peacemaking and humanitarian operations, with armed forces from a number of nations working together under the aegis of the UN.

The greatly changed political and strategic environment of the 1990s has obliged France and its partners within the Atlantic Alliance and the European Union to reassess major aspects of their foreign and defence policies. NATO has had to reform its strategy and command structure, and has taken on new rôles – acting for the United Nations in Bosnia, for example, and promoting friendship and co-operation with the former Warsaw Pact states.

Governments of NATO members have had to consider what response to give to the expressed wish of Central and East European states to join NATO, given that Russia has opposed such a move. They have had to consider what rôle should in future be played by nuclear weapons, given that Russia poses no immediate threat (while still possessing a vast arsenal of nuclear weapons), but that other countries, at present officially non-nuclear, may develop nuclear weapons. NATO countries have also had to decide to what extent they can cut military budgets and what steps they should, and can afford, to take to adapt manpower and equipment to the type of peacekeeping operation which is increasingly common after the Cold War.

France's problems of adjustment have, if anything, been greater than those of its allies, because of the very distinct posture which it has had, little changed in its fundamentals since the time of President de Gaulle.

Because of its absence from NATO's integrated command structure, France has sometimes been unable to influence major changes in NATO policy and organisation, for the simple reason that it was not present in fora where decisions were taken. As a result of its policy of independence and self-reliance in defence, another legacy of de Gaulle's presidency, France has over several decades given priority to development of nuclear weapons, to the detriment at times of its conventional forces. In the post-Cold War environment, this deterrent force has lost some of its importance. At a time when there is pressure to reduce military budgets, French governments have been faced with the need simultaneously to continue with major military equipment programmes initiated in the 1980s, to provide for the changed manpower and equipment requirements of the 1990s and to modernise the nuclear force. Another aspect of its policy of independence has been that France long sought, as far as possible, to be self-sufficient in production of equipment for its armed forces. The result was a major armaments industry in France which, to be economically viable, needed to export much of its output. The scaling-down of military budgets in recent years and growing international competition have created difficulties for the French arms industry, which is a major employer (see Buchan 1995 and Isnard 1995a); this led President Chirac to announce on 22 February 1996 a major re-structuring of the industry.

Many of France's political leaders have come to realise the disadvantages of pursuing a defence policy whose broad outlines were drawn up in the 1960s, in very different international circumstances. The policy, although initially controversial, gradually acquired wide public acceptance in France, and it has been difficult for politicians to advocate the jettisoning of important planks of de Gaulle's defence strategy.

While defence policy still bears, with modifications, the imprint of de Gaulle, the same is much less true of foreign policy. One important aspect, his attempt to carve out a special independent place for France between the two opposing blocs led by Washington and Moscow, and indeed to bring an end to the bipolar system, met with little real success in his own time, and has since been overtaken by events. The bloc system – or at least the Eastern bloc – has gone, but this is due to the failure of communist régimes and has little to do with the policies of de Gaulle.

Where Europe is concerned, there is a wide measure of agreement among French policy makers. De Gaulle was fiercely opposed to any form of European integration which smacked of supra nationalism and would erode France's full independence and freedom of decision. His successors have gradually moved away from this approach, to the point where Mitterrand, and after him Chirac, have been strong supporters of a common foreign and defence policy for the European Union and advocates of a single currency. In their enthusiasm for European integration and readiness to accept elements of supranationalism, French governments of the 1980s and 1990s have been more akin to governments of the Fourth Republic.

POLICY UNDER THE FOURTH REPUBLIC

During the Fourth Republic some of the major Western economic and defence organisations were founded. French governments played a considerable, at times catalytic, rôle in this.

After the Second World War, security was a major preoccupation of West European governments. There was a determination, especially on the part of France, to ensure that never again would Germany have the urge, or the opportunity, to behave aggressively towards its neighbours. Furthermore, the onset of the Cold War led to concern about Moscow's intentions. In 1947, Britain and France signed a defence treaty, the Treaty of Dunkirk. This was followed in 1948 by the Brussels Treaty, whose signatories – Britain, France, Belgium, the Netherlands and Luxembourg – agreed that, if any of them were attacked, they would 'afford the party so attacked all the military and other aid and assistance in their power'. Both treaties were ostensibly designed to counter any future aggression by Germany, but the participating governments must also have had in mind the danger from the East. A number of countries also wanted the United States to help defend Western Europe. Negotiations between the governments concerned led to the signing in Washington in 1949 of the North Atlantic Treaty. The founder members of NATO were the five signatories of the Brussels Treaty of 1948, plus the United States, Canada, Denmark, Iceland, Italy, Norway and Portugal. The Washington Treaty was designed to provide protection not against Germany but against the Soviet threat.

French anxiety about the return of Germany's industrial might set in train the process of economic integration still in progress within the European Union today. France, one of the four occupying powers in Germany (along with Britain, the United States and the Soviet Union) was reluctant to see Germany regain control of the industries of the Ruhr, whose coal and steel production would be important in any war in which Germany might engage. The West Germans, however, found it unjust that their production alone should be subject to control, and Britain and the United States proved unwilling to restrain the output of coal and steel from the Ruhr.

In 1950, France put forward an imaginative and far-sighted plan which met both German and French concerns. French Foreign Minister Robert Schuman proposed that all French and German coal and steel production should be placed under a common High Authority, in an organisation open to other countries of Europe. As a result of this proposal, the European Coal and Steel Community (ECSC) came into being in July 1952 with six members – France, West Germany, Italy, Belgium, the Netherlands and Luxembourg. Among the aims of the Community were creation of a common market in coal and steel and modernisation and expansion of production. The promoters of the ECSC were also very conscious that international economic integration would help bind the member countries closer together and thus make it less likely that they would ever go to war against each other again.

By its success, the ECSC laid the foundations of a broader and deeper community, the European Economic Community (EEC), which was established by the Rome Treaty of 1957 and came into being in 1958.

The ECSC consisted of a High Authority with considerable supranational powers, a parliamentary assembly with very limited powers, a council of ministers and a court of justice. The EEC followed the same pattern, with the Commission playing a rôle similar to that of the High Authority, although with fewer supranational powers.

The reduced supranationalism of the EEC when it was established can be seen as a consequence of the failure of another initiative, the European Defence Community (EDC) put forward by French Prime Minister René Pleven in October 1950.

Pleven's proposal was a response to pressure from NATO allies for West Germany to contribute to Western defence, and was designed to overcome strong opposition in France to the idea of German rearmament. The proposed EDC was supranational in concept. It would have involved creation of an integrated European army, under the operational control of NATO, which would have replaced national armies. In this way, German forces could have participated in the defence of Europe without coming under German control. A treaty instituting the EDC was signed in Paris on 27 May 1952 by France, Germany, Italy and the Benelux countries. Despite this, the EDC was never established, because the French National Assembly, which had previously supported Pleven's proposals, voted in August 1954 against ratification of the treaty. Among reasons for rejection of the treaty were continuing fear of German rearmament and hostility to the supranational aspect of the EDC. With failure of the EDC project in mind, the drafters of the Rome Treaty instituting the EEC did not include defence within its remit.

After the abandonment of plans for a European Defence Community, another way had to be found for the Federal Republic of Germany to participate in Western defence. The solution which emerged was based on the Brussels Treaty of 1948 and was formalised by the signing of the Paris Agreements on 23 October 1954. Under the terms of the Agreements, the three occupying powers in West Germany – the United States, Britain and France – ended the occupation régime and recognised the sovereignty of the Federal Republic of Germany (they retained rights only in regard to Berlin and an eventual reunification of West and East Germany); the Federal Republic agreed that the three former occupying powers should continue to station armed forces on German soil; the Federal Republic of Germany and Italy acceded to the Brussels Treaty; the Brussels Treaty organisation was strengthened and expanded, and the modified body was called the Western European Union (WEU); the Federal Republic agreed not to manufacture atomic, biological and chemical weapons; the members of the WEU were to work in close co-operation with NATO; and the Federal Republic of Germany was to be admitted to NATO, with the whole of its armed forces coming under NATO command. The Paris Agreements therefore contained provisions designed to allay fears about German rearmament.

DE GAULLE AND THE POLITICS OF *GRANDEUR*

When General de Gaulle came to power in 1958, France was therefore already a member of NATO and the EEC. The attitude which he adopted towards both bodies was markedly different from that of governments of the Fourth Republic. Since the Second World War, relations between the countries of Western Europe and North America had been characterised by growing co-operation and interdependence, with the emergence in Europe of international bodies embodying a degree of supranationalism. De Gaulle, however, believed strongly in the importance and primacy of the nation-state and the need for France to play an independent and major rôle in world affairs. He wrote:

> All my life I have had a certain idea of France. This is inspired by sentiment as well as reason. The emotional side of me naturally imagines France . . . as having an outstanding and exceptional destiny. I feel instinctively that Providence has created it for complete successes or exemplary misfortunes. . . . But also, the positive side of my mind convinces me that France is really itself only when it is in the front rank; . . . that our country . . ., if it is to avoid mortal danger, must aim high and stand straight. In short, to my mind, France cannot be France without greatness.
>
> (de Gaulle 1954: 1)

The policies which de Gaulle pursued were inspired by the desire to see France 'in the front rank'. They reflected his own convictions, but were also intended to raise the low morale of a nation which had suffered humiliating defeats by Germany in 1940 and the Viet Minh in Vietnam in 1954, which had been divided by the war in Algeria and whose political life, during much of the Fourth Republic, had been marked by instability and short-lived coalition governments. De Gaulle sought to pursue policies of *grandeur* (greatness) which would raise the status of France in the eyes of the world and of the French themselves, policies which, in his view, required independence in the political, military and economic spheres. He opposed anything which would limit France's sovereignty and freedom of action, whether it be the workings of one of the international bodies to which France belonged, or the bipolar system of international relations which characterised the Cold War, in which two blocs confronted each other, each, as he saw it, under the hegemony of one of the two superpowers. In de Gaulle's view, leadership of the Western democracies had lain since the Second World War with *les Anglo-Saxons* – the United States and Britain – and France had been unjustly excluded from this inner circle. He was hostile to the influence which he felt the United States had over Western Europe, and tried in many ways to counter this. He felt that the bloc system diminished the sovereignty of the individual European states and that it was necessary to reduce the influence of the United States and the Soviet Union in Europe, so that the bipolar system could be attenuated and would eventually disappear. France, he believed, was best placed of the European nations to initiate this process and take a lead in asserting European interests.

The European Economic Community was established to promote economic integration among its members, but there were also other objectives in the minds of the founders – reconciliation between France and Germany, the binding of Germany to the other West European democracies and the development of political co-operation, leading perhaps to a federal Europe.

There were also supranational aspects to the EEC, such as provision for qualified majority voting in the Council of Ministers.

Federalism and supranationalism were anathema to de Gaulle, and he had opposed the Treaty of Rome, but when in power he accepted French membership of the EEC because of economic benefits which it brought to France. He did, however, resist developments which would have added to the supranational content of the EEC or diminished French sovereignty. De Gaulle also vetoed in 1963 Britain's first application for EEC membership, stating as one of his reasons that Britain was too closely linked to the United States.

Shortly after issuing this veto, de Gaulle signed a treaty of friendship and co-operation with Konrad Adenauer, Chancellor of the Federal Republic of Germany – the Elysée Treaty of 22 January 1963. The treaty was the culmination of a period of growing *rapprochement* between the two countries, and has provided the framework for the close links in many fields and at times close coordination of policy which have continued and expanded down to the present day. Among de Gaulle's motives was a desire to have a close continental ally who might be persuaded to back his plans for French leadership of what he termed 'a European Europe' in which *les Anglo-Saxons* would have diminished influence. It soon became clear, however, that, while the Federal Republic wished to strengthen relations with France, it had no intention of loosening its ties with the United States, the guarantor of its security.[3]

De Gaulle also sought to pursue a policy of *rapprochement* with the Soviet Union and its satellite régimes in Eastern Europe, in keeping with his aim of weakening the bloc system and ending the division of Europe. In June 1966, shortly after France's withdrawal from the integrated command structure of NATO, de Gaulle travelled to Moscow, where he called for the establishment of a new European order, based on a new type of relationship between states, to replace the confrontation of the blocs. A joint statement was issued saying that the two governments had decided to consult together regularly on international problems. The Kremlin leaders were pleased with France's semi-detached attitude to the Atlantic Alliance and keen to encourage divisions in the Western camp, but they gave little in return. Although a kind of special relationship existed between France and the Soviet Union in the late 1960s and during the 1970s, Moscow and the other Warsaw Pact states – with the exception of Romania – showed no inclination to dissolve the bloc which they together constituted.

Nor did any Western country follow France's example where the Atlantic Alliance was concerned. De Gaulle's attitude to defence was that, although a country might belong to a military alliance, it had, ultimately, to be able to stand alone in its own defence. He had not opposed the establishment of the Atlantic Alliance, or France's decision to join it, but he strongly opposed the integration of forces and strategies involved in the operation of NATO, saying that it had created 'a bad protectorate' in which the United States dominated the European allies, who had to play a dependent and subordinate rôle. This view of France's defence needs led him to take two major decisions which still form the basis of French policy today: to create a French nuclear deterrent force, and to withdraw from NATO's integrated command structure.

This withdrawal was effected in stages, beginning with his announcement on 7 March 1959 that certain French naval forces in the Mediterranean would no longer come under NATO command in time of war. The process was concluded by measures taking effect in 1966 and 1967. The remaining French forces still destined to come under NATO command in wartime, including French forces stationed in Germany, were no longer to be subject to that command, and French officers were withdrawn from NATO's integrated structure; NATO was no longer to use French air space, and all allied forces, equipment and administration, including the NATO headquarters in Europe, had to leave France. De Gaulle said that, through these measures, France had regained its freedom of action and decision where defence was concerned. He stressed, however, that France remained a member of the Atlantic Alliance.

When de Gaulle came to power, France was already engaged in research designed to lead to manufacture and testing of an atomic bomb. It was de Gaulle, however, who decided to develop a full nuclear deterrent force – the *force de dissuasion* or *force de frappe* – based on ground-, air- and sea-launched weapons. In his view, France had to have nuclear weapons if it was to ensure its security through an independent defence policy. He argued that the advances made by the Soviet Union meant that Washington could no longer use nuclear weapons to defend Europe without risking destruction of the United States itself, and that America's nuclear guarantee to Europe's NATO members could therefore no longer be relied upon. Another motive for creation of the *force de dissuasion* was that it would bring prestige and enhance France's position as a world power.

The nuclear doctrine on which the deterrent force was based remained basically unchanged throughout the Cold War and has continued in some essential respects until the present day. It has similarities with the NATO doctrine of massive retaliation abandoned by the Alliance in the 1960s, in that it is based on the threat of rapid escalation to the use of long-range nuclear weapons if France's territory or vital interests are directly threatened. NATO replaced the strategy of massive retaliation with one of 'graduated response', which would have involved protracted battles in Europe with conventional forces and possibly tactical (short-range) nuclear weapons before any decision was made to use long-range, and much more powerful, nuclear weapons. Although France developed tactical nuclear weapons, official policy was that these were not intended for use as battlefield weapons; instead, the firing of a tactical nuclear weapon was to be a final warning (*ultime avertissement*) to an aggressor that, unless he desisted from attack, France would rapidly launch long-range nuclear weapons against his homeland. The number of nuclear weapons possessed by France was very small compared with the Soviet arsenal, but the Gaullist argument – the doctrine of proportional deterrence (*dissuasion du faible au fort* – deterrence of the strong by the weak) – ran that France could still inflict such devastation on the country of an aggressor that this would outweigh any advantage obtained by invading France. The *force de frappe* was a weapon solely for the defence of France – 'the national sanctuary' – and Paris was never prepared to guarantee that it would be used in defence of France's NATO allies against a Soviet threat.

With defence based on nuclear deterrence, the rôle of conventional forces was reduced. The rôle of French forces in Germany was not to fight protracted battles but simply to engage an aggressor as a 'test' of his intentions, to act as a tripwire which could lead to launching of France's long-range nuclear weapons. In keeping with its refusal to accept integration with NATO forces, France refused to commit itself to defence of any particular section of the inter-German border and said that it would decide in the light of circumstances at the time when, where, and indeed if to commit itself to battle in the event of massive attack by Warsaw Pact forces along the central front. Gaullist defence theorists distinguished between this first 'forward battle' and a second battle which would become necessary if NATO failed to hold the line – the battle for France itself.

THE EMERGING CONSENSUS ON DEFENCE

When de Gaulle resigned in 1969, his successor, the Gaullist President Georges Pompidou, stated his intention of continuing with the broad lines of the General's external policies. Where defence policy is concerned, there was indeed little change. Pompidou continued the policy of *rapprochement* with Moscow and independence *vis-à-vis* the United States, although he sought to avoid the overt anti-Americanism characteristic of so much of de Gaulle's policy. As regards European policy, Pompidou took a positive and constructive attitude to development of the EEC, in contrast to de Gaulle's sometimes negative and obstructionist approach. He lifted de Gaulle's veto on British membership of the Community, with the result that Britain, Ireland and Denmark became members in January 1973.

On the death of Pompidou in 1974, Valéry Giscard d'Estaing was elected president. Although he had been a government minister under de Gaulle and Pompidou, he was not a Gaullist. Pro-European, he took a number of initiatives designed to further co-operation and integration between EEC member states. There had been a few meetings of EEC heads of state and government during the 1960s and early 1970s, but in 1974, on the proposal of Giscard d'Estaing and with the support of West German Chancellor Helmut Schmidt, it was decided to institutionalise these meetings, which from then on were held three times a year (later reduced to twice yearly). The

71

European Council, as these summits came to be called, provided a relatively informal forum for discussion of policy issues. Giscard d'Estaing and Schmidt also played a major part in the establishment of the European Monetary System, designed to control exchange rate fluctuations.

Where defence was concerned, Giscard d'Estaing began by questioning some basic tenets of Gaullist policy. He expressed the view that it was unwise to have a defence strategy based solely on nuclear deterrence and that France should be able to fight a war with conventional forces if necessary. He rejected as unrealistic the idea of two distinct battles – the 'forward battle', in which France might or might not participate, and the battle for France itself. In a speech on 15 March 1976, the chief of staff of the armed forces, General Méry, said that it would be very dangerous for France deliberately not to participate in the forward battle, and indicated that France should commit itself to defend not only its own territory but also that of its neighbours. Believing that France should take part in the forward defence of Europe, Giscard d'Estaing reorganised and restructured the army to make it more mobile, and increased spending on conventional equipment. He also suggested that tactical nuclear weapons could be considered not only as an integral part of France's strategic deterrent – the 'final warning' – but also as battlefield weapons.

Giscard d'Estaing's attempt to modify aspects of Gaullist policy soon ran into opposition. This came from members of the Gaullist Rassemblement pour la République (RPR) and from other sectors of opinion, for by the mid-to-late 1970s, de Gaulle's defence policy, which in his day had remained controversial, was beginning to gain wide acceptance. Indeed, by the end of the decade, after the Communist Party in 1977 and the Socialist Party in 1978 had reversed their opposition to the *force de frappe*, there could be said to exist a broad consensus in favour of Gaullist defence policy. Giscard d'Estaing was accused of leading France towards reintegration into NATO's command structure and of abandoning the nuclear doctrine of massive retaliation in favour of the policy of graduated response long since adopted by NATO but rejected by France. Faced with strong criticism from various quarters, opposed by many Gaullists within the ruling parliamentary majority and facing elections in 1978 which the Left seemed to have a good chance of winning, Giscard d'Estaing abandoned his efforts to modify Gaullist doctrine and reverted to a more conservative stance (although his reorgan-isation of the army continued in force).

The lesson of Giscard d'Estaing's failure to modify aspects of Gaullist defence policy was not lost on other political leaders. With these policies now widely accepted and popular, it was very difficult for any politician to break the emerging national consensus on defence. With the *force de dissuasion* now in existence after years of expense and effort, it was almost a political impossibility to suggest that it should be scrapped, particularly as it was felt to have brought France prestige and independence. Similarly, any move to bring France back into NATO's integrated command structure would immediately be portrayed as abandoning French independence in order to return to dependence upon the United States.

BUILDING ON THE GAULLIST LEGACY

The foregoing explains why the change in 1981 from rule by the Centre-Right to rule by the Left did not involve any major change in defence policy. Electoral considerations played a part in the decisions of the Socialist and Communist parties in the late 1970s to accept the nuclear strike force. Mitterrand, too, who had been one of de Gaulle's strongest opponents and had voted against the General's decision to take France out of NATO's integrated command structure, accepted the new national consensus around de Gaulle's policies. Indeed, he proved a stout defender of the essentials of de Gaulle's defence policies, appearing at times more Gaullist than the leaders of the Gaullist RPR themselves. During the 1986–8 period of *cohabitation*, for example, Gaullist Prime Minister Jacques Chirac and Defence Minister André Giraud advocated that France's short-range nuclear weapons be redesignated as 'tactical' – that is, battle-fighting – weapons. They eventually abandoned this position, however, in the face of strong opposition from Mitterrand who insisted, in keeping with long-standing Gaullist policy, that these weapons should be used, not for battle-fighting, but solely as a 'final warning'; France's nuclear weapons, he said, were designed to prevent war, not to win it (Howorth 1992: 46 and Gordon 1993: 155).

Although Mitterrand always refused to reintegrate French forces into NATO, he took a more strongly pro-NATO, anti-Soviet line than his predecessors had done. He strongly condemned the Soviet occupation of Afghanistan; relations with NATO and the United States became closer and more cordial; and he proved a staunch defender of NATO's 1979 decision to station Pershing II and cruise missiles in several European countries as a response to Moscow's development of intermediate-range SS-20 missiles targeted on Western Europe. Strong opposition within the countries – particularly West Germany – where the 'Euromissiles' were to be based had given rise to fears that certain governments concerned might back away from this decision. The irony of Mitterrand's position was that France itself, because of its stance *vis-à-vis* NATO, had never agreed to accept any 'Euromissiles' on French soil.

There are several reasons why Mitterrand should have taken a strongly pro-NATO attitude. To begin with, East–West relations had worsened considerably in the late 1970s/early 1980s and, following a relentless build-up, Warsaw Pact forces now outnumbered those of the West in many fields. Second, the Socialists had invited the Communist Party to provide ministers in a coalition government, and Mitterrand may have wished to indicate to the

United States and other allies that this did not mean the French government would be more tolerant of Soviet policies abroad. Lastly, there was a fear in France during the early 1980s that Germany might be tempted by neutralism. French policy has long been to bind West Germany closely to its West European neighbours through integration within bodies such as NATO and the European Community. Another irony of French policy has been that although France itself has refused integration within NATO's military command structure, it has been strongly desirous that the Federal Republic of Germany should remain fully integrated into NATO. For France, Germany in NATO provided a buffer, protected by NATO, between France and the forces of the Warsaw Pact.

Mitterrand gave high priority to further development of the *force de dissuasion*, reversing the trend initiated by Giscard d'Estaing, who had reduced the proportion of the defence budget allocated to nuclear weaponry. The socialist president was equally faithful to Gaullist orthodoxy in his refusal to give any prior commitment that French forces would automatically come to the aid of France's allies were they to be attacked (France's commitments under the Brussels and Washington treaties notwithstanding).

While Mitterrand did not abandon the broad outlines of Gaullist defence strategy, he did add an important new element to French policy – closer European defence co-operation. This can be seen as part of a gradual shift in emphasis of French external policy. Notwithstanding continuing rhetoric about national independence, French policy has increasingly been based on the assumption that France, a medium-sized power in an increasingly interdependent world, can best achieve its objectives and protect its interests by acting together with its neighbours and allies. Under Mitterrand, France was the major proponent – often jointly with Germany – of many initiatives designed to broaden and deepen the competences of the European Community and thus to further the process of European integration.

The closer European defence co-operation promoted by Mitterrand fell mainly into two categories: Franco-German defence co-operation and the gradual development of a European defence identity within the framework of the Western European Union.

As stated above, the Western European Union had been established in 1954, based on a modification of the Brussels Treaty of 1948. For some thirty years the organisation lay virtually dormant. Then, in September 1983, Mitterrand proposed that the WEU should form the basis of a 'European identity' in defence matters. On the basis of proposals put forward by France and West Germany, the seven member organisations (the six original members of the EEC, plus the United Kingdom) agreed in October 1984 to give new life to the organisation. Further meetings of WEU foreign and defence ministers took place, leading to the adoption of a 'Platform on European Security Interests' at The Hague in October 1987 which both expressed support for NATO and spoke of the need to construct an integrated

Europe as regards security and defence. Membership of the WEU increased with the accession of Spain and Portugal in 1988 and Greece in 1995. The WEU has played a rôle in several conflicts. It has, for example, coordinated the activity of member countries' naval forces in the Gulf following Iraq's invasion of Kuwait in 1990 and in the Adriatic from 1992 to help enforce the embargo against Serbia-Montenegro.

The Maastricht Treaty on European Union signed in February 1992 provides for the establishment of a common foreign and security policy for the Union, a policy which 'shall include ... the eventual framing of a common defence policy, which might in time lead to a common defence', and in this connection creates a formal link between the European Union and the WEU. On the basis of proposals put forward jointly by Mitterrand and Chancellor Kohl of Germany, the Maastricht Treaty states that the EU 'requests the Western European Union, which is an integral part of the development of the Union, to elaborate and implement decisions and actions of the Union which have defence implications'. The Intergovernmental Conference held in 1996 to review certain provisions of the Maastricht Treaty, including the Common Foreign and Security Policy, has to give further consideration to a possible common defence, and to clarify the future status and rôle of the WEU, given that not all EU member states belong to the WEU and that the 1948 Brussels Treaty on which the WEU is based lapses in March 1998.

French political leaders frequently state that if the European Union is to have political weight in the world, it must develop a common defence. For France, the WEU is well-suited for such a purpose, given that its full members[4] all belong to the European Union and that France participates fully in its activities. The United States was at first suspicious of French moves to promote the WEU and a European defence identity, fearing that this could lead to the break-up of NATO, but French spokesmen are nowadays at pains to stress the importance that they attach to the continued existence of NATO and their belief that the WEU must collaborate closely with NATO and in no sense constitute a rival organisation. Since the WEU acquired its special status vis-à-vis the European Union, much has been done to strengthen its organisation and decision-making capacities and to define its missions, and NATO has agreed to make some of its facilities available for use by the WEU (Cutileiro 1995: 11).

Since the early 1980s, defence co-operation has become an increasingly important aspect of the special relationship between France and Germany. In 1982, the two countries set up a Franco-German defence commission and have since engaged in an increasing number of joint military manoeuvres. January 1988 saw the establishment of the Franco-German Defence Council and the announcement that a mixed Franco-German brigade was to be created. The brigade, consisting of 4,200 men, was to be stationed in Germany.

Shortly before the Maastricht summit of 1992, Mitterrand and Kohl announced plans for the creation of a European Corps. This was to be based on a strengthened Franco-German brigade and forces from any other member state of the WEU which wished to participate. Preparations went ahead for the establishment of the Eurocorps and, by 1994, Belgium, Luxembourg and Spain had announced their intention to join. The corps, whose headquarters are in Strasbourg, became operational with some 50,000 troops in November 1995. It is intended that it will be available to participate in the defence of Europe, should any NATO-member country be attacked, and also in peace-keeping and humanitarian missions. It may act within the framework of NATO or the WEU, and on 21 January 1993 an agreement was signed defining the conditions under which the corps would operate under NATO command. Criticism has been levelled at the Eurocorps to the effect that its creation was primarily symbolic and that for a number of practical reasons it is not well-suited to all the missions which have been envisaged for it,[5] but it can also be seen as the embryo of a future European army, and as such constitutes a development of considerable political and military significance.

On 7 December 1995, France and Germany took military co-operation a stage further by agreeing to develop jointly two 'spy' satellite systems.

ADJUSTING TO THE POST-COLD WAR ERA

The ending of the Cold War necessitated far reaching changes in the foreign and defence policies of France and its partners within the Atlantic Alliance and the European Union. For a variety of reasons, the readjustments required posed particular problems for France.

One consequence of the fall of Soviet-backed régimes was the reunification of Germany. This entailed the gaining of complete sovereignty by the Federal Republic and the ending of the residual rights of the four former occupying powers – the United States, the Soviet Union, Britain and France. For France, this meant the loss of a position which, it felt, enhanced its international status. Furthermore, as long as Germany remained divided, France could feel that its relationship with the Federal Republic was one between equals – that the greater economic strength of the FRG was offset by Bonn's lack of full sovereignty which contrasted with the position of a fully independent France armed with nuclear weapons. Reunification brought a larger, fully sovereign and potentially more independent-minded Germany to which Paris had to readjust. France's response was to seek to bind Germany more closely to France and its other West European neighbours by furthering the process of European integration.

The danger of attack by the Soviet Union had also provided the justification for France's development of a nuclear strike force which not only could be used for massive retaliation against an aggressor but also was designed to bring France prestige and influence in its international dealings. The end of the Cold War brought into question French military strategy, based primarily on nuclear deterrence, and begged questions about the purpose and utility of a nuclear force which had long absorbed about a quarter of the defence budget, to the detriment of France's conventional forces.

By the 1990s, the arguments which de Gaulle had employed to justify France's withdrawal from NATO's integrated structure had lost much of whatever cogency they might once have had. The system of blocs had gone and America was reducing its military presence in Europe. It might have been thought that this would provide the perfect context in which France could re-examine its relations with NATO. The Alliance was reviewing its structure, strategy and missions, and France, by participating in discussions within NATO, could have contributed to re-shaping the organisation in a way more to France's liking.

France did in fact join the Legge Group (set up by NATO in 1990 to consider the future strategy of the Alliance), but its continuing refusal to participate in the work of other NATO committees meant that it was powerless to influence the decisions made there. France initially took a generally hostile attitude to proposals aimed at giving NATO a more political and economic rôle or expanding NATO geographically. French opposition tended to be based on a belief that such proposals were designed to further American influence in Europe and would hamper the development of European bodies better suited to carry out the tasks in question. The centre-right government elected in 1993 tended, however, to take a more positive attitude towards changes in NATO's rôle (Gordon 1993: 169 and Meimeth 1994: 84).

Thus, although French leaders stress the importance of NATO for European defence, they have not been prepared to break the Gaullist taboo against reintegration into NATO's military structure. It has been clear, none the less, that a complete boycott of NATO committees is contrary to French interests, and the French government stated in 1994[6] that it was logical to ensure French participation in meetings of NATO committees where French interests were at stake and the engagement of French forces was involved; it said that the participation of French representatives in meetings of NATO bodies would be decided on a case-by-case basis. On 5 December 1995, France went a stage further by announcing that in future French representatives would participate fully in all meetings of NATO's Military Committee.

Despite French sensitivities about French forces being subject to United States control, France took part in the 1991 Gulf War under overall American command. Its participation revealed weaknesses in French conventional forces caused by the priority given over many years to spending on the *force de frappe*. Thus, France's capacity to transport men and equipment to the Gulf was found to be inadequate, as were its intelligence-gathering facilities. Outdated equipment also meant that French aircraft sent to the Gulf were limited in the missions which they could perform. The decision by President Mitterrand that conscripts would not be sent to the Gulf also meant that France, with an army nearly twice as big as Britain's, could send only 16,000 ground troops as compared with 35,000 sent by Britain, thus fuelling the arguments of those pressing for an end to conscription and the complete professionalisation of the French armed forces (Heisbourg 1995: 76). That those arguments had finally won the day was shown by the announcement by President Chirac on 22 February 1996 that he intended to phase out compulsory military service and to end conscription within six years.

France has been seeking to remedy the other deficiencies revealed by the Gulf War, a remedy which is all the more necessary as force projection capabilities are a prerequisite for any country wishing to take part in peacekeeping and humanitarian missions. France sets great store by its status as a permanent member of the UN Security Council and sees participation in United Nations peacekeeping missions as one of the duties which flow from this position – and, perhaps, as one way of ensuring that it retains its permanent membership. In 1994, France made the biggest national contribution to UN forces (some 7,500 troops).

The ending of the Cold War has brought other changes in French attitudes to security issues. The growth of Islamic fundamentalism in the Middle East and North Africa has created growing concern in France about a possible threat to security from across the Mediterranean. Political instability in Algeria, the knowledge that a number of Arab or Islamic states have been seeking to acquire nuclear weapon and missile technology and fears that such technology and weaponry may be obtainable from the Soviet Union's successor states because of inadequate controls have heightened this concern. In September 1992 the then French Defence Minister Pierre Joxe spoke of the need to adapt France's nuclear forces and to develop arms systems which were lighter, more flexible and more precise. A report produced by the Defence Commission of the National Assembly in February 1994 took a similar view, saying that France's nuclear forces must not be limited to a strategy of *dissuasion du faible au fort* and must permit a range of actions including the capability for limited and very precise strikes (Keiger 1995: 270). France, Italy and Spain have agreed to establish a joint maritime force, Euromarfor, open to other members of the WEU, to strengthen security in the Mediterranean.

It was concern about the danger of growing nuclear Proliferation which finally induced France to adhere in 1992 to the Nuclear Non-proliferation Treaty of 1968, something which it had long declined to do. France had also refused to have anything to do with the Mutual Balanced Force Reduction (MBFR) talks held during the period of the Cold War, on the grounds that they were bloc-to-bloc negotiations, but subscribed to the CFE (Conventional Armed Forces in Europe) Treaty, which was negotiated under the auspices of the Conference on Security and Co-operation in Europe – like the failed MBFR talks, the CFE Treaty was designed to limit and reduce conventional forces throughout Europe – and which came into force in 1992. France had also long declined to adhere to the Partial Test Ban Treaty agreed by the United States, the Soviet Union and Britain in 1963, but has announced that it expects to adhere to the Comprehensive Test Ban Treaty likely to be signed in 1996. According to the French government, the series of nuclear tests ordered by President Chirac in 1995 was designed in part to try out test-simulation procedures which can be conducted in laboratories in place of the underground nuclear explosions conducted on the Pacific atolls of Mururoa and Fangataufa since 1974.

One of the paradoxes of French politics is that during the late 1980s and early 1990s it was political heirs of de Gaulle, leading members of the RPR, who were inclined to propose deviations from Gaullist orthodoxy in defence policy while the socialist President Mitterrand insisted that France adhere to a Gaullist line where nuclear strategy and relations with NATO were concerned.

The main centre-right parties fully supported Mitterrand, however, as regards the major new element which he added to French policy – closer European defence co-operation. This new emphasis in French strategy made even more glaring the contrast between traditional Gaullist defence policy, framed during the Cold War, and France's security requirements in the 1990s. France was committed to the further integration of the European Union, the development of a common foreign and defence policy for the Union and, ultimately, a common European defence, yet at the same time French defence policy was supposed to be based on the principle of national sovereignty and independence of decision and action. The financial burden of the defence budget, at a time when other nations were substantially cutting defence spending following the end of the Cold War, and when France needed to restrain government spending in order to meet the criteria for introduction of the EU's single currency, also increased pressures for an overhaul of French defence policy.

Political leaders have thus had the task of gradually adjusting French policy – and public opinion – to political and economic reality while not appearing to scrap aspects of Gaullist policy which had become popular with the voters. This accounts to some extent for the apparently schizophrenic nature of official pronouncements on defence during the 1990s, with nationalistic assertions of military independence mingling with calls for development of a European defence identity.

The coming to power of the centre-right Balladur government in 1993 led to the publication in 1994 of a White Paper, the *Livre blanc sur la défense*. This analyses the new strategic context and seeks to outline French defence needs for the next twenty or so years. It states that, while France will continue to maintain a nuclear force, the rôle of nuclear weapons will become less crucial, and that of conventional forces more central. Although France's refusal to rejoin NATO's integrated military structure is reaffirmed, the emphasis throughout is upon French forces acting in concert with those of partners and allies, with whom, it says, there is growing interdependence of interests. Now that there is no longer a question of a major confrontation, it maintains, the prevailing concern will be the prevention and management of crises of varying intensity, often situated far from France. Such actions, it says, will usually be undertaken in co-operation with allies, with French forces serving as part of a multinational force under the aegis of bodies such as NATO, the OSCE, the UN or the European Union. The White Paper places great stress on the European context of French defence and on the need for increased military co-operation with France's European allies. It calls for the further strengthening of the WEU, to complement the rôle of NATO, and speaks of bringing French defence policy into line with the 'common defence' alluded to in the Maastricht Treaty. French policy, it states, is defined primarily in terms of its capacity to contribute to peace and stability in Europe and it rejects the Gaullist concept of *sanctuarisation* (a defence policy limited to the defence of France alone). Europe will have no autonomy in defence, the White Paper argues, unless it is defended by nuclear weapons based on a European nuclear doctrine. To this end, it says, the Franco-British talks on nuclear defence issues which began in 1992 must continue (see Isnard 1995b). The *Livre blanc* can thus be seen as an important step in redefining French defence policy and adapting it to the post-Cold War environment.

The emphasis on European defence continues to be prominent in policy statements by leaders of the governing Centre-Right. Speaking as Foreign Minister in January 1995,[7] Alain Juppé expressed support for the eastern enlargement of the European Union, and added that this process would be accompanied by an expansion of the WEU and so, in turn, since 'European defence will not be built outside the Atlantic Alliance', by enlargement of NATO. He counselled, however, against hasty expansion of the Alliance. In a speech on 31 August 1995 (*Le Monde*, 1 September 1995), President Chirac referred to the possibility of the French nuclear deterrent force playing a rôle in future defence arrangements of the European Union.

Although Gaullist rhetoric subsists alongside European rhetoric, it is clear that most of France's political leaders see their country's future as lying within an integrated European Union which, eventually, will have an integrated defence system in which France will play its part. While declamatory statements about France's rank among the nations and international rôle still abound, there is a realisation that, in the world of the twenty-first century, with ever-growing interdependence and integration between states, the goals which de Gaulle once held out to his compatriots can no longer be achieved by France acting alone. Increasingly, Europe is seen as the vehicle for achieving French ambitions.

80

CONCLUSION

The defence policy which de Gaulle introduced, against considerable opposition, came to enjoy strong popular support, and French politicians have been wary of publicly rejecting its main elements. Nonetheless, Gaullist defence strategy, which always contained inconsistencies and contradictions, has appeared increasingly ill-suited to the world of the 1990s and, after initial hesitations, French governments have been making determined efforts to adapt defence policy to the changed political and strategic environment. While believing that NATO is essential for European defence for the foreseeable future, France, more than any other country, has been determined to develop a European defence entity and sees the WEU as the best vehicle for achieving this, hoping that the WEU can eventually be merged with the European Union. The emphasis on European defence reflects the basic foreign policy choice which a succession of French governments have followed – that of ever-closer integration within Europe. Increasingly, the ambitions and aspirations which French men and women held out for France are being transferred to the European Union. Alain Juppé expressed this shift of perspective very clearly when he said in January 1995: 'We must in future have also "a certain idea of Europe" which encompasses and extends a certain idea of France.'[8]

DEFENCE POLICY: CHRONOLOGY

1947   (March) France and UK sign Treaty of Dunkirk.

1948   (March) France, UK and Benelux countries conclude Brussels Treaty.

1949   (April) Twelve states sign Washington Treaty establishing North Atlantic Treaty Organisation.

1950   (May) French Foreign Minister Robert Schuman puts forward proposals for European Coal and Steel Community (ECSC).
        (October) French Prime Minister René Pleven proposes European Defence Community (EDC).

1951   (April) ECSC Treaty signed in Paris by France, Federal Republic of Germany, Italy and Benelux countries.

1952   (May) EDC Treaty signed in Paris by six ECSC members.

1954   (August) EDC Treaty rejected by French National Assembly.
        (October) Creation of Western European Union on basis of modified Brussels Treaty.

1957   (March) Six ECSC members sign Treaty of Rome establishing European Economic Community (EEC).

1958   (January) EEC comes into being.
        (June) De Gaulle returns to power as prime minister.

1959   (January) De Gaulle proclaimed president of Fifth Republic.
        (March) De Gaulle begins first of several stages of withdrawal from NATO's

integrated command structure – some French navy ships no longer subject to NATO command.

1960   (February) First French atomic bomb exploded in Sahara.
1963   (January) UK's application for EEC membership vetoed by de Gaulle.
        Franco-German Treaty of friendship and co-operation signed (Elysée Treaty).
1966   (February) De Gaulle explains reasons for withdrawing remaining French troops from NATO's integrated command structure.
        (March) De Gaulle asks for removal of all NATO personnel and facilities from French soil by 1 July 1967.
        (June) De Gaulle visits Moscow.
1969   (June) Georges Pompidou elected president
        (July) Pompidou announces not opposed in principle to UK's EEC membership.
1973   (January) Denmark, Ireland and UK become members of EEC.
1974   (May) Valéry Giscard d'Estaing elected president.
1978   (January) Socialist Party ends opposition to France's nuclear force.
1981   (May) François Mitterrand elected president.
1982   (October) Franco-German Commission on Security and Defence established.
1984   (October) Member governments agree to revitalise and expand Western European Union.
1988   (January) Franco-German Council for Security and Defence established.
        Formation of Franco-German brigade announced.
1989   (September–December) Collapse of communist rule in Central and Eastern Europe.
1991   (January–February) French forces participate in Gulf War.
1992   (February) Treaty on European Union signed at Maastricht.
1995   (May) Jacques Chirac elected president.
        (November) European Corps (proposed by France and Germany in 1991) becomes operational.

NOTES

1 Military personnel – 505,546, composed of army – 240,372; air force – 89,853; navy – 64,170; paramilitary *gendarmerie* – 91,841; common services – 19,310 (French government figures).
2 For fuller discussion of the *domaine réservé*, see Chapter 1.
3 When ratifying the Elysée Treaty, the *Bundestag* (Lower House of the West German parliament) added a preamble in which it stressed the Federal Republic's continuing strong attachment to the Atlantic Alliance and desire to maintain close co-operation with the United States.
4 The WEU also has associate members (Iceland, Norway and Turkey), observers (Austria, Denmark, Finland, Ireland and Sweden) and associate partners (Bulgaria, Czech Republic, Estonia, Hungary, Latvia, Lithuania, Poland, Romania and Slovakia).
5 See the report on the European Corps made by Michel Caldaguès on behalf of the Foreign Affairs, Defence and Armed Forces Commission of the French Senate (Senate Document No. 48, Annex to the proceedings of the session of 20 October 1993).
6 *Livre blanc sur la défense*, 1994: 34 (English language edition).
7 Speech on 30 January 1995 on the occasion of the twentieth anniversary of the *Centre d'analyse et de prévision* (Centre for analysis and forecasting) of the French Foreign Ministry (Document no. SFC/95/22 issued by the French Embassy, London).
8 See Note 7.

DEFENCE POLICY: REFERENCES AND RECOMMENDED READING

* Archer, C. (1994) *Organizing Europe*, London: Edward Arnold.
  Historical analysis and up-to-date information about the major international organisations in Europe.
* Bozo, F. (1991) *La France et l'OTAN*, Paris: Masson.
  A very detailed account of France's relations with NATO from the foundation of the Alliance until 1991.
Buchan, D. (1995) 'France's defence industry halted by inertia', *Financial Times*, 20 October.
* de Carmoy, G. (1967) *Les Politiques étrangères de la France 1944–1966*, Paris: La Table Ronde.
  French foreign and defence policy from the Liberation until de Gaulle's withdrawal from NATO's integrated command structures.
Cutileiro, J. (1995) 'WEU's operational development and its relationship to NATO', *NATO Review*, 5/95: 8–11.
De Gaulle, C. (1954) *Mémoires de guerre – L'Appel 1940–1942*, Paris: Librairie Plon.
* Gordon, P. (1993) *A Certain Idea of France*, Princeton, N.J.: Princeton University Press.
  An analysis of de Gaulle's defence policy and the extent to which it has influenced French policy making into the 1990s.
Heisbourg, F. (1995) 'La politique de défense à l'aube d'un nouveau mandat présidentiel', *Politique étrangère*, 1/95: 73–83.
Hoffmann, S. (1987) 'Mitterrand's Foreign Policy, or Gaullism by Any Other Name', in S. Hoffmann, G. Ross and S. Malzacher (eds) *The Mitterrand Experiment*, Cambridge: Polity Press.
Howorth, J. (1992) 'François Mitterrand and the "domaine réservé": from cohabitation to the Gulf War', *French Politics and Society*, 10,1: 43–58.
Isnard, J. (1995a) '50,000 emplois seraient menacés en 1996–1997 dans l'industrie de défense', *Le Monde* 28 October.
—— (1995b) 'Entre Paris et Londres, un dialogue sur la dissuasion ininterrompu depuis 1992', *Le Monde* 29–30 October.
Keiger, J. (1995) 'France and international relations in the post-Cold War era: some lessons of the past', *Modern and Contemporary France*, NS3,3: 263–73.
Meimeth, M. (1994) 'France gets closer to NATO', *The World Today* 50,5: 84–6.

4

THE REGIONS IN THE MARKET PLACE

Richard J. Lund

France's policy of *aménagement du territoire*[1] has recently come under review at the national level. The central issue is to what extent French regions, individually and collectively, are sufficiently well placed to maximise the opportunities the European market offers. Despite thirty years of *aménagement du territoire*, regional economic disequilibria persist, measured *inter alia* in terms of population and employment structure and distribution, migration flows, industrial structure and distribution, and regional incomes. The fast-growth years of the 1960s and early 1970s witnessed the development of a policy devised and implemented centrally by successive right-wing governments through the regional development agency *Délégation à l'aménagement du territoire et à l'action régionale* (DATAR), created in 1963, with limited regional consultation. Decentralisation at the beginning of the 1980s, under left-wing governments, introduced an approach with clearly defined areas of responsibility passing, to a large extent, to the twenty-two regions themselves.

For foreign capital, France has proved in the past to be an attractive location with low inflation and moderate wage levels. Business and corporation tax (*la taxe professionnelle* and *l'impôt sur les sociétés*) have fallen, energy is relatively cheap, the communications networks are highly developed and France remains very much the country of the *grand projet*. With a population of some 58 million, France represents a major market within the European Union, and her geographical location gives her a central position at the crossroads to Spain, the United Kingdom, Northern and Southern Europe.

Conversely, for many goods and services, the European market has become increasingly saturated, and a process of *délocalisation*, the establishment of manufacturing facilities and service activities outside France, particularly with regard to the emerging markets of the Far East, is evident. Within the European Union itself the force of gravity is shifting towards Eastern Europe, thereby generating the concern that some French regions risk becoming increasingly marginalised, being peripheral to the core markets.

The question is, therefore, in a France plagued by the social ills of over 3

84

million unemployed, poverty and homelessness, urban disquiet and racial disharmony, yet enjoying the economic stability linked to a strong currency, single-figure inflation, steady growth and a balance of trade surplus, will the regions of France remain suitable sites for domestic and foreign investment and attractive areas to create jobs and stimulate self-sustaining growth? Will the call for *solidarité*, made explicit in the 1990s debate on the policy of *aménagement du territoire*, guarantee the position and influence of France's regions in the European market place and beyond?

This chapter will examine the policy chronologically yet focusing on the main issues and changes in policy orientation which have characterised *aménagement du territoire* from its inception in a period of rapid growth and progressive opening-up of the French economy, to a period of slower growth in an increasingly European, if not global, context.

DIFFERENTIAL SOCIAL AND ECONOMIC GROWTH

The main impact of nineteenth-century industrialisaton was to the east of an imaginary line running from Le Havre to Marseille, particularly in the *départements* of Nord and Pas de Calais. Here the development of the textiles industry, aided by the introduction of the steam engine, and the development of the waterways, together with the local deposits of coal, brought about the flourishing of the textile towns of Lille, Roubaix and Tourcoing, the mining towns of Lens, Béthune and Douai, and the iron and steel towns of Valenciennes and Denain. This early picture of a rapidly industrialising eastern half of France and a more sparsely populated, under-industrialised, agriculturally backward France to the west, with Paris dominating political and economic life, has persisted well into the twentieth century. Gravier (1964) has provided one of the clearest *exposés* of this, France's 'regional problem'.

Of the attempts at explaining differential regional economic growth, it is interesting to consider which are pertinent to the French experience. Two particular approaches would seem to underpin the policy of *aménagement du territoire* aimed at a fairer distribution of economic growth across French regions.

Christaller (1966) was primarily concerned with understanding the geography of retail and service activities. Different types of business activity require different population thresholds to sustain them and hence require different sizes of trade area, with purchases being made with variable frequency. Low-order centres would require a low threshold but high frequency of purchase, whilst high-order centres would require a high threshold yet low frequency of purchase. This then suggests a hierarchy of centres based around a central place. Financial services were thus likely to be located in large towns and cities whilst shopping for basic necessities could be undertaken in locations of much smaller size.

Such static theories assume economic space to be uniform, but in reality

85

regions differ in their endowment of natural resources and the quantity and quality of labour and capital. The extent and impact of government intervention will vary. Furthermore, regions can be characterised by the sophistication of their communications infrastructure, topographical features and the extent to which firms will tend to cluster to achieve economies. All these factors will contribute to a distorsion of any neat location pattern suggested by central place theory.

A more dynamic explanation is provided by Perroux (1991) based on the notion that growth occurs unevenly at points in geographical space, *pôles de croissance*, with varying intensity and variable effects on the economy as a whole. The 'pole' is the motor of the growth process and is seen as a single firm, an industry or an industrial complex which exerts a direct impact on other sectors, *effet d'entraînement*, that is to say, attracting other activities to the area. As a result, there is an *effet d'agglomération*, a clustering of complementary activities around the 'pole'. This then permits an *effet de jonction*, as linkages are established and the interrelated activities increase their supply of/demand for one another's inputs/outputs.

The first twenty years of *aménagement du territoire* are a reflection of the main ideas espoused by the above theories; that is, the concentration of resources geographically to develop major centres as part of a sophisticated urban hierarchy, each tier of which enjoys a zone of influence. This can initially be seen in the 1960s policy of *métropoles d'équilibre*. At this time France was experiencing high growth rates, rapid population increase, immigration, a constant *exode rural* as mechanisation and modernisation in agriculture meant less labour input and greater capital intensity, all this in an increasingly open economy. The aim was to deflect expansion away from Paris to eight *métropoles*, thus establishing more balanced growth: Lille–Roubaix–Tourcoing; Rennes; Nantes–St.Nazaire; Bordeaux; Toulouse; Marseille; Lyon–St.Etienne–Grenoble; and Strasbourg. It is worth noting the geographical situation of these regional centres, located as they are on the periphery and hence lending support to the point about the uneven distribution of resources spatially. By diversifying the economic base of these centres, increasing job opportunities and generating flows of people, goods and services over an identifiable area, a zone of influence could be established. Government economic decentralisation and foreign inward investment gave impetus to this process; the aerospace industry was set up in Toulouse, for example, and in Grenoble American companies such as Hewlett Packard, Caterpillar and Becton Dickinson catalysed the development of economic activities which had few historical ties with the area.

Measured by the rates of population growth, the impact was significant. The urban areas with a population of 200,000 or more grew by 20.1 per thousand of the population during the intercensal period 1962–8, approximately 8.0 being due to natural increase and 12.0 to in-migration (*Ministère de la Solidarité, de la Santé et de la Protection Sociale* 1989: 32). This compares with a population growth rate of 11.4 per thousand for France as a whole over this period.

As the *métropoles* began to experience the same congestion as Paris, development of the medium-sized towns, those with a population of between 20,000 and 100,000, became the new focus of attention. Instituted in 1973, the *contrats de villes moyennes* were financial contracts negotiated with central government for funding to improve the qualiy of urban development through housing renewal, the revival of *anciens quartiers*, investment in social infrastructure and public transport, and assistance with the establishment of new business, whilst safeguarding the environment. Through self-sustaining growth, closer links between place of residence and place of work, lower housing densities, less pollution and traffic congestion, and a greater sense of community, it would be possible to stem the rural–urban out-migration process. Whilst, between 1968 and 1975, the French population grew by 8.2 per thousand of the population, the urban areas with a population of over 200,000 grew by 11.9, those of 50,000 to 100,000 by 15.2 and those of 20,000 to 50,000 by 12.8, natural increase being more significant than migration during this time period.

By the mid-1970s the effects of the oil crisis and the beginnings of change in the character of labour markets were manifest. Oil prices had quadrupled at a time when France still depended on external sources for some 75 per cent of energy supplies. Cost-competitiveness in key sectors of traditional industries such as textiles and shipbuilding had declined. The fall in demand left plant and equipment in the iron and steel industry under-utilised and raised unemployment to previously unanticipated levels. Hence a brake was put on investment in infrastructure, industrial zones and urban renovation programmes. Keeping the French population in situ was paramount and, to this end, a new tier of the hierarchy took on significance. The small towns policy which resulted (1975) again focused on the capacity of towns, this time with a population of between 5,000 and 20,000 people, to create a *zone d'attraction*. Such towns were largely located to the west of the Le Havre–Marseille bi-sector. They were characterised principally by population decline and changes to the age distribution of the population. Average per capita incomes were lower and there was a dependency on a single industry. The census data shows that for the period 1975–82, whilst the growth of the French population as a whole had slowed to 4.6 per thousand, urban areas with a population of 10,000 to 20,000 grew by 6.3, with natural increase being the dominant factor, and those with a population of 5,000 to 10,000 inhabitants by 9.0 with migration being the more dominant factor. Conversely, for all urban areas with a population exceeding 20,000 there was significant out-migration.

Today, an integral stage in the spatial function of a *métropole* is its development as a *technopole* based around a *technopôle*. The *technopole* is the city itself within which a more dynamic scientific and technological base is evolving, whilst the *technopôle* is the precise location within or adjacent to that city which embraces complementary high-tech activities on a single site. The stimuli to their development have been *synergie, partenariat* and *spécialisation*. The notion of *synergie* is the collaboration between industry, research institutes and higher education; *partenariat* is the partnership between local organisations to promote the *technopôle* as an integral part of economic development; and *spécialisation* recognises the key dynamic sector(s) peculiar to that *technopôle*.

For example, Sophia Antipolis near Nice, established in 1972, has become a centre specialising in telecommunications. Digital Equipment, IBM, Texas Instruments and AT&T all located there. By the early 1990s Sophia Antipolis comprised more than 850 firms, three-quarters of which were engaged in advanced technologies, and employed 15,000 workers on site, plus 4,000 researchers in local public or private institutes and universities.

One danger facing the *technopôles* could be a present-day version of the single-industry trap which accounted for the demise of the coal, steel and textiles towns of northern France due to a high degree of regional specialisation in declining sectors. Sophia Antipolis, despite its focus on telecommunications, would seem to be sufficiently diversified, its base comprising computers, electronics, telecommunications; health, chemicals, biotechnology; alternative sources of energy, the environment; higher education and training.

REGIONAL MANAGEMENT AND LOCAL AUTONOMY

A fundamental issue in regional economic development has been the degree of autonomy enjoyed by the regions in the shaping and promotion of their own business and economic environments.

The decree of 14 March 1964 gave the regions a clearer administrative structure. The position of *préfet régional* was introduced to effect the government's policy on regional development. As representative of the state, this person constituted the link between central authority and the region. *Tranches opératoires*, four-year forecasts of the finance necessary for projects in the fields of housing, town planning and communications, for example, were prepared by the *préfet régional* in conjunction with the *mission régionale*, civil servants who undertook the necessary studies. Final decisions on the amount and regional distribution of expenditure were made centrally, these constituting the PRDE, *plan régional de développement économique*, considered in the regions by committees, CODERs (*commissions de développement économique régional*), consultative bodies comprising the local mayors, representatives of trade, industry and agriculture, and members of the employers' and trade unions.

The law of 5 July 1972 elevated the region to the status of *établissement public régional*. The CODER was split into a *conseil régional* and a CES, *comité économique et social*, the former being a deliberative assembly of elected politicians and the latter a consultative body principally of representatives of professional organisations and employers' and trade unions. Some local taxes provided a small element of regional finance, distributed by the *préfet de région*. Within the framework of the national plan, regions participated in regional economic and social development through the *programmes d'action prioritaire d'initiative nationale* (PAPIN) and *programmes d'action prioritaire d'initiative régionale* (PAPIR). The PAPIN comprised categories of infrastructure expenditure determined by the government, whereas the PAPIR were drawn up by the regions themselves within credit limits set by the national planning authority, the *Commissariat général du Plan* (CGP). The priority programmes were jointly financed by central government, the regions, the *départments* and the *communes*.

All in all, the reforms of 1964 and 1972 represented little more than the deconcentration of regional administration, thus formalising the notion of regional management. Yet it was the law of 2 March 1982 which constituted the major piece of legislation in the field of regional development. Heralding administrative decentralisation, this move represented a major plank of the socialist government's economic planning and raised the status of the region to that of *collectivité territoriale*. Regional sources of funding and responsibility were expanded to encompass economic development, regional planning and training. The *conseil régional* became directly elected with responsibility for drafting a regional plan and the *Comité economique et social* (CES) gave its opinion on the regional plan and the regional budget. The president of the *conseil régional* was vested with a more executive function, preparing the regional budget, voted by the *conseil régional*, and then implementing it. To protect the national interest, a *commissaire de la République* was appointed as the representative of the state in the region, thereby assuming in slightly modified form the rôle previously performed by the *préfet*. It could thus be said that the principal rôle of decentralisation was, in a period of slow growth and scarce resources, to replace the unrealised ambition of a more equitable distribution of the fruits of growth by more autonomous choices.

Here the shift in emphasis is towards greater individuality and identity. Two important tools are the regional plan and the planning contracts between the state and the regions, *contrats Etat-Région*. The regional plan sets out the strategic choices and objectives for a given region's medium-term economic, social and cultural development. The regional plan must be coherent in that it espouses the joint development of economic activities and associated infrastructure and is not at odds with the objectives of the national plan. The priority programmes necessary to give meaning to the regional plan derive from the planning contracts, and together the regional plan and the negotiated contracts provide a unique prospective of a given region in the medium term.

The planning contracts continued the notion of co-financing. The first generation focused on manpower training, the technological environment for firms, research and innovation, living conditions and regional accessibility.

The second generation saw government funding increase by 22 per cent to over 50 billion f. complemented by around 45 billion f. from the regions. The four main categories of expenditure were comunications, regional development, economic development and employment, training and research. For the most recent *tranche* (1994–8), government funding has been increased by 30 per cent to 67.5 billion f. and its distribution is determined by three main criteria: the region's tax base, its unemployment rate and employment change. To date, the principal beneficiaries have been the less-favoured regions (Nord Pas de Calais and Lorraine, for example), and their share has been increased by 23.5 per cent. The Ile de France, on the other hand, has experienced a reduction due to a downward readjustment of Paris' population growth rate by the year 2015 and the anticipated fall in its relative shares of students and R&D activity. (These latter points are discussed later.)

The 1980s saw the French regions endowed with a veritable armoury of devices to attract investors and foster self-sustaining growth. Measures included the *prime régionale à l'emploi*, a regional employment subsidy, and the *prime régionale à la création des entreprises*, a grant to encourage new firm formation. Firms could apply for temporary exemption from *taxe professionnelle* (business tax), and a reduction in *droit de mutation* (capital transfer tax). Finance could be sought from the *sociétés de développement régional* (SDR), regionally based organisations established in 1955 to consolidate businesses' operating capital. Loan guarantees as well as price and rental of sites could be negotiated with local government, whilst access to the regional *centre régional d'innovation et de transfert de technologie* (CRITT), established in 1982, improved the awareness of business and enterprise to the contribution of technology to the modernisation process. *Pépinières d'entreprise*, start-up factories geared to local economic development, providing the essential secretarial, accounting and computing services, enabling those launching projects to minimise the risk of failure and benefit from advice and an exchange of ideas, were established.

Partenariat, partnership, was instrumental in attracting new investment. In Grenoble, for example, the *Centre de formalités des entreprises*, housed in the *Chambre de commerce et d'industrie*, assisted with new firm formation whilst the then *Bureau pour l'implantation des entreprises nouvelles* provided a database on the area and the *Services économiques* of the individual *communes* courted potential investors with information on site availability, price and rental. The *Société d'aménagement et de développement industriel* furnished the sites, the regional SDR *Sud-Est* provided funds to consolidate firms' own resources, and the *Conseil Régional Rhône-Alpes* made decisions on projects which would attract grants and exemptions.

Success in stimulating new investment brings with it new jobs, increased tax receipts, greater regional wealth and enhanced attraction. But everyone was now playing the same game.

THE 1990s: NETWORKS, COHESION AND SOLIDARITY

The beginning of the 1990s only served to confirm the existence of some long-established constraints preventing a more even spatial distribution of resources and opportunities. The Ile de France accounted for 19 per cent of the population on 2 per cent of the territory; 22.5 per cent of jobs, 40 per cent of which were managerial; almost 40 per cent of new jobs; 23 per cent of public employees; 28 per cent of students in higher education; and 27 per cent of gross domestic product. Higher-order services, 60 per cent of researchers and 78 per cent of the head offices of France's leading 200 companies were located in the capital. Many towns were still suffering from the legacy of the single-industry trap, others from poor accessibility which would render them less attractive to business and industry in relation to the ease with which goods might be transported to markets, for example, and others from structural unemployment due to the mismatch between vacancies and available skills.

Questions were raised about the viability of the size of the regions and their budgets by comparison with European partners. In 1987 Midi-Pyrénées had a budget of some 100 million ecus, Tuscany 6,000 million ecus and the Rhine-Palatinate 7,000 million ecus. Should the lines be redrawn? Within the regions the financial strength lay in the cities. The forecast budget for Midi-Pyrénées for 1992 had been 2.3 billion f. whilst that for its capital, Toulouse, had been 3.1 billion f.

Critics maintain that whilst certain responsibilities have been decentralised, the necessary funding has not. An article in *L'Express* of 25 April–1 May 1996 entitled 'Comment ils dépensent votre argent' examines the deficits that have ensued; the Rouen tramway cost 2 billion f., three times the city's annual budget, and 70 billion f. were spent by the regions between 1986 and 1993 on the *lycées*. Deficits invariably have to be met by tax increases which vary by region. The highest per capita housing tax, *taxe d'habitation*, in 1995 was 2,010 francs in Nice, with the average for France at 1,351 f. The highest property tax, *taxe sur le foncier bâti*, in 1995 was 2,542 f. in Bordeaux, with the average for France at 1,476 f.

Furthermore, research conducted at the end of the 1980s revealed that France's major towns and cities fell short of the critical mass necessary to be major players on the European stage. The work, conducted by GIP-RECLUS (1989) focused on towns whose population exceeded 200,000 inhabitants, located within the then European Community, Switzerland and Austria. The key indicators used were: international links, communications, economic strength, research and technology, cultural rôle, industrial specialisation, presence of international congresses and trade fairs. In the resulting 'league table', Paris came second, Lyon twentieth. These were by far the best performances by major French towns and cities in the study.

New measures came on stream in response to this situation, suggesting networking at the regional and local levels. The *loi Joxe* of 6 February 1992 introduced *ententes interrégionales*, a strengthening of the co-operation between two to three contiguous regions where major regional development projects were concerned; *communautés de villes* enabled closer co-operation between urban communes to achieve economies of scale in the provision of urban public services; *communautés de communes* espoused the association of rural communes with a view to joint rural development projects. Investment in the motorway and high-speed rail networks was increased to improve accessibility, *désenclavement*. Moderating the influence of the capital was envisaged by relocating 30,000 public employees and 9 per cent of public research activity from the capital by 1995. The launch of *Université 2000* heralded the creation of new, multi-site universities in order to reduce the share of Paris in the field of higher education to 25 per cent of all university and IUT students by the year 2000.[2]

With regard to foreign investment, the location decision was becoming increasingly strategic in response to developments within Europe and the move to a single market. The eastern frontier regions absorbed a large slice of investment and in 1993 Rhône-Alpes, Nord Pas de Calais, Lorraine and Alsace accounted for 40 per cent of the projects and 56 per cent of the ensuing jobs. Computers, electronics, telecommunications, pharmaceuticals, chemicals and biotechnology led the fields in which foreign investment was concentrated. Together with the attraction of the capital, the key factor was proximity to European member states and to the core European market. The infamous *banane bleue*, stretching from London to Milan and incorporating the zone of greatest population density in the then European Community, the largest flows of capital, goods and services and the highest levels of regional gross domestic product (GDP), was beginning to exert an influence on the design and direction of France's policy of *aménagement du territoire*.

The key objective is that all regions must contribute to the development of resources and to the creation of wealth in an increasingly competitive regional context in which there are winners and losers. To this end, the idea of a hierarchical urban structure appears gradually to have been replaced by one based on networks. Such networking needs to be established between regions, towns, cities, businesses and industries in order to achieve greater cohesion across national space. Partnership, synergy and communication have removed obstacles to the development of such relationships by linking points in space and thereby enabling the establishment of networks. In the words of Veltz (1994: 71): 'The network of motorways, the high-speed rail system, a supply of telecommunications services which today is somewhat in excess of the average requirements of firms, significantly facilitate the operation of multi-site systems of production.'

Brunet (1994) discusses the argument in favour of developing relationships between clusters of towns, pooling local resources and co-ordinating the management of the regional economy, requiring the redistribution of local finance through tax reforms. The key words which would now seem to underpin thinking on the direction of *aménagement du territoire* and the contribution of the French regions to economic and social advancement are: *réseaux*, systems of linked points in national, regional and urban space; *connexité*, the cohesion resulting from the linkages made possible by the existence of networks; *connectivité*, the extent to which points within a region are interconnected; *accessibilité*, the integration of a region into continuous economic space, avoiding polarisation due to the inadequacy of nodes on major national systems of communication.

The reasoning behind a new approach would in part seem to be a response to the increasing divisions manifest in France (high unemployment, *exclusion* etc.), the geographical location of French towns, cities and regions in relation to core European markets and the increased competition both internally and externally occasioned by market forces. Politically and administratively the responsibilities of the *collectivités territoriales*, (*région, département, commune*), have been overlapping despite the region's presumed rôle as the motor of economic development. In addition, a certain degree of central control over the scope and destination of funding through the *contrats Etat-Région* was evident. Given remarks already made concerning the size and financial muscle of the regions, it would appear that it is the metropolitan level, the city and networks of towns and cities, which will be the motors of regional economic development. France is a highly urbanised country with some 80 per cent of the population inhabiting the towns and cities, their suburbs and peripheries. The 1990 census revealed a return to significant rates of population growth in the large towns and in particular in their suburbs. Those towns and cities with a population of more than 200,000 grew by 0.38 per cent between 1982 and 1990 compared with 0.17 per cent between 1975 and 1982. This would seem to suggest that the economies and international importance of the *métropoles* be strengthened.

Another important variable in designing policy is the French concern for *l'immédiat*, their immediate environment. Annual surveys conducted by the *Observatoire interrégional du politique* (1993) established a close link between geographical mobility and social milieu. The 1991 survey showed that 84 per cent of French people live and work in the same region and that it is only those with higher order, managerial jobs who are mobile. The French then are deeply rooted in their home region and this would again suggest investment in *équipement de proximité*, local infrastructure, universities, communications networks, and so on.

In 1993 a right-wing government came to power and a complete review of *aménagement du territoire* was undertaken. It seems that the issues at the heart of how to re-design France's policy of *aménagement du territoire* were threefold. How do you simultaneously maintain Paris as a major European capital whilst not exacerbating existing regional disequilibria, foster self-sustaining growth intraregionally, and harness the assets inter-regionally to the process of national economic development?

The debate on regional development policy in France began in October 1993 (DATAR 1994). It concluded with the publication of the law of 4 February 1995 and addressed these apparent contradictions (*Journal officiel* 5 February 1995). The principal objectives of the new law are to enable French regions, collectively, to play a full part in the nation's battle against international competition whilst giving them the opportunity to progress more equally individually. It aims to avoid the conflict between urban and rural, between large and small towns or cities, between Paris and the provinces, between areas of strong and weak labour markets. It proposes to develop infrastructure, local economies and human resources to encourage the growth of business, enterprise and employment and avoid the marginalisation of France in a European context.

Amongst the principal measures proposed were the establishment of a *schéma national d'aménagement et de développement du territoire*, an outline of aspects of regional development policy of national interest based around the notions of *pays* (towns and communes in rural areas) and *réseaux* (networks), and the establishment of a *schéma régional d'aménagement et de développement du territoire*, an outline of the main regional infrastructure programmes, ensuring coherence with the *schéma national* and ensuring the coherence of projects within the region. The *contrats de plan* remain the physical expression of the aims of the *schéma*. In addition, *schémas sectoriels* will constitute the framework of the *schéma national*. For example, in higher education a more even distribution of centres of higher education is sought and in particular the development of specialist universities located in medium-sized towns as part of a network, and with research interests linked to an area of specialisation.[3] In the field of research, 65 per cent of all public sector research workers are to be located outside Paris by the year 2005. The interconnectedness of France will be assured, since no part of France is to be more than fifty kilometres or forty-five minutes by car from a motorway or the high-speed rail network by the year 2015. Within the same time period telecommunications networks will be accessible throughout France to all populations, firms, *collectivités* and rural areas. The establishment of a *schéma directeur* for the Ile de France will seek to strengthen the position and influence of Paris as a European capital. A *fonds national d'aménagement et de développement du territoire* will allocate government funding to regional development, the restructuring of old mining areas, the relocation of business, local employment initiatives and the development of rural and mountainous areas. New priority areas will be defined under two headings: *zones d'aménagement du territoire*, areas of poor economic development with an inadequate industrial/tertiary base, and *territoires ruraux de développement*, rural areas of poor economic development where capital transfer tax, *droit de mutation*, is reduced in towns of fewer than 5,000 inhabitants.

There will be changes to the system of local taxation by the year 2010, with reforms to the *taxe professionnelle* and the setting up of a *fonds de péréquation* (equalisation fund), and an extension to the *ententes régionales* enabling a region to belong to more than one *entente*.

CONCLUSION

In the last thirty years, *aménagement du territoire* has evolved from a policy which sought to effect the relocation of business and industry to less favoured areas of France in an effort to bring about a more equitable distribution of economic potential, to one which put French regions firmly in the market place, through greater freedom in decision making, based on the premise that individual regions were most keenly aware of their medium-term economic and social needs and had the capacity to market themselves more aggressively.

In its latest phase, the notion is that the efficient utilisation of the sum total of the resources of the regions collectively is, in the current European and international climate, of greater consequence than the economic strength of a single region operating at the expense of any other region. This amply demonstrates France's ambivalence between economic liberalism and interventionism, since the latest strategy would suggest a return to a more *dirigiste* approach, with central government seemingly wresting the initiative and, once again, dictating the content and direction of the policy, thereby assuming reponsibility for *le bien collectif*.

Given that the ultimate objective is to strengthen and increase the attractiveness of all French regions, with *aménagement du territoire* not merely a complementary policy for redistributing resources but part of a coherent national strategy, it is hardly surprising that the single word which has come to infiltrate current thinking on many aspects of contemporary French life, and which has now invaded the increasingly rich vocabulary of regional development, is *solidarité*.

THE REGIONS IN THE MARKET PLACE: CHRONOLOGY

1963   Creation of DATAR: *Délégation à l'aménagement du territoire et à l'action régionale.*

1964   Regionalisation of planning: *le décret du 14 mars.*
       Delimitation of the 21 regions: *circonscriptions d'action régionale.*
       Nomination of the *préfets de région.*
       Establishment of the CODER: *Commissions de développement économique régional.*

1965   Implementation of the policy regarding the *métropoles d'équilibre.*

1972   Regions assume the status of *établissements publics régionaux*: *la loi du 5 juillet.*

Division of the CODER into *Conseils régionaux* and *Comités économiques et sociaux* (CES).

Setting up of the *technopôle* in Sophia-Antipolis.

1973 Beginning of the medium-sized towns policy: *la politique des villes moyennes.*

1975 Beginning of the small towns policy: *les contrats de pays.*

1982 Regional decentralisation: *la loi du 2 mars.*

Regions assume the status of *collectivité territoriale.*

The *Conseils régionaux* become directly elected.

Regionalisation of the budget.

Regionalisation of certain grants: *la prime régionale à la création d'entreprise* and *la prime régionale à l'emploi.*

Establishment of the CRITT: *Centres régionaux d'innovation et de transfert de technologie.*

1984 First tranche of *Contrats de plan Etat–Régions.*

1985 Easing of the development controls in the Paris region.

1986 Establishment of the *zones d'entreprise.*

1989 Second tranche of *Contrats de plan Etat–Régions.*

1992 Introduction of the *ententes régionales: la loi Joxe du 6 février.*

1993 National debate on the policy of *aménagement du territoire.*

1994 Third tranche of *Contrats de plan Etat–Régions.*

1995 Publication of *la loi du 4 février* on the policy of *aménagement du territoire.*

NOTES

1 The expression *aménagement du territoire* is neither easy to define nor to translate, encompassing as it does regional development, regional policy, urban development and regional decentralisation. Regional development provides the framework of social and economic development in the regions, largely in the form of appropriate infrastructure, whilst regional policy concerns the financial and fiscal incentives and disincentives likely to influence the location of business, industry and enterprise. Urban development focuses on the role of towns of various size as anchors in the development process, and the degree of regional decentralisation is a reflection of the extent to which decision making which impacts on regions is taken centrally or locally.

2 Further details of the *Université 2000* project and the rôle of the regions in it can be found in Chapter 5 (section entitled 'Government policy since 1988').

3 See Chapter 5.

REFERENCES AND RECOMMENDED READING

* Bernady de Sigoyer, M. and Boisgontier, P. (1988) *Grains de technopole*, Grenoble: PUG.
    Discusses the key factors that have enabled Grenoble to sustain its dynamic industrial sector, including the role of the technopole, synergy and partnership.
Brunet, R. (1994) *La France, un territoire à ménager*, Paris: Editions no. 1.
Christaller, W. (1966) *Central Places in Southern Germany*, London: Prentice Hall.
DATAR (1994) *Débat national pour l'aménagement du territoire: Document d'étape*, Paris: La Documentation française.
GIP-RECLUS (1989) *Les villes européennes*, Paris: La Documentation française.
Gravier, J-F. (1964) *L'aménagement du territoire et l'avenir des régions françaises*, Paris: Flammarion.

* Hough, J.R. (1982) *The French Economy*, London: Croom Helm.
   Provides a chapter covering the direction and content of the state-led regional policy
   in France prior to 1982 and the shift to a policy of regional autonomy.
Journal Officiel (1995) *Loi no. 95–115 du 4 février 1995 d'orientation pour
   l'aménagement et le développement du territoire*, 5 février.
Ministère de la Solidarité, de la Santé et de la Protection Sociale (1989) *Dix-huitième
   rapport sur la situation démographique de la France*, Paris.
* Montricher, N. de (1995) *L'Aménagement du territoire*, Paris: Editions La
   Découverte.
   Reviews the main stages of the policy of *aménagement du territoire*, the key issues
   and constraints, the achievements, the European context and future challenges.
* Morvan, Y. and Marchand, M-J. (1994) *L'Intervention économique des régions*,
   Paris: Montchrestien.
   Assesses the efficacy of decentralising responsibilities and finance to the regional
   level and the examines the evolving relationship between region and state.
Observatoire interrégional du politique (1993) *Le Fait régional et l'opinion publique*,
   Paris: La Documentation française/DATAR.
Perroux, F. (1991) *L'Économie du XXe siècle*, Paris: PUG (3rd ed.).
Veltz, P. (1994) *Des Territoires pour apprendre et innover*, Paris: Editions de l'aube.

5

HIGHER EDUCATION

Rob Turner

It is widely recognised among industrialised countries that educating the maximum numbers in the population to the highest level possible is a vital element in maintaining international competitiveness. Citizens too recognise that, for the individual, successfully traversing the education system to graduate level opens up the best employment and career prospects. The commitment in France to education is particularly strong among government and people alike, with François Mitterrand making education the priority of his second presidential term in office and Jacques Chirac, his successor, promising to make a referendum on educational reform the centre-piece of his domestic policies. Yet the education system is seen as a problem area, with higher education in particular considered to be in a state of crisis. The central issues which currently confront policy makers, that is, the distribution of students between the different sectors of higher education, the acute logistical and academic problems of the universities and the necessity of a shift to vocational education responding to the needs of industry, derive from the distinctive features of the French system, most particularly the rapid increase in student numbers and the diversity of the establishments which receive them.

THE INCREASE IN STUDENT NUMBERS IN FRANCE

If the drive to expand higher education is common to all industrialised countries, the scale and pace of the growth of student numbers in France makes it unique among its European neighbours. There exists a strong ideological consensus in France on the importance of education, and the republican principles of 1789 included a commitment to free universal schooling which was finally to be implemented by Jules Ferry in the Third Republic. Higher education, however, remained the preserve of the middle and upper classes until the 1960s, when a combination of population growth, public demand for access to education at all levels (a phenomenon known in France as *scolarisation spontanée*), and the 1959 reform extending compulsory secondary education resulted in a twofold increase in numbers continuing schooling to the level of the *baccalauréat*, the French 'A' level-equivalent (Durand-Prinborgne 1991: 28). This increase in numbers in turn fed directly through into higher education and particularly into the open-access, non fee-paying university system. This trend has continued up to the present, with numbers in higher education rising in direct proportion to the number of successful *baccalauréat* candidates, known as *bacheliers*, emerging from the secondary sector. France today, as a result, has a mass higher education system with one in four young people receiving a university education, and this figure is set to rise to one in three by the end of the century. The number of university students has risen from 800,000 in 1980 to 1,285,000 in 1994 and is set to rise further to one and a half million by the end of the century (*Le Monde de l'Education*, October 1994). Higher education in total in France already takes in more than two million students and numbers will rise to two and a half million by the year 2000 (Goedegebuure 1994: 121). To put these figures in a comparative perspective, France currently has 36.4 per cent of an age group in higher education as against 28.7 per cent in Germany and 21.6 per cent in the UK, and France's lead seems set to lengthen by the turn of the century (Flory 1993: 20). Indeed, France is only just behind the world leaders in the field – the United States and Japan.

This expansion is essentially a response to the factors already mentioned – the government's desire for a highly trained work-force and the popular demand for higher education which has been sharpened by France's high level of youth unemployment. It has gathered unstoppable momentum, however, as a result of a combination of political decisions and the particular structure of French higher education. In 1985 Jean-Pierre Chevènement, the then Minister of Education, proclaimed the goal of 80 per cent of young people gaining the *baccalauréat*. This objective, which was considered far-fetched at the time by many observers, was subsequently incorporated in the educational framework law of July 1989 and is now the subject of a wide political consensus. Since all *bacheliers* enjoy the right of automatic entry into the university system – a right which was also enshrined in law in the Savary legislation of 1984 – and since 93 per cent of *bacheliers* do in fact opt to continue their studies in the higher education system (Bédarida 1994: 15), the influx seems irreversible. An attempt to limit the right of access for *bacheliers* was made in 1986 when the right-wing Chirac government introduced the Devaquet Bill but student protest forced its withdrawal. A further failed attempt was made by right-wing parliamentarians in 1995. After these débâcles any further attempt seems off the political agenda for the foreseeable future. The trend is further strengthened by the fact that although it was envisaged that most of the vocational stream *bacheliers techniques* and *bacheliers professionnels* who will make up the bulk of the increase in numbers passing the *baccalauréat* would enter the labour market directly they, too, are entering higher education in substantial numbers (80 per cent and 15 per cent respectively) (Lavroff 1995: 17).

Apart from the increase in entrants into the system, overall numbers are swelled by two factors which affect French higher education on an unparalleled scale. In the university system, despite recent reforms, pass rates in the 'first cycle', which in theory is constituted by the first two years of open-access university courses, run at a rather mediocre 55 per cent (Bédarida 1994: 67). However, the first cycle qualification, the *diplôme d'études universitaires générales* (DEUG) is, as Lavroff points out, normally gained only after one or two resits. Indeed, all the statistics are based on a three-year period. Even then only six out of ten students progress into the second cycle after three years, with 11 per cent taking longer and 19 per cent failing (Lavroff 1995: 18). This phenomenon continues into the second cycle with the average time taken to complete the two cycles to the end qualification, the *maîtrise*, being seven and a half rather than the prescribed four years! (Allègre 1993: 18). Although definitive pass rates do not compare too badly with other European systems, as Allègre points out, the system is having to cope with double the number of students it would have if qualifications were achieved in the time intended.

Finally, France is experiencing a marked and increasing tendency for students to prolong their studies to gain additional qualifications. In 1993 the 9 per cent increase in numbers of second-cycle students was for the first time greater than that of first-cycle students at 4.8 per cent (*Le Monde Campus*, 1 December 1994). This phenomenon is driven by high levels of graduate unemployment and the devalued status of first degrees on the job market. Since these factors in turn result not only from economic difficulties but also from the increased numbers of graduates on the labour market, a kind of vicious circle ensues, with the level of qualification required to ensure good job prospects being forced ever higher.[1] Indeed, this phenomenon is reaching into the third cycle with an increasing number of students staying on to *bac + 5* level (i.e., five years post-*baccalauréat*) to gain the vocational *Diplôme d'études supérieures spécialisées* (DESS).[2] It may also be that the hierarchical, heavily stratified nature of the French higher education system and rigidities in the labour market into which it feeds encourage students to prolong studies to gain the highest level of qualification possible, since this is likely to predetermine their career pattern. As Maria Vasconcellos (1993: 90) puts it: 'In France the link between qualifications and social status is relatively close. Right from the beginning of a career qualifications seem to determine promotion possibilities in a clear and precise manner.' If this tendency to prolong the length of studies can be observed elsewhere, it is far more marked in France than in its major European competitors, with numbers of students continuing their studies remaining stable in the UK and even falling in Germany (Flory 1993: 47).

The scale and rapidity of the increase in numbers that has been outlined is such that absorbing the flow of students and distributing them between different sectors has become the dominant issue in government policy making for higher education. Indeed, so overwhelming are the problems it generates that policy has become essentially reactive. As Claude Allègre, former adviser on higher education to Lionel Jospin during his spell as education minister puts it: 'The future of higher education in France lies in controlling student flows to and between institutions and routes' (Allègre 1993: 171).

THE DIVERSE NATURE OF FRENCH HIGHER EDUCATION

The issue of distribution of student flows is complicated not only by the large numbers involved but by the range and diversity of institutions and routes which make up the system. As Kaiser and Neave point out (in Goedegebuure 1994: 116) the diversified and fragmented nature of French higher education can be explained by a tendency to create new institutions to meet specific new demands rather than reforming existing institutions, a daunting prospect given the notorious inertia of the French public sector. As a consequence of this accretive process of change France has acquired a uniquely multi-faceted system.

Alone among its European neighbours France retains a substantial proportion of students within the secondary system. Created in 1959 to provide an outlet for the reformed and extended technical stream in secondary education and substantially expanded in the first half of the current decade the *sections de techniciens supérieurs* (STS) number 235,000 students training for industrial and commercial careers at technician level in over 1,700 *lycées* of the French public and private secondary education sector (*Le Nouvel Observateur*, 30 November 1995: 8). Studies last for two years and are recognised by the award of the *brevet de technicien supérieur* (BTS). Students are selected for entry on the basis of academic record and performance in the *baccalauréat* by the head teachers of the *lycées*. The majority of students have followed the *baccalauréat technologique* stream which provides an appropriate foundation for STS courses. Graduates are sought after by employers for direct entry to technician and middle management posts.

In the *classes préparatoires des grandes écoles* (CPGE) the *lycées* also prepare 72,000 students for the *concours* or competitive entry exams for the *grandes écoles*, the prestigious institutions which train high-level entrants for management and professional posts (Lavroff 1995: Annexe A3). Again they are selected by head teachers on the basis of academic record and performance in the *baccalauréat*. Because of the prestige and selectivity of the *grandes écoles*, only the strongest students are accepted into the CPGE and this logic percolates further down the system, with the strongest students in the *lycées* entering the science and maths-based *baccalauréat* streams which feed into the CPGE. The content of the two-year courses varies according to the type of *grande école* to which entry is sought but maths- and science-based courses predominate, given the large numbers of engineering and scientific *grandes écoles* with 64 per cent of students. Economics, which is necessary for entry into business schools, comes second with 18 per cent, and literary courses, which prepare students for entry into the *écoles normales supérieures*, third with 13 per cent. Virtually all CPGE students progress into a *grande école*, if not necessarily that of their first choice.

There are approximately 300 *grandes écoles* which take some 200,000 students (numbers are approximate since there is no watertight definition of a *grande école*). The first *grandes écoles* appeared under the *ancien régime* and were established to provide a technically proficient officer corps for France's armies. Napoleon Bonaparte, in addition to recognising the need for scientific military training, extended the rôle of the *grandes écoles* to training the administrators required by the empire. The incipient industrialisation of the Third Republic saw the establishment of an increasing number of engineering and business schools. From the beginning the *grandes écoles* were designed to provide a high-level vocational education and to produce France's administrative and business élites. This social function is clearly incompatible with the provision of mass higher education and remains the major factor dividing the *grandes écoles* from the universities. Entrance to all the *grandes écoles* today is selective, mainly by competitive examination (or *concours*) and despite post-war moves to increase numbers, particularly in engineering and business, in response to demand from employers they continue to count their students in hundreds rather than the thousands of the universities. All the *grandes écoles* provide professional training, with the two largest groupings being the engineering schools and the business schools. It should be noted, however, that the more prestigious schools provide general management training rather than a narrowly vocational education, since their graduates are expected to move directly into top management posts. A third group of *grandes écoles* prepares graduates for entry into the upper reaches of the civil service, a category which in France includes not only central and local government but the teaching profession, the police and the magistracy.

While the majority of *grandes écoles* are in the state sector, a substantial minority come within the private sector, with many being linked to chambers of commerce or professional associations. Despite their disciplinary and statutory diversity the *grandes écoles* have in common the considerable prestige and influence which they enjoy by virtue of their historical vocation to train the élites of French society. A striking but not atypical example is provided by the 1973 group of graduates from the *Ecole nationale d' administration* (ENA) which included future leading politicians Laurent Fabius, Gérard Longuet and François Léotard along with the future managing directors of Elf Aquitaine and Suez (*Le Nouvel Observateur*, 16 February 1995: 4). Thanks to their graduate associations, the *grandes écoles* constitute a very powerful lobby. Furthermore, their prestige has inevitably made them the model for new developments in vocational education in France. Their status has not wholly protected the *grandes écoles* from criticism, however, which centres mainly on the nature of their recruitment procedures which, although they may appear superficially meritocratic, in reality tend to *'favoriser les étudiants favorisés'* or favour the privileged (see Bourdieu and Passeron 1964) because of the content, location and expense of the *classes préparatoires*. Certainly the student body in the *grandes écoles* remains disproportionately middle class, white and masculine.

In many respects the universities would appear to be at the opposite end of the spectrum from the *grandes écoles*. Although French universities were some of the earliest to be created in medieval Europe, they were abolished under the Revolution and the First Empire. When they were revived under the Third Republic in the shape of loosely connected faculties rather than true universities they had permanently lost the rôle of training the nation's élites to the *grandes écoles*, their rôle being restricted to ensuring the transmission of bourgeois culture and to providing recruits for the liberal professions – doctors, dentists, pharmacists and lawyers from the medical and law faculties and teachers from the arts and science faculties, along with middle-rank civil service entrants for whom a degree is a prerequisite for sitting the entrance examinations. The universities became the main beneficiaries of the surge of numbers in higher education which took place in the 1960s, since their courses placed no restrictions on entry for *bacheliers*. The influx of students, however, placed massive strain on the archaic faculties. Teaching methods, facilities, course content and administration proved inadequate for the demands placed upon them and the traditional career outlets could not absorb the increased numbers of graduates. All these aspects of the system, along with many others, were called into question in the earthshaking student revolt of May 1968 which nearly toppled the Gaullist régime.

The government response was the 1968 framework law which sought to modernise the system, creating true, autonomous universities, administered by presidents and governing bodies jointly elected by staff and students. Modifications to the traditional faculties permitted by 1976 the development of cross-disciplinary courses such as Applied Modern Languages and Social and Economic Administration which prepared students for new career opportunities. Further reforms followed, with the 1984 Savary law attempting to instil vocational relevance into a wider range of disciplines and encouraging the reform of many of the courses in the initial two-year cycle in the shape of the *DEUG rénové* (the reformed DEUG).

However, these attempts to modernise course content and teaching and to improve career opportunities for graduates were undermined by the relentless increase in numbers. To cope with this expansion, a number of new universities have been created, particularly in the Paris region, and there are presently seventy-nine public sector universities along with a number of satellite campuses. However, new building has barely kept pace with increasing numbers. The system remains under stress and, with many traditional literary and arts courses remaining of a non-vocational nature and new more vocational courses often swamping a limited job market, no definitive solution to the universities' problems has yet been found. Since traditional career outlets have been saturated by rising numbers, it is clear, as a series of government reports have stressed (see particularly Laurent 1995: 29 and MESR 1994: 26), that universities must look to the industrial and business sectors to absorb their graduates. In an attempt to boost the proportion of vocational education in the universities which, whilst well established at second-cycle and third-cycle level in the range of *maîtrises technologiques* and the DESS, was virtually absent from the first cycle (apart from the medical faculties), new establishments, the *instituts universitaires professionnalisés* (IUP) were created within the universities at the beginning of 1990s. As yet, however, numbers in the IUPs remain insignificant.

The mismatch between university graduates and the job market had been apparent from the moment that numbers began to increase substantially in the 1960s and an early initiative to address this problem came in 1966 with the creation of the *instituts universitaires de technologie* (IUT). They were intended to relieve some of the pressure of increasing numbers in traditional university courses by siphoning off in particular the increasing numbers of *bacheliers techniques*, to correct the imbalance in favour of general rather than vocational education in the universities and to respond to employers' demands for highly trained technicians and middle management entrants on to the job market. These institutions, set up with special status within the university system, recruit students immediately following the *baccalauréat*, selecting them on the basis of their academic record. The intensive courses last two years and are heavily vocational in nature, with teaching delivered partly by professionals from the world of industry and commerce and with all students undertaking work placements. Courses are classified as either industrial or commercial and often directly reflect the structure of the local economy in the specialisations offered.

Demand for IUT places soared in the difficult employment climate from the mid-1970s onwards and a second wave of IUTs was created in the early 1990s in towns with no previous university presence. The 116 IUTs numbered 98,000 students in 1995 (Lavroff 1995: 16), and substantial though this number is, it is well below the 25 per cent of total numbers in the university system that the IUTs were intended to absorb. Their numbers are also no less than half those in the STS which were initially expected to be supplanted by the IUTs over the long term. The status of the IUTs remains rather ambiguous, since their structure and organisation was clearly based on that of the *grandes écoles* and indeed it was anticipated that they would develop into second-rank *écoles* training the echelon of middle management below the *grande école* graduates. However, surveys consistently reveal that employers rank STS and IUT graduates on the same level and government has recently implicitly validated this judgement by allowing both types of establishment to offer the same third-year qualification (the *diplôme national de technologie supérieur* or DNTS). This would seem likely to put a brake on the IUTs' ambitions to compete with the middle-rank *écoles* since they are now bracketed with the STS, which as extensions of the secondary system cannot realistically aspire to the status of *école*.

The picture presented by the French higher education system as a whole is remarkably diverse and fragmented. *Lycées* and universities compete for post-*baccalauréat* students. The selective IUTs and STS and the hyperselective *grandes écoles* coexist with the open-access university system. The vocational courses of IUTs, STS and *grandes écoles* contrast with the generalist culture offered by the open-access university courses. The university system itself is split, with new vocational courses practising selective entry contrasting with the traditional open-access courses and with eleven of the twelve new universities of the 1980s and 1990s being granted exemption from the legal requirement for open access (the sole exception being Le Havre). These various sectors are further differentiated by teaching methods: the universities are still heavily dependent on the *cours magistral*, the formal lecture to a mass audience, while the selective sectors can make more use of small-group teaching and the student participation it permits. There are also differences in course content with the vocational sector adopting a more practical, less theoretical approach, often based on case studies taught by professionals. Finally, the better-financed selective sector, with controlled numbers, enjoys more favourable staff–student ratios. In this system the loser is clearly the traditional open-access university sector. Drained of the best students by the selective and vocational sector, it is swamped by students who are often ill-motivated and ill-equipped for the type of courses it offers and for whom its facilities are inadequate. Those students who do manage to emerge successfully from the university system find their qualifications less saleable on the job market than those from the more prestigious selective sector.

PROBLEMS IN THE UNIVERSITY SECTOR

The two essential characteristics of the French higher education system which have just been described – the rapid increase in student numbers and the fragmentation and diversification of the system – pose particular problems. Many universities experience immense difficulty in coping logistically with the stresses imposed by the open-access system. A constant refrain in the media through the 1980s and 1990s was the imminent collapse of the university system with apocalyptic stories of students attending lectures in cinemas and marquees or even drawing lots to take their place in the lecture theatre.[3] The staff–student ratios in the universities are the worst in Europe. France, with approximately twice the number of university students as the UK, currently has approximately the same number of university teaching staff (Flory 1993: 42). With, for example, over fifty students to each member of staff in Law departments, teaching methods remained heavily based on the traditional formal lecture, a teaching method especially unsuited to the increasing numbers of *baccalauréat technique* students. Many of these problems clearly reflect the chronic underfunding of the university sector in comparison both with its European counterparts and with domestic competitors.[4] The higher level of funding in the selective sector allows better staff–student ratios and more effective teaching and results in the higher pass rates enjoyed by the IUTs and STS. Those university students who do successfully complete their studies and emerge on to the labour market with the DEUG or even the *maîtrise* find that their chances of remaining unemployed are almost twice those of IUT or STS graduates (MESR 1994: 22). Catherine Bédarida in her recent study of the problems of the university sector sums up the situation of university first-cycle students as follows:

> This clientèle with its destabilising aspirations is offered a completely unchanged education by the university system. All the protagonists know that lectures are badly organised, courses badly designed and content and syllabi partly out of date.

> (Bédarida 1994: 212)

She also summoned up the spectre of an apocalyptic scenario which must haunt French governments still traumatised by the memory of what student dissatisfaction led to in May 1968: 'the scenario for the year 2005: the education system explodes, the state collapses.'

GOVERNMENT POLICY SINCE 1988

If the alarming prospect of serious student unrest is to be avoided, French government policy in the 1990s has to deal with two imperatives: managing the growth in numbers, particularly in the first cycle of the universities, and adapting university courses to the demands of the labour market. Lionel Jospin's *'université 2000'* project, masterminded by his adviser on higher education, Claude Allègre, was a serious, if not radical attempt to achieve these objectives by the turn of the century. When Jospin moved into the Ministry of Education in 1988 he found himself in a relatively strong position since education had been designated the top priority of Mitterrand's second presidential term. He was able to have funding increased by 90.5 per cent over the period 1984 to 1992 and central government allocated 16,000 million francs to the *université 2000* reform over a five-year period, a figure which was matched by local authorities.

The involvement of the regions in the expansion of higher education was a key part of Jospin's strategy since the cost of his plans would have been politically unacceptable if borne by central government alone, whereas one of the distinctive and favourable aspects of France's position, as Laurent points out (1995: 16), is the strong demand from local authorites to be involved in higher education. This is particularly the case of the regions which are seeking a distinctive role and which recognise the importance of a trained work-force to the local economy.[5] Jospin brought central and local government together with the universities to draw up contracts covering resource needs based on projected numbers.

Although the regions were given no formal involvement in running the universities, a step which would have threatened the principle of autonomy enshrined in the 1968 legislation and which would have provoked strong opposition from staff and student bodies, they were given a *quid pro quo* for their funding in the shape of the creation of a new wave of IUTs in provincial towns which previously had had no university presence. The increase in numbers of IUT students was also in line with the government's strategy, since it would relieve pressure on the universities and correct the imbalance in provision of vocational education as against the still dominant generalist first-cycle courses.

In an attempt to reduce failure rates in the university first cycle, which Jospin himself termed unacceptable, the DEUG, in a reform implemented by Jospin's successor Jack Lang, was in effect transformed into a modular foundation course, centred on a limited number of major subjects but with a selection of 'minor' options allowing students to try out a range of subjects and change direction if they wished before specialising in the second cycle. An American-style credit-accumulation system was introduced, allowing more students to avoid resitting an entire year. Finally, the exposure of students to *cours magistraux* was delayed with class numbers being held down in the first months of the course. In a pale imitation of Anglo-American tutorial systems advanced students were drafted in to act as tutors to DEUG students. The results of these reforms, if not spectacular, represented modest progress. Pass rates in the DEUG rose from just below 50 per cent to over 55 per cent, although remaining well below the 77 per cent achieved in the IUTs.

In the field of vocational education Jospin and Allègre moved first to alleviate some of the rigidities in educational and career structures which have already been noted. Although the engineering schools had, at the behest of government, somewhat reluctantly abandoned their traditional Malthusianism and increased their recruitment by 25 per cent in the 1980s (Vasconcellos 1993: 79), employers were still calling for increased numbers of trained engineers. At the same time the graduates of IUTs and STS found their careers blocked at technician level (Durand-Prinborgne 1991) because of lack of a higher qualification. In response to the proposals of a Villetaneuse university professor, the eponymous *filières Decomps* or *nouvelles filières d'ingénieurs* were created, allowing technician-level employees to upgrade their qualifications to engineer level through sandwich course studies. The courses which were made available both in university engineering schools and certain *grandes écoles* also recruited students who had completed the university first cycle. This represented a radical enlargement of the recruitment pool for engineers beyond the normal boundaries of the CPGE. Jospin pinned high hopes on these new routes, but recruitment on post-experience courses is notoriously difficult and it remains to be seen whether the ambitious objective of training an extra 10,000 engineers per annum can be achieved.

The centre-piece of the government's efforts to promote vocational higher education was the creation within the universities of *instituts universitaires professionnalisés* (IUPs). As had been the case in the past with the creation of the IUTs and university engineering schools, the model for the IUPs was clearly the *grandes écoles*. Recruitment takes place one year post-*baccalauréat* and is selective. Courses follow the normal university pattern of DEUG, *licence* and *maîtrise* but are heavily vocational in content and taught partly by professionals brought in from outside the university. Students also gain the qualification of *ingénieur maître*. It took a hard-fought battle to wring this concession from the engineering profession, which feared the dilution of the prestige (and concomitant status and salary) of the title of qualified engineer which remains reserved for the graduates of traditional engineering schools. It is likely that the new diploma will rank somewhere between the DUT (*diplôme universitaire de technologie*) and BTS and the *diplôme d'ingénieur*. The creation of the IUPs went ahead at a remarkable rate with over 80 put in place by 1992 (Allègre 1993: 176), often absorbing existing vocational courses such as the *diplôme d'études Universitaires scientifiques et technologiques* (DEUST). But, although the numbers of institutions grew rapidly, the numbers of students enrolled remained disappointingly small and fell far short of the half of first-cycle students which Allègre had intended. This may be attributed partly to the institutional inertia which has traditionally bedevilled French universities and partly to inadequate funding which meant that the IUPs could only be developed at the expense of existing courses.

Although the Jospin/Allègre reforms can best be characterised as an attempt to fine-tune the existing system rather than a radical reform, they did halt the deterioration in the system and achieve some modest improvement in the productivity of the university first cycle as well as laying the foundation for expansion of post-*baccalauréat* vocational education. Furthermore, it can be argued that this type of gradualist and piecemeal approach offers the best hope of overcoming the formidable coalitions of vested interests which can oppose change in the system.

When the right-wing government of Edouard Balladur came to power in 1993 its policies of financial stringency put the effort required to continue the funding of the *université 2000* reforms beyond it. The 1994 budget of the new Minister for Higher Education, François Fillon, created 1,050 new teaching posts when planning experts reckoned 2,800 were required, and indeed the number of staff increased by only 2 per cent as against the number of students which increased by 3.4 per cent (Bédarida 1994: 193). It seems unlikely that the 2,000 new staff per annum necessary to keep up with the increase in numbers up to the turn of the century will be found. Furthermore, it seems probable that any financial benefit from a reduction in the numbers of students resitting years in the DEUG will be counteracted by increased numbers progressing into the more costly second cycle. The benefits of stable forward planning were eroded as provisions for staffing were removed from the state/university contracts. By 1995 commentators such as Bédarida were once again predicting the collapse of the system.

With the high levels of spending of the Jospin era ruled out by the Balladur administration the Right sought other methods for keeping the development of the university first cycles under control. In some right-wing quarters there had long been a visceral objection to the principle of open access, but the Devaquet débâcle had made government reluctant to risk the open introduction of selection. However, in the first flush of victory right-wing deputies introduced a bill to allow all universities to opt out of the open-access system on a voluntary basis, following the example of the recently created universities of the Paris region which had been granted exemption from the provisions of the Savary legislation banning selection. However the bill fell foul of the *Conseil constitutionnel* which abrogated it in its entirety, making it clear that a fundamental change of principle of this kind required a major piece of legislation. The new secretary of state for higher education, François Fillon, then postponed any major changes until he had received a series of reports on the university system. His caution was reinforced by the reception accorded to the first of these, produced by Daniel Laurent, president of the selective university of Marne-la-Vallée and entitled: *Universités: relever les défis du nombre* (Laurent 1995). Laurent's recommendations to reform the university calendar, increase fees and create local university colleges stirred up a storm of protest on all sides. All in all the report's reception amounted to an object lesson in the power of staff and student lobbies and of their resistance to change other than increased spending on the universities (*'Fillon, du pognon!'* chanted the demonstrating students demanding increased spending). Fillon rapidly distanced himself from the report's findings, and further postponed any major changes until after the presidential elections.

Laurent however highlighted a factor specific to French universities which seemed to provide a new interpretation of the problems of the university first cycles and to open up the possibility of a new solution. He emphasised that the bulk of the increase in *bacheliers* which was feeding through to the universities was made up of *bacheliers technologiques* and *bacheliers professionnels*. It had always been envisaged that *bacheliers technologiques* would enter the STS and IUTs and *bacheliers professionnels* would enter directly on to the labour market. In fact, however, whilst 47.5 per cent of *bacheliers technologiques* do in fact enter the STS only 9.1 per cent enter the IUTs as against 21.1 per cent who enter university first cycles, particularly in Law, Economics and Social Sciences (Laurent 1995: 19). A similar, less marked but growing trend could be observed amongst *bacheliers pro-fessionnels* (ibid.: 21). Laurent argued that these students were inadequately prepared for university study and even with improved teaching methodology would be subject to an unacceptable failure rate, pointing to the example of the University of Toulouse Le Mirail which had implemented all the improvements in teaching and tutorial back-up put forward by the Lang reforms but still only achieved first time pass rates of 30 per cent (ibid.: 20).

Laurent's analysis was confirmed and refined by the report on university first cycles produced three months later in March 1995 by Dmitri Lavroff, which revealed that under 30 per cent of *bacheliers technologiques* passed the DEUG, whereas their pass rates in the STS and IUTs were over 75 per cent. Lavroff also revealed that if the results of *bacheliers technologiques* were abstracted from the results in university first cycles the situation improved dramatically with 68 per cent of science stream *bacheliers généraux* gaining the DEUG and 65 per cent of literary and economic stream *bacheliers généraux* passing.

Clearly, if the STS and IUTs reverted to their original vocation of absorbing *bacheliers technologiques* and left university first cycles to recruit *bacheliers généraux*, then prospects would improve for *bacheliers technologiques* and pass rates in university first cycles would also rise to acceptable levels. The system is distorted, however, by *bacheliers généraux* who are attracted by better conditions and facilities in the IUTs and to a lesser extent in the STS and who, as they are academically more able, displace *bacheliers technologiques* in the competitive entrance procedures to the IUTs and STS.

A further distortion is produced by the fact that over half these students continue their studies, moving over into the universities, whilst the proportion of *bacheliers technologiques* who do so is considerably less, although still substantial. Clearly the preponderance of *bacheliers généraux* in the IUTs is subverting them from their original vocation of providing the direct entrants on to the labour market for which industry and business are calling. As Jallade (1991: 75) and Flory (1993: 43) both point out the situation in France is the opposite of that which obtains in other countries, where the most academically able students undertake long courses of study and the weakest undertake short courses.

François Fillon attempted to take direct action to rectify this situation, publishing the Bardet directive which withdrew the automatic right of entry of IUT graduates into the second year of university vocational courses in the *instituts universitaires professionnalisés*. This measure was intended to discourage *bacheliers généraux* from entering the IUTs with the prior intention of switching to the university system to continue their studies. It was also intended to encourage all IUT students, whether *bacheliers technologiques* or *généraux*, to enter the labour market directly on completion of their studies in the IUT. But Fillon, like so many of his predecessors, came up against the power of student protest, which in a few weeks of fury forced the withdrawal of the directive. This left Fillon only with the more expensive and probably less effective alternative of introducing an optional third year of study in the IUTs, recognised by the award of the *diplôme national de technologie spécialisée* (DNTS) in the hope that this would keep students in the IUTs and away from longer university courses. It is questionable, however, whether this diploma will prove to be sufficiently prestigious to achieve this objective, particularly since it is also offered in the STS.

Fillon also proposed to boost the rôle of the IUPs within the university, expanding them to encompass all the *filières technologiques*, including the DEUST and DEUG *technologiques*, up to the selective vocational *maîtrises*. This move to create a single, coherent vocational route within the universities which would also enjoy the advantages of selection and cater for the academically strongest *bacheliers généraux* had several advantages. It would eliminate the *illisibilité* or baffling fragmentation of the various university vocational courses which might well be partly responsible for the mismatch of students and courses and consequent failures or drop-outs. It would also restore the IUTs to their vocation of producing *bac + 2* entrants on to the labour market and, as the IUPs expanded, hold down growth in the open-access first cycles. But Fillon came up against the *grandes écoles* lobby which is particularly influential in right-wing circles and who feared that the new heavyweight IUPs might prove to be too strong competition for the less prestigious *grandes écoles*. He also came up against opposition from the directors of the successful *maîtrise technologique* courses who had no wish to be absorbed into the IUP structure. As a result the IUPs were divested of both the DEUST and the *maîtrises technologiques*. Once again the power of vested interests had halted innovation in the system.

The Juppé government which came to power after Chirac's success in the presidential elections maintained this cautious approach, largely endorsing the Lavroff report and it was made clear that no radical measures, such as the introduction of selection or increases in fees, were contemplated. Lavroff had in fact specifically excluded the possibility of any simple solutions to the problems of the first cycle and had suggested the development of a better system of student guidance, greater flexibility permitting students to transfer between courses and the creation of a wider range of vocational first-cycle courses. These proposals are intended to steer students into the institutions and on to the courses best suited to them and consequently to reduce failure rates. This cautious approach, which amounts to managing the problems of the first cycle rather than eliminating them, is very reminiscent of that adopted by Jospin and Allègre, although the Right arrived at it rather more slowly, painfully and reluctantly than the Left. Even the Right's commitment to financial stringency was eroded by the student protests of autumn 1995 which won increases in the universities' budgets.

CONCLUSION

This brief survey has shown that the very characteristics which make French higher education unique – the rapidity of the increase in student numbers and the diversity of the institutions involved – have generated unique problems. These problems, concentrated above all in the university first cycles, are not the result of the absence of selection *per se* but of the coexistence of the open-access university system with the selective CPGE and *grandes écoles* and the IUTs which were modelled on them. The selective sector drains the best students and the lion's share of resources from the open-access sector. Even the virtue of open access is questionable since the reality is, as many observers have commented, that *de facto* selection in the university system takes place after entry into the system, as a result of the high failure rates.

The obstacles to reform which we have noted also result from the distinctive aspects of the French system. The unique and prestigious *grandes écoles* form a powerful lobby which has held back the development of vocational education in the university sector to protect its own status. University staff at times use the self-governing autonomy they gained from the 1968 reform to demonstrate corporatist attitudes and resistance to change. Above all, the long shadow cast by the student revolt of May 1968, reinforced by memories of more recent government climb-downs following student demonstrations, means that a whole range of policy options to which part of the student body has ideological objections is effectively ruled out. As Claude Allègre ruefully pointed out, when there are more than two and a half million students, not to mention *lycéens*, only a relatively small proportion of them need to take to the streets to put government under enormous pressure.

It is ironic that a country which is characterised by the high priority given by both public and government to higher education should be so ill-served by the institutions which cater for the great mass of its students and should appear to have so little prospect of seeing any improvement.

HIGHER EDUCATION: CHRONOLOGY

1959   Creation of STS.
       School leaving age raised.
1965   Technological *baccalauréat* created.
1966   First IUTs created; reform of university qualifications creating first cycle leading to DUEL/DUES followed by second cycle leading to *licence* and *maîtrise*.
1968   Student revolt; Faure legislation reforming university structures.
1971   Introduction of 'numerus clausus' at the end of first-year medical studies.
1973   DEUG replaces DUEL/DUES at end of first cycle.
1974   Creation of DEA and DESS.
1984   Savary legislation reforms the DEUG.

1985　Creation of *baccalauréat professionnel*.
　　　Chevènement sets target of 80 per cent of age group passing the
　　　baccalauréat by the year 2000.
1986　Demonstrations force the withdrawal of the Devaquet Bill introducing
　　　selection in the universities.
1989　Creation of first IUPs.
　　　Creation of selective universities in the Paris region.
1990　Student revolt over conditions in the universities.
　　　Launch of '*Université 2000*' project by Lionel Jospin.
1992　Reform of DEUG implemented by Jack Lang.
1995　Private Members' Bill introducing selection into universities abrogated;
　　　student unrest over conditions in the universities.

NOTES

1　See 'Inflation de diplômés, pénurie des emplois', in *Le Monde*, 15 March 1995.
2　See *Problèmes économiques*, No. 2410, 8 February 1995: 5.
3　See, for example, *Le Nouvel Observateur*, 30 November 1995: 8.
4　Funding is 32,900 f. per capita per annum in DEUG as against 50,300 f. in the
　　STS and 53,000 f. in the IUTs (Laurent 1995: 18).
5　See Chapter 4.

REFERENCES AND RECOMMENDED READING

Allègre, C. (1993) *L'Age des savoirs*, Paris: Gallimard.
* Bédarida, C. (1994) *SOS Université*, Paris: Seuil.
　A comprehensive and up-to-date survey of the problems of the university system.
Bourdieu, P. and Passeron, J-C. (1964) *Les Héritiers, les étudiants et la culture*, Paris:
　Minuit.
Durand-Prinborgne, C. (ed.) (1991) 'Le Système éducatif', *Cahiers français*, 249,
　Paris: La Documentation française: numéro spécial.
* Flory, M. (1993) *Etudiants d'Europe*, Paris: La Documentation Française.
　A useful, well-documented comparative study.
Goedegebuure, L.C.J. (ed.) (1994) *Higher Education Policy: An International
　Comparative Perspective*, London: Pergamon.
Jallade, J-P. (1991) *L'Enseignement supérieur en Europe*, Paris: La Documentation
　Française.
Laurent, D. (1995) *Universités: relever les défis du nombre. Rapport remis à Monsieur
　le ministre de l'Enseignement supérieur et de la Recherche*, Paris: Ministère de
　l'Enseignement supérieur et de la Recherche.
* Lavroff, D. (prés.) (1995) *Rapport de la commission sur l'évolution du 1er cycle
　universitaire*, Paris: Ministère de l'Enseignement supérieur et de la Recherche.
　This report is likely to be the basis of future reforms.
MESR (1994) *Rapport du groupe de travail sur les filières technologiques de
　l'enseignement supérieur*, Paris: Ministère de l'Enseignement supérieur et de la
　Recherche.
Vasconcellos, M. (1993) *Le système éducatif*, Paris: La Découverte.

6

TELEVISION

Sheila Perry

The development of television in France has been similar to that of many of its Western European neighbours: it first began with a single public service channel, financed and regulated by the state, and has expanded rapidly to become a dual system of both public and private channels on a number of technological supports (terrestrial transmission, satellite and cable), offering programmes twenty-four hours a day (the expansion of terrestrial channels in France can be seen in Figure 6.1).[1] What is specific to each of the European countries which have followed this path is the way in which reform was introduced and the extent to which the public sector has been preserved: in France change has been highly controversial and politicised, characterised by a large number of successive reforms, and the shift from the public sector to the private, with its concomitant shift from the public service ethos to commercially motivated programming, has been radical.

France is in fact the only European country to have privatised a state channel (TF1 in 1987), as opposed simply to creating new, commercial channels alongside the state-run system; it is also – and the two are not unrelated – the first to have lost a channel (La Cinq) through bankruptcy. On the other hand, it is also true that the channel with the largest national market share in Europe is French: TF1, previously France's first state-owned channel, now commands an average of 40 per cent of French audiences. Likewise, one of the most financially successful channels is also French, namely, the subscription channel Canal+, created in 1984 (the first encoded channel in Europe), and now investing in six European countries and Africa. In spite of this, however, French television viewers are not particularly satisfied with their television, which is not renowned for its quality and is dominated by American imports.

Nor is it by any means certain that the legacy of French television's political past is entirely overcome: when the head of Canal+, André Rousselet, was ousted from the channel by a power struggle on the board of directors, rumours circulated accusing Prime Minister Edouard Balladur of deliberately organising the episode in order to get rid of Rousselet, seen as François Mitterrand's man – rumours fed, incidentally, by Rousselet himself with his

1936	First TV broadcast						
1945	RTF						
1963	RTF 2 channels						
1964	ORTF 2 channels						
1973	ORTF 3 channels						
1974	TFI	Antenne2	FR3				
1984	TFI	Antenne2	FR3	Canal+			
1985	TFI	Antenne2	FR3	Canal+	La Cinq	TV6	
1987	TFI (privatised)	Antenne2	FR3	Canal+	La Cinq (reallocated)	M6 (reallocated)	
1989	TFI	Public channels under single chairmanship Antenne2/FR3 (+ La SEPT)		Canal+	La Cinq	M6	La SEPT (on FR3, awaiting satellite)
1992	TFI	France Télévision France 2/France 3		Canal+	La Cinq (ceases 12/04)	M6	
1992	TFI	France Télévision France 2/France 3		Canal+	From 28/09 ARTE (formerly La SEPT) (from 7 pm)	M6	
1994	TFI	France Télévision France 2/France 3		Canal+	La Cinquième (daytime) ARTE (evenings)	M6	

Key: ▨▨▨ Public sector; ▧▧▧ Private sector

Figure 6.1 Expansion of French television channels, 1936–94 (excluding satellite and cable)

article in *Le Monde* (17 February 1994) entitled *'Edouard m'a tuer'* [sic].[2] In other words, although control of television by the government has supposedly been relinquished, there are strong suspicions of behind-the-scenes manipulation. At the same time, commercial channels complain bitterly about unrealistic government-inspired constraints on their programming (e.g., quotas for French or European Union productions) and they are frequently sanctioned (usually in the form of fines) by the regulatory body, the *Conseil supérieur de l'audiovisuel* (CSA), for not respecting these.

Television, in spite of repeated reforms over the past ten years or so, is still a highly controversial subject in French society.

The issues involved in any mass medium such as television are threefold: political, economic and socio-cultural. Politically, a democratic system requires its media to be free from government control, unbiased and fair in their reporting and to provide a forum for wide public debate. They are also an important economic sector, providing employment and various products (in the case of television, the programmes themselves, but also technological products such as television sets, satellite dishes and decoders) and (in most countries) an advertising market providing outlets for other economic products. But media output also has a cultural impact, which has an effect on other aspects of society, such as pluralism of opinion, freedom of access, representation of minorities, language and cultural identity. This means that some form of regulation may be considered necessary on the grounds that a totally free market economy cannot be relied upon to provide the necessary balance in these areas.

One could argue that in France there has not been a successful mix of these different elements, that in the desire to shake off the increasingly untenable state monopoly of television, for example, there has been insufficient regard for the dangers of economic freedom, or that the government's belated attempt to regulate a largely commercial system is tainted by the old habit (or suspicion) of government intervention designed to keep a given party in power. In particular, '*l'alternance*', or the switching of power from the Right to the Left and back again during the period of expansion of television, has made it a political football between adversarial forces which have approached television in blatantly ideological terms, or simply used it for crude electoral purposes.

The following sections will treat each of these three aspects in turn, in order to show how they have each contributed and interacted with each other to create French television as it is today.

THE POLITICAL: THE SHIFT FROM GOVERNMENT CONTROL AND CENSORSHIP

A major turning-point in the development of French television came in 1982. For nearly forty years prior to that, the state exercised a monopoly of control over the broadcasting media (both radio and television). The relatively short period since 1982 has seen a somewhat frenzied attempt to reform the system, often for short-term political gain at the expense of long-term strategic planning.

Although there were reforms of the system prior to 1982, none of these broke the state-controlled monopoly inherited from the immediate post-war period, as the *Radiodiffusion-télévision Française* (RTF) then the *Office de la radiodiffusion-télévision Française* (ORTF), were directly responsible to government ministers (see Chronology at the end of this chapter). As for de Gaulle, he put his position of power to good personal use, arguing that an antagonistic regional press meant that his control of the air waves simply redressed the balance of opinion.[3] This control held another attraction: it meant he could address the French people directly, and this corresponded to his style of government, which was to go over the heads of parliamentary parties (which he held responsible for the instability of the Fourth Republic) and claim his legitimacy directly from the people.[4]

Meanwhile, the opposition got little or no coverage, as television news was vetted directly by government ministers (from 1964 through the *Service des liaisons interministérielles pour l'information* (SLII)). Censorship was direct: each morning there was a meeting with the minister to draw up the news agenda. It was also indirect: given that the government was the employer, journalists who wished to keep their jobs were careful not to suggest topics or coverage which would not get government approval; the risks were too great and the item was unlikely to get through anyway, and so self-censorship was rife. This is hardly surprising, given that each change of government brought in a change of top media personnel.

This stranglehold on the media was useful to those in power, but not without its drawbacks. Cayrol (1986: 36) tells of how the unprecedented appearance on television of opposition candidates for the presidential election campaign led to de Gaulle's failure to win outright in the first round. Furthermore, the government stranglehold on television was blatant, and therefore open to criticism, published largely in the regional press, and this was its second drawback. Many caricatures of de Gaulle with a television screen replacing his head, and other such representations of his dominance, appeared in the papers. Reaction against the authoritarian Gaullist state and against television as an arm of government, reached a pitch in the events of May 1968, in which, initially, contrary to the other media, television supported the government and failed to report on the extent of the revolt. The question of freedom of television was on the agenda. It was not to produce concrete results for some time – television journalists did finally join the ranks of other striking workers, but there was a major crackdown immediately after the 'events' and many lost their jobs – nevertheless the subject had been raised and was not going to go away.[5]

Neither Georges Pompidou nor Valéry Giscard d'Estaing broke the state monopoly over broadcasting. The former tolerated a period of greater freedom on the first channel while Chaban-Delmas was prime minister, but this was short-lived, and ceased with the departure of the premier. It was Georges Pompidou (in a press conference on 2 July 1970) who coined the oft-quoted definition of television news as 'the voice of France', using it to justify state control.[6] In 1974 Valéry Giscard d'Estaing brought in a major reform, leading to the separation of the various elements of the ORTF into seven autonomous units, each responsible for a particular function (production,

117

transmission, conservation, etc.: see Chronology). Although this occasioned a major shake-up in the way in which all of these functions were performed, and political control became more indirect, control nevertheless remained. The much-trumpeted autonomy and independence of the various constituent parts of the former ORTF, and in particular of the three television channels, was independence from each other rather than from the state. The state was still the sole shareholder and responsible for determining the level of the licence fee (approved by parliament) and fixed the ceiling on the proportion of advertising allowed. Perhaps more importantly, from the point of view of political control and censorship, the state was still the sole employer, and in particular named the heads of each of the channels.

The Left in opposition had complained bitterly that they were disadvantaged by the government's control of the media, so when they came into power under François Mitterrand in 1981 one might have expected them to abolish what they had constantly berated as an abuse of power. Freedom of the media was, indeed, a promise of François Mitterrand's electoral campaign. But as had been the case for de Gaulle, the temptation to use this power which had been denied for so long proved too great for the newly elected president, and he reformed the media only after certain undesirable elements had been disposed of: replacements were made for all the heads of the channels, all the news editors and sub-editors and many journalists. Habits were so ingrained in this sector, Serge Bauman wrote, speaking of the number of heads which rolled in the broadcasting media, that 'It was *logical* that the news world should be affected by the change in Majority brought about by the presidential and parliamentary élections' (Bauman 1981: 9; our emphasis), whereas the opposite might have been expected. François Mitterrand justified this by arguing it was the country (rather than the government) which wanted a radical change, and that this would only be possible in these circumstances. Eventually, the new president did commission a report, the *Rapport Moinot*, to make proposals on media reform.

Largely in keeping with the recommendations of the *Rapport Moinot*, the reforms which François Mitterrand introduced followed two strands. The first was the creation of a regulatory body, *La Haute Autorité de la communication audiovisuelle*, intended to act as a buffer between government and the media (both radio and television) and thus break the umbilical cord which had kept the media at government's beck and call. The second was to break the state monopoly by allowing the creation of privately owned channels.[7]

The regulatory body as a buffer to government control

La Haute Autorité de la communication audiovisuelle was set up to mitigate the government's control of the media by assuming some of the powers previously exercised by politicians. It was this body, and no longer the prime minister, the minister of information or the *Elysée*, which was to control and

Table 6.1 Broadcasting regulatory bodies in France, 1982 to date

	La Haute Autorité	*La CNCL*	*Le CSA*
Dates	1982–6	1986–8	1989 to date
Parliamentary majority	Left	Right	Left 1988–93 Right 1993 to date
Members	9	13	9
Mandate	9 years	9 years	6 years
Nominated by	3 President of Republic	2 President of Republic	3 President of Republic
	3 President of National Assembly	2 President of National Assembly	3 President of National Assembly
	3 President of Senate	2 President of Senate	3 President of Senate
		1 *Conseil d'Etat*	
		1 *Cour de Cassation*	
		1 *Cour des Comptes*	
		1 member of *Académie française*, chosen by that body	
		3 professionals coopted by 10 preceding members	

Key
CNCL *Commission nationale de la communication et des libertés*
CSA *Conseil supérieur de l'audiovisuel*

regulate French broadcasting and to ensure that the public service obligations (discussed below) were met. In particular, the regulatory body chose the heads of public sector television channels and radio stations who, as a result, were no longer dependent on politicians for their jobs.

Since the *Haute Autorité* was created in 1982 there have been three regulatory bodies in succession, and Table 6.1 shows the difference in composition between them.

The most striking fact that emerges from this table is that neither of the first two bodies survived a change in parliamentary majority, in spite of the fact that in both cases, in order to protect the body's independence, its members had a longer mandate than deputies (who have five years) or the president (seven years). In other words, the attempt to break away from the tradition whereby each change of parliamentary majority or president brought in a corresponding change in media professionals had failed. The new right-wing government of 1986 had no legal right to oust the members of the *Haute Autorité* chosen by the two socialist presidents (of the Republic and of the National Assembly), but they found a simple solution to this problem: they simply introduced legislation to disband the *Haute Autorité*! In 1988, when the Left regained power, they played tit for tat and reconstituted the *Haute*

119

Autorité (at least in terms of its composition) under a different name. There has been one positive development on this front, however: the CSA has survived both a change of parliamentary majority (in 1993), and of president (in 1995). This owes as much to effects of reform fatigue as any other motive, but the broadcasting sector badly needed this stability.

The CSA's powers are extended from those originally given to the *Haute Autorité* in 1982, and this has also reduced government control. Although the first regulatory body was responsible for allocating broadcasting rights to local stations, the government had retained this right on a national level. This meant that the *Haute Autorité*, rather than government, had responsibility for the burgeoning local radio stations. However, as far as television was concerned, little had changed: it was the government which had the freedom to allocate the three new television channels which were created during the period in which the *Haute Autorité* functioned,[8] and in two of the three cases, broadcasting franchises went to friends of François Mitterrand (André Rousselet for Canal+ and Jérôme Seydoux for La Cinq). It is symptomatic of the ironic twists and turns in French politics that when the Right removed the power to allocate franchises from government (and so from themselves) in the 1986 reform, and gave it to the new regulatory body, the CNCL, it was so as to replace Mitterrand's men with some of their own. La Cinq was taken from Jérôme Seydoux and allocated to the right-wing sympathiser and press magnate Robert Hersant (whose expansionist tactics the Left had tried to curtail in their 1984 reform, which limited press take-overs and ownership).[9] Lyonnaise des Eaux, which took the largest share of M6, was headed by the Gaullist Jérôme Monod. Ostensibly the reform was to increase media independence but, in effect, right-wing sympathies among the CNCL's members ensured that the government continued to be well served.

This example illustrates that it is dangerous to trust too readily to the declared intentions of those advocating reform, and that the structures set in place when reform is carried out do not always indicate clearly where real power lies. Table 6.1 shows that of the three regulatory bodies, the CNCL had the lowest proportion of members chosen by politicians, and yet it is the one whose reputation for independence was the most quickly tarnished. Admittedly, the flames of the fire against the CNCL were fanned by François Mitterrand, annoyed that 'his' organisation had been replaced, but this was with some justification, as the reallocation of franchises mentioned above shows.[10] These precedents led the CSA to fight hard to establish its own legitimacy by being, and being seen to be, independent of government, but this has often been difficult. It appointed, for example, Phillippe Guilhaume to the chairmanship of France-Télévision in 1989, although he was known not to be a government supporter at the time. Under government pressure Guilhaume resigned fifteen months later and was replaced by someone more sympathetic to the government, Hervé Bourges, who in turn was replaced by Jean-Pierre Elkabbach when the Right returned to power in 1993.[11] However, the CSA's continued existence is gradually helping it to gain authority and at least the principle, if not the practice, of independence is firmly established.

The creation of new channels

When Mitterrand came to power in 1981 there were three state-owned television channels. By the time he left in 1995, there were seven terrestrial channels (both public and private), cable and satellite offering a wide range of channels and services, and local television channels in several major cities. The impetus for creating new channels did not spring exclusively from the desire to distance the media from government control, but this desire was, nevertheless, a factor in favour of such a move. It is perhaps ironic that it should have been a left-wing government, after twenty-five years of right-wing rule, which brought private capital into television. Indeed, it was fear of the influence of the forces of capitalism which had posed a dilemma for the politicians of the Left in their arguments against government control of the media when they were in opposition: although they did not like de Gaulle, or Pompidou or Giscard d'Estaing exercising this control, neither did they have any great desire to see it go into the hands of capitalists.

So why did they suddenly double the number of channels with, first of all, a subscription channel (Canal+), for which they could be accused of élitism (it was available only to those who could afford to buy a decoder and pay a monthly fee on top of the licence fee), and then with two fully commercial channels? A generous answer would be to say that this was to meet the increasing demand from the public for wider choice without increasing the licence fee beyond the bounds of most people. A more cynical view, borne out by the mad rush to launch the later two channels before the parliamentary elections of March 1986, is that the Left's motivation was to win back support by adopting a popular measure. It could also be argued that before the Left came to power, liberalisation of the media had already brought commercial practice into the public sector.[12]

Successive governments have continued to increase the number and types of channel available, including cable and satellite. The nature and effects of these changes will be discussed in the sections below: as far as political control of the media by government is concerned, suffice to say that both the creation of a regulatory body and the multiplication of the number of private channels mean that the institutional link which previously existed between government and journalists no longer exists, except in the much reduced public sector, and even there it is not as direct as it was. Political control, where it exists, is exercised behind the scenes[13] and no longer has political legitimacy – except, of course, in times of war, when information is controlled at source, as in the Gulf War of 1991.

THE ECONOMIC: THE SHIFT FROM PUBLIC SERVICE BROADCASTING TO COMMERCIAL TELEVISION

Although many would argue that television, as a cultural product, is not a commodity like soap powder or cars, and cannot be given the same treatment, nevertheless, it still has economic value. Even in public service broadcasting, there are elements which link television to the nation's economy, such as employment or the production of the technological supports for transmission. Government has to take these factors into consideration when legislating on television.

Political pressure to break the French state monopoly with the introduction of alternative sources of finance was accompanied by economic pressure, due to rising costs and the demand for television expansion. France, like most countries, introduced a licence fee, but where France differed from, say, Britain, is that as television expanded and costs rose, the extra finance needed was raised not from the creation of a private sector (introduced in Britain in 1954) nor from raising the licence fee, but with the introduction of advertising on public sector broadcasting, in 1968. This meant that increases in the licence fee could be kept to a minimum, with its obvious political advantages for those in power, naturally loath to increase an unpopular levy.

So although when François Mitterrand came to power in 1981 the French had an entirely state-owned system, this had already been partially commercialised with the introduction of advertising. Furthermore, the 1974 reform introduced by Valéry Giscard d'Estaing, which split the ORTF into seven separate units, stipulated that the three television channels should be in competition with each other. In other words, the elements of commercial television were already laid down even before the creation of the first private channel.

François Mitterrand had a further economic motivation for the introduction of private channels. He wanted to make France a modern, technological nation, at the forefront of developments which could then be exported to the rest of the world, and one way to do this was to invest in new broadcasting technology. Pressures from outside were also becoming unavoidable. Control of the air waves was difficult enough: inhabitants of the border regions of France could escape the state monopoly over broadcasting by turning their aerials in the direction of surrounding countries in order to receive Swiss or Belgian programmes. With the advent of satellite, television was to become even more internationalised, and the geographic prerequisite for circumventing the monopoly was no longer necessary. The French government attempted not only to accept the inevitable, but to turn it to France's advantage by becoming a leader in the field.

Unfortunately, the ventures undertaken failed to have the anticipated results. The sale of satellite dishes in France has been markedly slow, in comparison with that of dishes in Britain, largely because in the early stages the financial outlay required of households was not compensated by the range of channels available. France's joint satellite venture with Germany met with serious technological problems and launch was delayed until October 1988, by which time alternative outlets had had to be found for some of the proposed programmes (e.g., La SEPT was given broadcasting slots on FR3's wavelength, to the dissatisfaction of both companies). Canal+ in particular has sought to make satellite more attractive by working on the principle of a 'bouquet' of thematic channels (film, sport, programmes for children, etc.).

In 1982, France also launched an ambitious programme for cable, whereby the whole of France was to be equipped within a few years. However, by choosing the technologically most advanced, but also therefore the most expensive, optic fibre, the programme ran into difficulties and was officially abandoned as a systematic development in 1987. By 31 March 1994 only 23.7 per cent of French households with access to cable were subscribers (La Lettre du CSA 56, May 1994: 2) whereas Germany had reached 70 per cent by the beginning of the decade (Regourd 1992: 59). One of the major difficulties for those developments requiring financial outlay from viewers was that terrestrial channels were expanding at the same time, at no extra cost. In addition, France's exports have suffered because the norms adopted for video recorders and television sets have not become the accepted standard throughout Europe.

The system was, therefore, through economic and political pressure, becoming variegated. By the time the Right came into power again in 1986, satellite and cable had been established, and there were three state-owned terrestrial channels (TF1, Antenne 2 and FR3), one 'hybrid' channel (Canal+, in which the state-owned Havas had a majority holding, but which was run on commercial lines through its subscriptions) and two private channels (La Cinq and TV6). In normal times, this might have been considered a well-balanced and sufficiently pluralistic system for matters to rest there for a while, particularly as the latter three were all less than two years old. These were not normal times, however, as the Right, ousted from power after 23 years of uninterrupted rule in 1981, had returned triumphantly to parliament and government. The desire to make their mark was very strong, particularly as François Mitterrand was still president, and this was the first period of cohabitation. Guided by the need to outdo the Left which had stolen their thunder by introducing private channels and by a commitment to the ideology of a free-market economy, the Right decided to privatise one of the state channels.[14]

It is now generally agreed, particularly in the light of the demise of La Cinq in 1992, that this privatisation led to an untenable imbalance in the system. It meant that the two new, smaller, channels (La Cinq and M6), which as yet, for technical reasons, did not have full national coverage, were competing for the same advertising revenue with the well-established and newly privatised giant. The advertising market had expanded massively with the introduction of television commercials, but it was not infinitely expandable, and as all the channels were general, as opposed to thematic,[15] they were all aiming for the mass market.[16] This market was too small to sustain the number of outlets[17] and La Cinq, able to gain only 10 per cent of the market share, could not earn sufficient revenue and collapsed.

It is generally agreed by commentators that when television channels compete for advertising revenue, this leads to a uniformity of programming. The principal aim of the company run on commercial lines is to make profits; this does not, of itself, preclude quality programming, but it does mean that the aim is to satisfy the greatest number, rather than minority groups, and the degree of satisfaction can become secondary to the number of people viewing, measured quantitatively rather than qualitatively. This runs counter to the ethos of public service broadcasting.

Public service broadcasting has three main objectives: to inform, to entertain and to educate. Francis Bouygues, who won the bid for TF1 when it was privatised, claimed: 'Ours is a commercial channel. There are things we do not wish to do, such as broadcast cultural, political, or educational programmes' (*Le Monde*, 23 June 1987). He was overstating the case, but the search for profit has led to a major increase in the number of variety shows and American imports, because these programmes are much cheaper than home-produced fiction or documentaries. American production companies can recoup their investment on the large home market and so offer their programmes at extremely low rates on the international market, making it impossible for European companies, with a much smaller domestic market, to compete.[18] The public service ethos also means respect for pluralism of opinion, equal access to air time, minority programming, but economic pressures mean that these programmes, where included, are pushed to less popular viewing times, since channels cannot afford to devote prime time, when the largest audience is available, to minority groups. Hence programming is dominated by what is commonly called '*la dictature de l'audimat*' (dictatorship of the audience ratings), that is, the pressure placed on television professionals to produce programmes attracting mass audiences.[19]

THE SOCIO-CULTURAL: FROM THE 'VOICE OF FRANCE' TO THE THREAT OF AMERICAN IMPERIALISM

Recently, as a result of technological progress, television has become increasingly international. Previously, however, television developed in parallel in many nations, and it did so in terms of the specific socio-cultural expectations of the country involved. The definition of television as 'the voice of France' by Georges Pompidou was a convenient political slogan, but it also showed how Gaullism perceived television as a manifestion of the nation's cultural identity. Indeed, Jérôme Bourdon argues (1990: 20) that government intervention took place as much in the cultural field as in the political, censoring what ministers perceived as inappropriate moral attitudes or language. This tradition has not been lost: when the *Haute Autorité de la communication audiovisuelle* was set up in 1982, one of its missions was to be a watchdog in matters such as protection of the French language. This role has been handed down from each of the regulatory bodies to the next, and the CSA currently prints in its monthly newsletter a column on the misuses of the French language which have been observed in the previous month and information on the correct usage. The prescriptive role assumed by the *Académie Française* in the seventeenth and eighteenth centuries lives on in the CSA of the twentieth century!

One of the largest threats to the French language, and to French culture in general, is believed to come from American imports.[20] Inexpensive American programmes occupy air time which might otherwise be given to French culture, and lead to underinvestment in French productions, making it even harder to develop a competitive industry. Under the state-run system in the 1950s and 1960s, production as well as broadcasting was financed by the public sector, and French television built up its reputation, inspired by the cinema, on adaptations of works of fiction. The production monopoly had been broken, but the independent sector was slow to get off the ground, having only the ORTF as an outlet. In 1986 the Right gave a boost to the independent sector by abolishing the obligatory quota of programmes from the SFP (*Société Française de production*) that channels were required to fund, but this was at the expense of the public sector and did nothing to increase the overall production budget, severely constrained by the shift to commercial rather than public service broadcasting.

On its return to power, the Left attempted to boost French production with the introduction of quotas for French and European productions as a whole, irrespective of whether this was from the public or private sectors (set initially at 50 and 60 per cent for the proportion of air time which was to be allocated to French and European Community productions respectively, modified in line with the European directive '*Télévisions sans frontières*' of 1989 to 40 per cent national and 50 per cent European). These, and all government-inspired obligations, were met with protest from the private channels. In their eyes, any constraints were too restrictive, and the government was accused of not understanding private television, and of wilfully trying to push channels into the red.[21] This seems a fairly clear indication of the direction French television would take if the market were not regulated by the state.

Indeed, in spite of government efforts, it still tends to drift in the direction of Americanisation. Much of the work of the CSA has been the sanctioning of television channels which have failed to respect the quota system. Sanctions usually take the form of fines, though as a last resort the CSA can temporarily or even permanently withdraw the right to broadcast. Similar wrangles have taken place between channels, government and the regulatory body on the broadcasting of programmes considered unsuitable for children. On the other hand, the protection of French cinema has been more successful, particularly with the investments made by Canal+ in return for more lenient broadcasting rights. In the terms of the channel's new contract, negotiated in 1995, this funding is due to rise progressively to reach 4.5 per cent of Canal+'s turnover by the year 2000 (*La Lettre du CSA* 69, June 1995).

In order to protect the public service ethos from further encroachment by commercialisation there are restrictions on the extent and nature of advertising. Some products, such as cigarettes and alcohol, are denied the right to advertise on television. When advertising was introduced in broadcasting, it was kept initially to a ceiling of 25 per cent of revenue for the sector. This was largely to placate the powerful press lobby, rather than to limit any supposed nefarious effects on television viewers, but it did mean that television companies had 'insufficient incentive to pursue the mass audience at all cost' (Kuhn 1995: 154). Currently, advertising is limited to twelve minutes in any given hour, and to one advertising break within films on the private channels (breaks are forbidden in the public sector). The issue of whether films should be interrupted at all proved to be highly controversial, on the grounds that a film is a work of art and to insert advertising is to spoil its artistic unity. The cinema lobby lost the battle, but that the fight took place at all is indicative of the high esteem placed on culture in France. The CSA now sometimes authorises a second advertising break if the film is particularly long, a fact which shows the extent to which channels fight to get the maximum revenue possible from advertising. The battle is being fought inch by inch.

The Right has, naturally, shown itself to be more sympathetic towards the commercial argument, whereas the Left has been more concerned by the 'pollution' which advertising can represent, as well as the influence it can exert on the programme makers. The line drawn between programme and advert is being gradually eroded, with more and more programmes being sponsored by major companies, although it is far from reaching the proportions of Italian television (where advertising companies can buy programmes and insert their own adverts), and advertising is clearly labelled as such or the CSA exacts fines for what it calls illicit advertising (*'publicité clandestine'*).[22]

Because commercialisation has led to a loss of educational and informative programmes, these have had to be introduced via another route, with the creation of La SEPT (which became Arte in 1992), a joint Franco-German venture financed largely by government money. This was originally intended for satellite transmission, but due to the delays in launching the satellite it was first given air time on FR3, and then after the bankruptcy of La Cinq was allowed to broadcast on the fifth terrestrial channel from 7 pm. It now shares this channel with another government-inspired venture, La Cinquième, an educational channel which began its exclusively daytime broadcasting on 13 December 1994. The system is now split, not between public and private sectors, but between low-budget, 'serious' channels (some would say recondite or boring) and high-budget entertainment ones (vilified by their opponents for being frivolous and of low quality): the difference is exaggerated, but nevertheless real. To illustrate this, Figure 6.2 shows the difference between channels in terms of genre for 1993 (before the creation of La Cinquième):

TF1	France 2	France 3	Arte	Canal+	M6
TV fiction 42.3%	TV fiction 23.5%	TV fiction 25%	Documentaries 55.9%	Cinema 46%	TV fiction 34.5%
Music, variety 15.8%	Music, variety 19.7%	Documentaries 24.5%	Cinema 16.1%	TV fiction 18.7%	Music, variety 26.3%
News and information 12%	News and information 19.3%	News and information 14.6%	TV fiction 13.5%	Documentaries 13.5%	Documentaries 20.1%
Documentaries 10.4%	Documentaries 18.8%	Music, variety 13.2%			

Figure 6.2 Programmes on each television channel, 1993 (showing genres which represent more than 10 per cent of total programming)
Source: *La Lettre du CSA* 64, January 1995[23]

Will France Télévision manage to overcome the dichotomy between rich and poor channels? France Télévision is the organisation which combines France2 and France3 (formerly Antenne 2 and FR3) in a unitary structure intended to foster complementarity, rather than competition, between the two channels, a reform brought in by the Left in 1989. Still part of the public sector, the two channels have as their mission respect of the public service ethos, and their complementarity means they can reach different sectors of the population and offer genuine choice, while together they are competing with TF1 for a larger market share. So, whereas the early days of expansion meant more channels but not necessarily greater choice, recent 'corrective' measures have sought to re-establish an element of genuine choice.

CONCLUSION

The three variables of television – political, economic and socio-cultural – are in perpetual conflict in France. Commercialisation was brought in to counteract excessive government power, but excessive commercialisation is threatening French culture, so the market has to be regulated by the state. The need to regulate the audiovisual market means that although the government has relinquished certain powers over the media, it has retained the right to initiate legislation in areas considered of national interest. Government no longer has a monopoly of power, as this is now split three ways, between government, the regulatory body and the channels themselves. All the powers now exercised by the channels or the CSA, such as matters relating to personnel or the distribution of air time during an election campaign, were once prerogatives of government, but government still has responsibility for determining the framework within which these powers are exercised, and so can ultimately be said to retain control. It is this three-way split that is the source of controversy, as there can be conflict of interest (or collusion) between any of the parties, and finding the real source of power can be difficult.

The demise of La Cinq is a good example of this. The cause may simply have been a case of poor commercial management, since the channel's chief shareholders, first Robert Hersant and then Hachette (who took it over in an attempt to save it), were accused of adopting an over-ambitious broadcasting strategy, in which La Cinq was competing head-on with TF1, in spite of being a much smaller company with a small market share. But the involvement of both government and the CSA muddied the waters, and La Cinq collapsed amid a storm of controversy. Before it went bankrupt, the channel was fined frequently and heavily for failing to respect the legal quotas for French and European productions. Since it was the CSA which exacted the fines, but the government which determined the quotas, both were blamed for the financial difficulties of the channel, and both denied responsibility. Suspicions ran high: did the government deliberately push the channel to its end? It seemed plausible enough, in that the channel was proving to be a political football between Left and Right: the Left had created it and awarded it to Silvio Berlusconi and François Mitterrand's friend Jérôme Seydoux, the Right had reallocated it, with the aid of the CNCL, to the right-wing sympathiser Robert Hersant; it was likely that the Left would get great satisfaction from seeing it wrested back again. Catherine Tasca, the Left's communications minister, also took pleasure in announcing at every available opportunity that there was a generalist channel too many, and to see one go bankrupt obviously vindicated her and gave weight to the implied criticism of the Right's privatisation of TF1. But of course the government did not in fact need to push, they simply had to stand back and do nothing, having put in place the quota system which La Cinq could not afford. So, was the CSA, by insisting that La Cinq respect the quotas, guilty of carrying out the government's dirty work, and did this call into question its much-acclaimed independence? Possibly. Its members said their job was simply to apply the legislation, not to create it, which was true, but they did have the power to negotiate terms with each of the channels, and could, for example, have given La Cinq longer to meet its legal obligations. On the other hand, if either the government or the CSA had stepped in to save La Cinq, what then? Its managers claimed they could not survive financially within the constraints the government had imposed on them: was the government to abandon its policy of protection of French culture, and allow market forces to take over?

The legacy of French television, and the highly politicised context in which extensive and rapid reform has taken place, means that it will take some time before the mistrust disappears, or indeed before the temptation to pull strings, even behind the scenes, is overcome. This is particularly so, since vested interests are at stake on both sides and rumour can be a powerful political tool in such circumstances. This is not to say, however, that no progress has been made. Direct censorship no longer exists. The CSA carefully catalogues all political interventions and attempts to ensure equal access to air time.[24] On the whole, appointments are now made on professional rather than political grounds, and this obviates the need for self-censorship. Political progress has not been matched by cultural progress, however, and television is suffering from a perceived decline in standards (*'nivellement par le bas'*) as a direct result of competition for audience ratings. Commercial television is not synonymous with neutral or objective television, and France, like other nations, has seen a dominant capitalist culture pervade its media with the profit motive, at the expense of alternative value systems. The system as a whole is more balanced now, with the introduction of Arte and La Cinquième, both of which are more concerned with educational and cultural considerations than financial (La Cinquième does not subscribe to Médiamétrie, the French company which assesses channels' market share), but it is debatable whether a total separation of the commercial and the cultural leads to quality programming. Perhaps France-Télévision, which is aiming to compete both commercially and qualitatively, will succeed in bridging that gap – unless it fails to please on either count! If television is still 'the voice of France', it is a very different, more fragmented France it now represents.

Even so, representation is still incomplete and unsatisfactory. For example, France has given little thought to questions such as the access to air time of ethnic minorities or women. Indeed, it may even be argued that the concern for 'Frenchness' has obstructed considerations of France as a multiracial society. As for women, some, such as Christine Ockrent, Anne Sinclair, Geneviève Guicheney and, latterly, Claire Chazal and Béatrice Schoenberg, have broken in to the male bastions of news reporting, but this has not changed women's role in other areas, where they continue to be used for their physical beauty, the criterion used to choose the very first *speakerines* (programme presenters) in 1949 (Rambert and Maquelle 1991: 172). Discussion programmes involving the public are organised according to socio-professional category and not gender or race, so debates are frequently made up exclusively of white men. What is more, these issues are not even on the agenda, and so it is unlikely that in the foreseeable future there will be much change.

TELEVISION: CHRONOLOGY

1945 (March) The RTF, under government control, exercises a state monopoly over all aspects of the broadcasting media.

1959 The RTF is financed by a licence fee but is still under direct government control, through the offices of the minister of information.

1963 (December) A second television channel is launched.

1964 The RTF is replaced by the ORTF, intended to be more autonomous. However, government representatives remain in a majority on the Board of Directors, and the state still has financial control.

1968 The introduction of brand advertising on television.

1973 Launch of the third television channel and first experiments in cable networks.

1974 (7 August) The ORTF is split into seven autonomous organisations directly responsible to the prime minister. These are: Radio-France; the three television channels (TF1, Antenne 2 and FR3) in competition with each other; the SFP, responsible for programme production; TDF, entrusted with the technical support of broadcasting; and INA, responsible for the archives and for research. State representatives are in a minority on the Boards of TF1, A2 and FR3 but the government appoints the managing directors (PDG), draws up the *cahiers des charges* (obligations the channels must meet) and decides on the distribution of the licence fee. Advertising is limited to 25 per cent of total income for the sector.

1982 Following the recommendations of the Moinot Commission, the Broadcasting Law of 29 July breaks the broadcasting monopoly and sets up the regulatory body, the *Haute Autorité de la communication audiovisuelle*. (November) An ambitious cable networking plan is launched alongside the development of the satellite TDF1.

1984 (November) Creation of the fourth television channel, Canal+, the first encoded subscription channel.

1986 Broadcasting rights are awarded for the fifth and sixth television channels, both private: La Cinq, (Jérôme Seydoux and Silvio Berlusconi) and TV6 (Publicis and Gaumont). Discussions begin for a seventh, La SEPT, a joint Franco-German venture.
Adoption, amid widespread controversy, of the Laws on the Liberty of Communication. The government is obliged by the *Conseil constitutionnel* to place restrictions on the holdings any single person or group may have in the broadcasting media. The SFP becomes a limited company with the state holding a majority of the shares, and no longer enjoys the privilege of obligatory orders from the state-owned channels. The privatisation of TF1 is prepared.

1987 The government brings an end to the systematic cabling of France. Broadcasting rights for La Cinq and TV6 (which becomes M6) are withdrawn from the previous owners and reallocated, La Cinq going to the press magnate Robert Hersant and Silvio Berlusconi, M6 to a consortium led by La Lyonnaise des Eaux and CLT.

TF1 is privatised, 50 per cent of the shares going to Francis Bouygues.

1988 Legislation replaces the CNCL with the CSA, which takes over on 30 January 1989.

1989 (April) The CSA allocates the five networks of the satellite TDF1 to six thematic channels, including La SEPT and Canal+.

(June) Creation of a single managing directorship (*présidence commune*) for A2 and FR3

1991 (31 December) La Cinq goes into receivership.

1992 (3 April) La Cinq is declared bankrupt and broadcasts its last programmes on 12 April.

(23 April) The government allocates the air network previously occupied by La Cinq to the Franco-German cultural channel Arte, which has replaced La SEPT, and which begins broadcasting (evenings only) from 28 September.

(7 September) Antenne 2 and FR3, still in the public sector, become France2 and France3 respectively.

1993 (25 August) The government gives the go-ahead for an educational channel to be broadcast on the same network as Arte until seven in the evening, to start in the Autumn of 1994.

1994 (February) Resignation of André Rousselet, head of Canal+. Publication in *Le Monde* of his article '*Edouard m'a tuer*' [sic], accusing the Prime Minister of having plotted against him.

(13 December) Launch of the educational channel La Cinquième.

NOTES

1 Further details can be found in Paracuellos 1993: 3–21. For a comparison of French and Western European television, see Regourd 1992.

2 Literally meaning 'Edouard [Balladur: the prime minister] killed me': Rousselet ensured the notoriety of his article by deliberately reproducing the grammatical error of a much-discussed contemporary murder case.

3 In France, the regional press has traditionally been stronger, and had a wider circulation, than the national (i.e. Parisian) press.

4 See Chapter 2.

5 For further details, see Guichard 1985; Comité d'histoire de la Télévision 1987; Bourdon 1990; Bourdon 1994.

6 In using this argument to restrain criticism of the government, of course, Pompidou was equating the nation-state with those in power at the time. Alain Peyrefitte, de Gaulle's spokesman and then minister of information from 1962 to 1966, claims (1994: 98) that Pompidou was simply repeating a favourite phrase of the General's, which seems perfectly plausible as it equates with de Gaulle's notion of the state and his role in relation to it.

7 For radio this occurred in 1981, though first without advertising, introduced only in 1984. For full details on the Moinot report and the legislation which followed, see Kuhn 1995: 172–8.

8 Canal+, La Cinq and TV6 (later M6): see Chronology.

9 The Italian media mogul Silvio Berlusconi managed to retain a small percentage share in the new franchise.

10 Mitterrand said in September 1987, 'The CNCL has done nothing to inspire the sentiment one calls respect'. In addition to the reattribution of the channels mentioned above, the CNCL was criticised for the appointment of the Gaullist

Claude Contamine as chairman of Antenne 2, and for the dismissal of Michel Polac, the presenter of a popular and controversial discussion programme, *Droit de réponse* (December 1981–September 1987). For a comparison of the first two regulatory bodies, see *Le Monde* of 15–16 June 1986 and 2 June 1988, and Blanc-Uchan 1987: 5–8.

11 The Giscardian Elkabbach, it will be noted, had been ousted by the Left in 1981. In spite of his known political preference, however, he has an excellent reputation as a media professional and was granted the honour of conducting François Mitterrand's last television interview as president. See Note 13.

12 A factor bitterly denounced by certain media professionals (Le Dos, Jezequel and Regnier 1986). The word 'libéralisation' is ambiguous, being used to signify the freeing of television from government control at the same time as refering to economic liberalism, the doctrine of a free market economy. It was this ambiguity which the Right exploited in 1986 when they called their regulatory body the *Commission nationale de la communication et des libertés*: their reform was conducted in the name of the political ideology of market freedom, but made attractive to the public in the name of political freedom.

13 For example, when on 4 June 1996 Jean Pierre Elkabbach was replaced by Xavier Gouyou Beauchamps at the head of France Télévision, *Le Monde* featured an article entitled '*Et dans la coulisse, l'Etat . . .*' in which it was argued that 'the rôle of the highest authorities of the state, although discrete, was none the less a determining factor', in both the resignation of Elkabbach and the appointment of his successor (*Le Monde*, 9–10 June 1996).

14 This was initially to have been two, A2 and FR3, but under pressure to limit it to one the government opted for the larger TF1.

15 M6 had started as a music channel (TV6) but had become generalist when it was reallocated by the Right in 1986 (though it has, to some extent, kept its emphasis on musical clips and its appeal to the young).

16 This is in sharp contrast, for example, with the privileged position given to Britain's Channel 4, which initially received subsidy from ITV and was able to target its own advertising to a specialised market sector in keeping with its programming style.

17 In 1990 the French television advertising market was only two-thirds the size of Britain's and a third of that of the USA (Paracuellos 1993: 13).

18 A similar situation pertains in the cinema: see Chapter 11.

19 New technology means that audiences can now be classified according to age, profession, and so forth, of individual viewers, almost by the minute: providing, of course, that they each remember to press the button as they enter or leave the room! For a discussion of evaluating audience figures, see Le Diberder and Coste-Cerdan 1991: 50–76 and Folléa 1992: 16–17.

20 See Chapters 10 and 11.

21 See for example *Le Monde* of 14 and 25 July 1989, for the government position and the response from M6.

22 For example, in the period October 1994–January 1995 (taken at random), the CSA brought action against M6, France 3 and TF1 (twice) for illegal advertising, and against France 2 for not respecting the rules for sponsorship (*La Lettre du CSA*).

23 For an explanation of television genre and further details on programming in France, see Jost and Leblanc (1994).

24 How equality is defined in this context is extremely complex and open to debate: see CSA (1995) for details relating to the 1995 presidential election, for example.

REFERENCES AND RECOMMENDED READING

Bauman, S. (1981) 'Quels changements dans l'information?', *Revue politique et parlementaire*, 894: 9–13.

Blanc-Uchan, O. (1987) 'Communication: les nouvelles lois', *Regards sur l'actualité*, 127: 3–16.

Bourdon, J. (1990) *Histoire de la télévision sous de Gaulle*, Paris: Anthropos/Economica.

* —— (1994) *Haute fidélité. Pouvoir et télévision 1935–1994*, Paris: Seuil.
The most comprehensive study of French television to date.

Cayrol, R. (1986) *La Nouvelle communication politique*, Paris: Larousse

Comité d'histoire de la télévision and FNSP (1987) *Mai 68 à l'ORTF*, Paris: La Documentation française.

CSA (1995) *Election du Président de la République. Rapport sur la campagne électorale à la radio et à la télévision (20 septembre 1994–7 mai 1995)*, Paris: CSA.

Folléa, L. (1992) 'De la boîte noire au bouton-poussoir. La Mesure de l'audience télévisée', *Le Monde Radio-Télévision*, 19–20 January: 16–17.

Guichard, J-P. (1985) *De Gaulle et les mass media. L'Image du Général*, Paris: Editions France-Empire.

Jost, F. and Leblanc, G. (1994) *La Télévision française au jour le jour*, Paris: Anthropos-Economica/INA.

* Kuhn, R. (1995) *The Media in France*, London and New York: Routledge.
The most up-to-date and detailed study of the French media available in English. Informative and enjoyable to read.

* Le Diberder, A. and Coste-Cerdan, N. (1991) *La Télévision*, Paris: La Découverte.
A general introduction to the medium of television from an economic perspective, outlining three main 'types': American, European and television in developing countries.

Le Dos, J-J., Jezequel, J-P. and Regnier, P. (1986) *Le Gâchis audiovisuel: histoire mouvementée d'un service public*, Paris: Editions Ouvrières.

* Paracuellos, J-C. (1993) 'Le Paysage audiovisuel français', *Regards sur l'actualité*, 191: 3–21.
An excellent analysis of the economy of television as it relates to political and socio-cultural issues, highlighting the specificity of the French system in comparison with other European countries and the USA.

Peyrefitte, A. (1994) *C'était de Gaulle*, Paris: Editions de Fallois/Fayard.

Rambert, C. and Maquelle, S. (1991) *Des Femmes d'influence. Pouvoirs et télévision*, Paris: Hachette/Carrère.

* Regourd, D. (1992) *La Télévision des Européens*, Paris: La Documentation française.
A thorough comparative study of television in the twelve countries of the European Union, from all angles: legalistic, cultural, economic, political, structural.

Part II

DEFINING SOCIO-CULTURAL IDENTITIES

7

WOMEN

Alison Holland

December 1993 saw a lively, not to say acrimonious debate in the French press which centred around the question of whether mothers (and fathers) should receive financial support if they decided to give up working outside the home in order to bring up their children. Some called the allowance in question the *salaire maternel*, others referred to it as the *salaire parental* and yet others termed it the *allocation de libre choix* (free choice allowance). The debate surrounding the *salaire maternel* is an important one as it crystallises the arguments to do with the rôle of women in France today and reveals the precariousness of women's situation. As the writers of the report prepared for the fourth United Nations world conference on women argue:

> If the fact that women work outside the home is, for the most part, widely accepted today, their right to do so is nevertheless questioned from time to time. The question 'should they work or not?' is always asked, individually and collectively of women and women alone. . . . women's right to work which is generally protected and promoted, is not, however, thought to be self evident in the same way that men's is.
>
> (Aubin and Gisserot 1994: 55)

This debate conflates the notions of womanhood and motherhood, the latter being of particular significance in the French context where concern with demographic issues continues to be acute.[1] It is also important to be aware that to speak of women as an undifferentiated class has the effect of masking differences and yet, differences of social class are particularly important.[2] The issues raised by this debate are of crucial importance, relating as they do to fundamental principles which underlie French society. The debate can only be understood if the context in which it took place is clearly defined.

The particular development of the feminist movement in France forms part of the wider context of this debate about the *salaire maternel*. Has there been an influential feminist lobby in France?[3] British and American writers on feminism in France contrast the activism and pragmatism of the movement in the UK and the USA on the one hand, and the intellectual and philosophical nature of the movement in France on the other. There certainly is such an 'exceptional' intellectual strand of feminism in France. Influenced by the ideas of the psychoanalyst Jacques Lacan, it is concerned with feminine difference or specificity and, in particular, with women's relationship to language.[4] However, as Simone de Beauvoir pointed out in 1974, feminist thought 'is in no way monolithic' (Beauvoir in Francis and Gontier 1979: 519) and this intellectual tendency exists in parallel with another, much more pragmatic, materialist strand represented by *Les Féministes révolutionnaires*, who were influenced by American radical feminists. *La Ligue du droit des femmes*, responsible for setting up centres for women victims of domestic violence and rape, was born out of this strand of feminism.[5] When speaking of the feminist movement it is important not to neglect all its strands and to recognise the debates that are taking place within it. The tradition of women's activism, which is identifiable in France, is something that links women all over the world, as demonstrated by the 1995 United Nations Conference on Women in Beijing.

In France today there still exist groups which 'continue the feminist struggle to defend and promote the rights of women' (Aubin and Gisserot 1994: 21). Of the 530 groups who are working to improve women's lives in every field and who took part in a survey carried out as part of the preparation for the Beijing conference, 60 per cent described themselves as 'feminist'. The women's movement today has not so much disappeared as it has been transformed. Aubin and Gisserot speak of the professionalisation of women's groups.

It is widely accepted that many of the improvements in the condition of women in France have been won as a result of feminist struggles. This is the view expressed in the report for the Beijing conference on women: 'The 1970s and 1980s were decades which saw a high profile, militant feminism, based in particular on the demand for sexual freedom and the right to contraception and abortion and which led to legislative reforms influenced to a great extent by women's groups' (ibid.: 20–1). Thierry Blöss and Alain Frickey (1994: 120) tell us, '[women] forced open the doors of emancipation' and write of 'the new rights they won'. On the macro socio-political level, feminists were the driving force behind the creation of *le secrétariat d'Etat à la Condition féminine* in 1974.[6]

Elisabeth Badinter, a self-professed and well-known feminist in France,[7] suggests, in line with commentators in the UK and USA, that France has entered a post-feminist era. She gave an interview to Elisabeth Schemla, published in *Le Nouvel Observateur* in May 1994 (Badinter 1994: 40–3). Making much of the fact that French women, unlike American women, have eschewed extremism, it was entitled *'Ici, en droit, nous avons tout obtenu'* (Here, in law, we have got everything). She assumes that there is nothing left to work for and that: 'Now everything is down to negotiations between individual men and women'. Elisabeth Badinter herself is photographed with Rodin's 'Le Baiser' and her question – 'In France today, what reason do we have to demonstrate in the streets?' – forms the caption. Is her analysis correct? What is the condition of women in French society today? The validity of Elisabeth Badinter's comments can be evaluated through an examination of women's economic activity and their domestic situation.

WOMEN AT WORK

The title given to Elisabeth Badinter's interview gives us a convenient starting-point; it is hard to disagree that, in terms of legislation, women have achieved equality in France (see Chronology for a list of laws affecting women's condition). Since 1946 when the principle of equality was first enshrined in the French constitution, legislation has progressively outlawed discrimination against women and promoted their rights. Yet this should not be allowed to mask the still disadvantaged position of women in French society. Gains have been made but women remain subject to discrimination. As Aubin and Gisserot (1994: 20) have pointed out, equality before the law may be an 'indispensable prerequisite' but it does not guarantee equality in practice.

The rôle of women has been transformed to the extent that women working outside the home has become the norm. Women make up 44 per cent of the work-force and the percentage of women aged 25–49 who work outside the home increased from 71 per cent in 1985 to 77 per cent in 1994.[8] Contrary to what some would have us believe, women show no signs of wishing to reverse this trend. A recent survey of 25–34-year-olds revealed that 80 per cent of the young women and men polled think it essential that women work outside the home both because their salary is indispensable to a household budget and because it affords women real autonomy and self-fulfilment (ibid.: 123–30). Increasingly, women continue to work after having children and take fewer and shorter career breaks (ibid.: 28–9 and Blöss and Frickey 1994: 111–13). Undeniably, paid work has been a factor of crucial importance for the emancipation of women. Yet, despite their commitment, women continue to be disadvantaged at work and in many ways their achievements are fragile. Even today women's working outside the home is popularly associated with any number of problems. As Blöss and Frickey say (ibid.: 91–2): 'Prejudice dies hard. This is particularly true regarding the idea that women have only really worked outside the home in recent years and that their sudden arrival in the job market has caused a string of untold problems.' In fact, women have always worked. What has happened is a progression from unpaid and so invisible work to paid work and thus greater visibility.[9]

It is illegal for employers to discriminate against women, although evidence shows that women continue to be disadvantaged in the job market. Employment is segregated both horizontally and vertically. Women are mainly concentrated in the tertiary sector, in low-status, low-paid, less secure jobs. A widening gap has been identified between women with qualifications (middle class), whose conditions of work are similar to men's, and women without qualifications (working class), whose working lives are characterised by insecurity and unemployment (Aubin and Gisserot 1994: 51). More women than men are working on temporary contracts. Women generally are more affected by unemployment than men and, once unemployed, they remain so for longer. Young women in particular, find it difficult to enter the job market and in January 1994, 24.8 per cent of women aged 15–24 were unemployed compared with 21.5 per cent of men of the same age (ibid.: 54). Part-time work is dominated by women, who do 85 per cent of all part-time work; 25 per cent of women workers work part-time, as opposed to only 4 per cent of men. Part-time work is not necessarily a bad thing in itself. In the current sexual division of labour where women carry the burden of childcare and housework, part-time work often allows them to reconcile work and family commitments. However, all too often part-time contracts are imposed rather than chosen and are linked with underemployment (women working less than they wish) and poor pay and conditions. Indeed, in spite of legislation which guarantees women equal pay for work of equal value,[10] women continue to earn significantly less than men, 24 per cent less in 1994, even if the gap has been narrowing (INSEE 1991: 126–9). This can be partly explained by *la non-mixité de l'emploi* (the fact that men and women do different jobs), but it is also true that important differences persist within socio-professional groups:

> in 1992 according to INSEE [French national institute of economic and statistical information] the average salary for senior male executives is 27 per cent higher than that earned by senior female executives; salaries for males in the caring professions and clerical jobs are 13 per cent and 10 per cent higher; the salary gap between men and women in manual jobs is 23 per cent.
>
> (Aubin and Gisserot 1994: 53)

These salary differences pertain to women and men of the same age with the same level of qualification and experience. Indeed, women's education and qualifications are not a sufficient explanation for their disadvantaged position at work.

In fact, girls succeed better than boys at every stage of primary and secondary education. More girls than boys obtain the *baccalauréat* (57 per cent) and since 1975 there have been more women in higher education than men, even though women are still in the minority in the prestigious *grandes écoles*.[11] The fact of the matter is that women are generally undervalued by employers and the same qualifications do not necessarily lead to the same jobs for women and men. Today, as qualifications are more widely required, women's situation is deteriorating and the gap between women and men is widening. For example, in 1972, two-thirds of female graduates became managers (*cadres supérieurs*) compared with three-quarters of male graduates, whereas, by 1985, only half of all women graduates obtained managerial posts and men graduates' position had hardly deteriorated at all (Blöss and Frickey 1994: 73). Women's experience over the last decade confirms the findings of the report written for the Minister of Women's Rights in 1982: 'It is a fact that, at every level of employment, women are frequently employed in lower status jobs than men with the same level of training and qualifications' (La Documentation française 1982: 37).

Nevertheless, the number of women executives is growing, albeit slowly. The rise is occurring not only in fields with a high proportion of women but also in areas where they are in a minority. In business, the percentage of women executives increased from 13 per cent in 1982 to 22 per cent in 1992 (figures quoted in Aubin and Gisserot 1994: 32). Overall, women's share of top jobs increased from 24.6 per cent in 1982 to 30.6 per cent in 1990, according to Alain Lebaube writing in *Le Monde*. He sees this increase, this 'conquest' as he calls it, as the major occurrence of recent years and one which is not unproblematic, raising fears as it does:

> More and more women have jobs that used to be reserved for men and, one after another, former strongholds are falling and old fears of 'feminisation', for some a synonym of decline, are being reawakened.
>
> (Lebaube 1995)

Maryse Huet, an expert on women's employment, is optimistic: 'The age of women pioneers is over. Access to skilled jobs and managerial posts has become widespread. Overall, the increasing number of women in management posts is indisputable' (quoted in Menanteau 1995). But, and it is a very big 'but', women executives are coming up against the so-called 'glass ceiling' which prevents their reaching the very top of the organisations they are working for. As the authors of the report for the UN Conference on Women point out: 'the fact that women now hold highly skilled positions with a high level of *responsibility* should not be confused with their gaining access to positions of *power*' (Aubin and Gisserot 1994: 32; original emphasis). Indeed, there is not a single woman at the head of one of the 200 top French companies (Menanteau 1995). Even within the civil service where there is a high proportion of women, fewer than 6 per cent of government appointments are held by women; thus 5.5 per cent of top administrative posts are held by women, and only 2.6 per cent of *préfets* and 3.7 per cent of ambassadors are women (Aubin and Gisserot 1994: 32–3). The *Association des femmes chefs d'entreprise*, is categorical that 'hierarchies are not changing' (quoted in Menanteau 1995). Women are excluded from the decision-making process. Unfortuately, to quote Margaret Maruani, head of research at the *Centre National de la Recherche Scientifique* (CNRS), 'power is masculine,' (quoted in Menanteau 1995).

The effects of policies to promote equality, favoured by the government, have been disappointing. For Maryse Huet this is due to a lack of commitment on the part of unions and employers, revealing that this is a question of gender rather than of economics. In an interview with *Le Monde*, she calls for women's concerns to inform all employment policy instead of being treated as a separate issue (quoted in Betbeder 1995).

The new direction called for here echoes the broad considerations at the heart of the report on women in France where the writers deplore the fact that shifts in women's economic activity have not been matched by parallel socio-cultural shifts. Referring to the fact that the common pattern of women's lives is now paid work combined with running a home and raising a family and no longer one marked by significant career breaks, this is what the writers say in their introduction:

> This phenomenon, which has not been hit by recession and high unemployment, is such that it might lead to fundamental changes not only as regards the status of women but also the structure and organisation of society as a whole. However, society has not yet taken on board all the implications of such a mutation.
>
> (Aubin and Gisserot 1994: 11)

THE *SALAIRE MATERNEL* DEBATE

It is within this context then, that the debate over the *salaire maternel* graphically illustrates the tensions which exist around women's rôle in French society. Why was this such a vexed question? Surely, given women's place in the job market (44 per cent of the work-force), no-one could seriously question their right to paid employment, could they? Unfortunately, the answer has to be 'yes'. Witness the editorial in *Le Point* where, before going on to rule out a *salaire maternel* in the name of free market economics, Philippe Manière demonstrates just how 'tempting' an option it is:

> On the one hand there are three million unemployed in France. On the other, France is one of the European countries with the highest number of women in the labour force. Now, the fact of the matter is that a large number of these women work without really wishing to do so, in low-skilled or unskilled jobs for very low pay . . . hence the straightforward idea that instead of paying benefits to the unemployed who do not wish to be unemployed whilst others who do not wish to work are working, why not pay an allowance to those women (or men) who would opt to give up working and so free up the equivalent number of jobs?
>
> (Manière 1993: 43)

He is confident that he is speaking for ordinary women whom he is defending against feminists – 'do-gooders who seek to liberate women through work' – who have failed to ask women if they really want to work long hours for low pay!

The views of Jacques Chirac, now President of France, at that time Mayor of Paris and leader of the right-wing Gaullist Party, appear to coincide with Philippe Manière's as far as the lot of women is concerned. He advocated the *salaire maternel* in an article in *Le Monde* (Chirac 1993) arguing that: 'Financial constraints that restrict mothers' choices must be removed as far as possible and as soon as possible'. Apparently motivated by a desire to improve women's lives (he sympathises with women who face a second day's work in the home after a hard day's work in the office and a gruelling journey to and from work), he would like women to be compensated either for the cost of childcare or for the loss of income should they give up work – clearly his preferred option as he is keen to promote the family as: 'the place where respect and love, a sense of solidarity and responsibility are learned . . . the crucible where knowledge and values that go to make the soul, the culture and the identity of a people, are transmitted from one generation to the next'. Chirac does mention that financial assistance would be available to fathers as well as mothers but, on the whole, his text tends to exclude them.[12] It is to women that he would like to give the choice: 'both to work and bring up their children, to be able to take a break and later to go back to work without having fallen behind or being handicapped in any way'.

Chirac was surprised and hurt by some of the responses to his article: 'Here they are, calling me a dreadful misogynist reactionary whose only intention is to send women back into the home' (Jacques Chirac, letter in *Le Monde*, 18 December 1993), feeling he had been misunderstood. Yvette Roudy, president of *l'Assemblée des femmes*, thought she understood only too well what was behind what she called 'this old grandad's fantasy': 'In a number of different disguises – one of the first being a concern about an alleged fall in the birth rate, which remains to be proved – is hidden the reprehensible attempt to bring about a fall in unemployment' ('*Renvoyées chez elles*', letter in *Le Monde*, 11 December 1993). Her views were diametrically opposed to Chirac's:

> Salaries for women who stay at home, a new resurgence of fascist nostalgia, are, above all, a dreadful trap for women resulting in a loss of economic independence, isolation and being cut off from the world outside the home. In short, a real backward step, culturally speaking, not to mention the fate that awaits them once their children have grown up and the danger that they might find themselves without any income whatsoever.
>
> (*Le Monde*, 11 December 1993)

Yvette Roudy found an ally in Simone Veil, then minister for health and social security and urban affairs. At a meeting of the *Conseil national des femmes françaises* on 14 December she ruled out any possibility of a *salaire maternel* as expensive and harmful to women. She went on to condemn: 'those who think that since, on the one hand, there are unemployed men, and on the other, women exhausting themselves working inside and outside the home, the way to solve the problem would be to send women back into the home' (*Le Monde*, 17 December 1993). Furthermore, Simone Veil was not convinced that women who stayed at home would, in fact, have more babies. However, and seemingly at odds with his minister, on 15 December Prime Minister Edouard Balladur, in presenting his policies to parliament, spoke of the need to 'encourage people to have more children so as to ensure the future of France and to make it easier for parents to choose freely whether to work or not' (reported in *Le Monde*, 17 December 1993). In fact, he was advocating the extension of a benefit in existence since 1987, namely, the *allocation parentale d'éducation* (APE) rather than proposing the creation of a new allowance. Until then the APE, 2,929 f. per month, was paid to a parent who gave up their job on the birth of their third child. Balladur wished it to be available to parents from the birth of their first child.

In February Simone Veil was to announce that the benefit would indeed be extended but, in the immediate future, only to parents with two children. Writing in *Le Monde*, Jean-Michel Normand (1994) felt this was being offered as a consolation prize to those on the Right who had been calling for the *allocation de libre choix*, which he considered to be a reactionary measure, seeking to exclude women from the labour market. Although the government undoubtedly hoped that some jobs would become vacant because of the extension of the allowance for parents, nevertheless the main aim of their policy was to increase the birth rate. The journalist reminded his readers that in spite of the rise in unemployment, the number of women working outside the home continued to increase and that encouraging them to stay at home went against the aspirations of all women, not only against those of women managers and the middle classes.

WOMEN AT HOME

Genuine concern for women's welfare would translate into action to redress imbalances not into inducements to leave the labour market. Women are in the labour market and are there to stay. Yet, unquestionably, women are paying a high price for the autonomy they are earning outside the home. Not only do they find thmselves in a disadvantaged position at work, but a majority of women also suffer from the double burden, '*la double carrière*', working outside the home and still taking full responsibility for home and family. Many commentators still consider the reconciling of work and family commitments to be a problem peculiar to women, as if men did not have families too! In practice, it is as if every policy, every structure put in place to promote the harmonisation of work and family, were addressed more or less exclusively to women. For example, women make up 98.5 per cent of those on maternity/paternity leave in the private sector and 99 per cent of those in the public sector. The fact that women generally assume family responsibilities is widely recognised and this is often cited as a handicap when it comes to women's employment prospects. It is well documented that women spend more time with their children than men – this obtains when both parents are in full-time employment. It is documented that the more children men have, the more time they spend at work away from them (Roy 1992: 34).

The question as to who does the housework naturally figures large in any discussion of women's condition. French women work longer hours both inside and outside the home than most other women in Europe, nine hours longer than British women, for example. On average, French women in full-time employment (that is 75 per cent of women in paid employment) work sixty-eight hours a week, forty of them outside the home and twenty-eight of them in the home. They still do the most housework – an average of five hours and twenty-four minutes a day compared with two hours and forty minutes for men – although the situation is evolving slowly, and over the last ten years the time spent on domestic chores by men has increased by ten minutes a day while for women it has decreased by five minutes a day (Dirn 1991: 91). Generally, women who work outside the home have one hour a day less leisure time than their partners. And yet, a widespread belief in equality within marriage coexists with these statistics. Geneviève Cresson and Patrizia Romito (1993: 43) have studied the way in which women undervalue their own work in the home so as to be able to maintain the illusion that their relationships are based on equality and a fair division of tasks and responsibilities.

As far as shared decision making is concerned, popular conceptions of greater equality in marriage may be more accurate, although attitudinal surveys are difficult to evaluate. Y. Lemel tells us that studies show how 'there is greater equality in terms of marital roles ... there seems to be greater equality now when it comes to making important decisions about bringing up children, deciding where to live, choosing friends etc.' (Dirn 1991: 93; see also Mermet 1994: 139). Janine Mossuz-Lavau, researcher at the CNRS, agrees: '[in France] there is a real harmony in relationships and men and women make important decisions together as equals' (quoted in Coignard and Guichard 1994: 46). Yet the high divorce rate, 30.5 per cent in 1987, contradicts this picture of marital bliss (Blöss and Frickey 1994: 113).[13] It suggests that, despite the good-humoured, bantering tone adopted by journalists in the popular media when they are discussing the rôles of women and men, women are, in fact, seriously dissatisfied with the *status quo*. Figures for domestic violence support the view that all is not well in the French home and fail to tally with the idealised picture close to Chirac's heart and quoted above. No accurate statistics exist but it is estimated that there are two million *femmes battues* (battered wives/women) in France (Mermet 1994: 138). Much of the violence against women remains hidden; however, a large majority of women's groups who participated in the survey which is part of the report

145

for the United Nations Conference on Women believe that over the past ten years domestic violence (*violences familiales et conjugales*) has increased. The writers of the report comment:

> It is noteworthy that to a great extent it is, on the one hand, all forms of domestic violence, occurring between partners, against children, and incest, and, on the other hand, rape and sexual assault that motivate a very large number of women's groups.
> (*Enquête auprès des associations féminines et féministes* in Aubin and Gisserot 1994: 118)

These women's organisations (there are 283 of them) are critical of the judicial system which can fail to take women's complaints seriously and which acts indulgently towards the male perpetrators of violence against women. They cannot agree with Elisabeth Badinter that '*Ici, en droit, nous avons tout obtenu*' and regret the lack of an anti-sexism law, particularly since, to their minds, existing laws are not merely badly applied, they are sexist too (Aubin and Gisserot 1994: 118).

L'EXCEPTION FRANÇAISE?

The picture of the condition of women that has emerged from the analysis so far, their disadvantaged position within the employment and domestic spheres, reveals the extent to which the concerns of French women activists, and indeed the concerns of French women generally, coincide with those of women activists elsewhere. Interestingly and quite paradoxically, the ongoing debate about the *salaire maternel*[14] is taking place in a self-congratulatory atmosphere, a context in which French commentators enjoy underlining what they see as the *difference* between the situation in other countries (notably the UK, the USA and Germany) on the one hand and France on the other. They emphasise the femininity of French women and their commitment both to love and romance and to the family. They compliment themselves on having achieved equality whilst having avoided what they define as the excesses of feminism. In short, they extol *l'exception française*.

This was the subject of a special report in *Le Point* in February 1994. Readers were gratified to read that: 'While the war of the sexes is raging on in the United States and in Germany, French women know how to create a special harmony in their relationships with men' (Coignard and Guichard 1994: 45). They were left in no doubt that *l'exception française* 'continues to grow', that it was not 'simply an intellectual notion, but something that can be clearly perceived in everyday behaviour'. The journalists who compiled this report did admit that '*l'exception française* [...] is not necessarily the same thing as equality' (this did not concern them unduly) and in the end *l'exception française* seems to boil down to little more than flirtatiousness or mutual seduction and 'being truly feminine', which they may well consider to be one and the same thing. The report as a whole, and the rosy picture painted of harmony at home and success at work, stand in contradiction to all that we have seen.[15]

Images of women in the media exemplify the symbolic status of women in French society. Women are most frequently portrayed in the home as wives and mothers. When women do appear at work, they are, according to Blöss and Frickey (1994: 121), 'either in a subordinate position or present simply for decorative purposes, as in the ludicrous situation where a sexy young woman, all of twenty years old, is portrayed chairing a board meeting'. Women's magazines do not actually tell women that their place is in the home, but articles on bringing up children frequently remind them of how important a mother's presence is·and dwell on the supposedly harmful effects of her being absent too often (Aubin and Gisserot 1994: 74).

More generally, representations of women perpetuate sexual stereotypes and thus encourage sexist behaviour. 'Women in advertising, in films and in magazines are almost always portrayed as objects to be possessed, acquired or seduced', argues the report for the Beijing conference (ibid.: 74). Moreover, the most extreme form of women's oppression, violence against women, is used as an advertising tool. Women combating violence against women criticise the media and advertising as they 'put great emphasis on rape and violent men. In this way they play a part in trivializing violence against women' (ibid.: 118). Christine Delphy describes a shameful example:

> There are billboards in the streets paid for by Barclays Bank – who would not dare do the same thing in Britain – showing the face of a battered wife/woman with the words: 'she is not crying because she is losing money, but she is'.
>
> (Delphy 1993: 1)

The anti-feminist stance of many commentators and the hostile, anti-feminist tone of much of the debate surrounding the rôle of women today deserve closer attention. Is it possible to identify an anti-feminist backlash in France? The call by some for a *salaire maternel* has been interpreted as a sign of such a reaction. This is the view of Elisabeth Badinter who finds evidence of a backlash, not only in the call for a *salaire maternel*, but also in the increased violence against women (Badinter 1994: 40). Christine Delphy tells us (1993: 1) that the anti-feminist, anti-woman backlash is getting worse all the time. She exposes the way in which French journalists refuse to acknowledge that sexism exists in France, preferring to locate it elsewhere, notably in Algeria:

> And in the eyes of *Le Monde*, sexism is only to be condemned when it is happening in Arab countries – when it provides a good reason to condemn them. When the struggle against sexism threatens these self-

same French journalists, then it is denounced and described as a foreign import.

(Delphy 1993: 4)

The media prefer to concentrate on the 'mutual seduction', 'special gentleness and complicity' that they see as typifying relations between the sexes in France and enjoy reporting the excesses of the 'sex war' happening elsewhere, secure in the knowledge that it 'can't happen here' (Coignard and Guichard 1994: 47).

CONCLUSION

The issues raised by the debate surrounding the *salaire maternel* are complex and reveal the tensions that attach to the rôle of women in France today. While women are ever more active in the work-force at every stage of their lives, nevertheless their opportunities are restricted in terms of type of work and status. It is suggested that the sexual divisions that persist in the workplace reproduce patterns of sexual domination that characterise gender relations in society as a whole (Blöss and Frickey 1994: 97). Proponants of the *salaire maternel*, such as Jacques Chirac, unquestioningly accept that women will continue to take responsibility for childcare and housework. Ostensibly, a *salaire maternel* would release women from the 'burden' of paid work and free them to fulfil their 'natural' rôle. The real effect of the introduction of such a measure would be to undermine the gains made by women through their increased participation in paid employment and to further entrench gender stereotypes. While the allowance for mothers may seem an attractive option for those women in poorly paid employment, ultimately it would be harmful to them, excluding them from the labour market and directing attention away from the need to restructure work practices and improve working conditions.

The notion of *l'exception française*, the idea that gender relations in France are essentially harmonious and that 'significant' inequality has been eradicated, does not stand up to scrutiny. Whilst concern with sexism and women's oppression is displaced to former colonies and other states, it is suggested in the media that radical activism to improve women's lives would disturb the existing harmony and serve only to increase masculine insecurity. One of the major preoccupations of the media is to avoid 'destabilizing masculine identity through women becoming too self-assured' (Aubin and Gisserot 1994: 74). In the special report on women in *Le Point*, Elisabeth Badinter encourages women to help men to find a new identity, to share power with men, not to seize it from them, and the women journalists agree: 'Indeed, the ultimate irony would be if women, this time, make too much progress too quickly, and leave men behind. We have not reached that point though!' (Coignard and Guichard 1994: 51).

The juxtaposition of the *salaire maternel* debate and the notion of *l'exception française* reveals the contradictions inherent in populist views of the condition of women in France. The proposal to introduce a *salaire maternel* was thrown out in February 1994 but the debate has not gone away. Whilst there is an ongoing concern with the birth-rate and unemployment, the rôle of women in modern society will continue to be contentious. There is still a place for women's activism in France. It is premature to reduce feminism to mere vigilance, as Elisabeth Badinter would have French women do. For, as an examination of women's condition in France shows, 'contemporary French history, after all is said and done, shows that women's emancipation has been regulated and kept within limits compatible with sexual identity, that is to say in line with their unequal status' (Blöss and Frickey 1994: 121). French women, like women all over the world, must continue to work towards ensuring that notional equality under the law is translated into structural equality in the workplace and the home.

WOMEN: CHRONOLOGY

1944   Women obtain the right to vote and to be elected.

1945   Recognition of the principle of equal pay for women and men doing the same work.

1946   The principle of equality of women and men in every sphere recognised in the constitution of the Fourth Republic.

1963   Co-education in secondary schools becomes the norm.

1965   Law reformed to give married women more power over jointly held property. Women can work outside the home without their husband's permission. *Comité du travail féminin* set up.

1967   Legalisation of contraception (*loi Neuwirth*). Formation of feminist groups, *Féminin-Masculin-Futur* and *Féminisme-Marxisme*.

1968   Mass unrest. Formation of *Psychanalyse et politique* (also referred to as *Psych et po* and *psyképo*).

1970   Smaller women's groups come together and consciousness of a women's movement emerges. MLF adopted as the name of the women's liberation movement in France. Law replaces 'paternal' authority with 'parental' authority within the family – mother and father share responsibility for moral and material welfare of their children.

1971   Women demonstrate for contraception and free abortion on demand.

1972   Law confers equality of status on legitimate and illegitimate children. Law guarantees women and men the same salary for work of equal value.

1974   Free contraception. Government sets up Secretariat of State for the Status of Women, headed by Françoise Giroud.

1975   Legalisation (provisional) of abortion (*loi Weil*). Divorce by mutual consent adopted. Adultery no longer a penal offence. Equality of opportunity in primary and secondary schools (*loi Haby*). Law against sexual discrimination, particularly relating to recruitment of women.

1977   *Congé parental d'éducation* for women (in companies with more than 200 employees).

1979   Split in the women's movement. *Psychanalyse et politique* renames itself *Mouvement de Libération des Femmes – Politique et Psychanalyse* and registers the name and logo *Mouvement de Libération des Femmes, MLF* as a trademark.
Abortion legalised definitively.
Certain women no longer prevented from working on night shifts.

1980   Law protecting pregnant women's employment rights.

1981   Secretariat of State for the Status of Women replaced by a ministry, a higher body.

1982   Abortion free.

1983   Sexual discrimination in employment outlawed (*loi Roudy*).

1984   Both parents eligible for parental leave.

1985   Law strengthens equality of women and men within marriage. Recognition of the right to add the mother's surname to a child's surname.

1987   Joint parental authority in case of separation. All women allowed to work nights in certain conditions.

1988   Secretariat of State for the Rights of Women replaces ministry.

1991   Advertising of contraceptives legalised.

1992   Laws against sexual harassment.

1993   Joint parental authority without regard to the marital status of parents. There has been no Secretariat of State or Ministry for the Rights of Women since this date (change of government after the parliamentary elections).

NOTES

1 See Introduction and Chapter 12.

2 So too are differences of race. The dearth of statistical data precludes the consideration of this here.

3 It is legitimate to ask what 'feminist' means. Monique Rémy (1990: 17) proposes the following definition: 'The term feminist will be used to designate everything that is spoken and written about the condition of women in society and every movement related to the condition of women in society if they denounce that condition as the outcome of the domination of one sex (female) by the other (male).' This is a much more satisfactory definition than the narrow one still found in the *Petit Robert* – 'A doctrine that aims to extend the rights and role of women in society' – which with the term doctrine confers on the movement a uniformity of vision it does not possess and confines it to a reformist rather than a radical or revolutionary role. Adopting the wider definition allows us to call 'feminist' all those who resist the oppression of women, even if they themselves refuse that label. This is important in the French context where the women's movement and feminism are not necessarily notions which coincide.

4 See Hughes (1993), for an overview of French feminist theories.

5 There is no space here to review in detail the development of feminism in France. See Rémy (1990), and Duchen (1990).

6 This body has undergone a number of changes in its name and status, becoming a Ministry for Women's Rights (a higher body) from 1981–8. See Chronology.

7 Some may wish to question her feminist credentials in view of some of the ideas she expresses (see note 3).

8 See INSEE (1991: 93–123) for further statistical data related to women's employment.

9 See Blöss and Frickey (1994) for a useful historical survey of women's role in the labour force.
10 1972. See Chronology.
11 This has the effect of cutting them out of the race for top jobs. See Chapter 5 for further details on the rôle of the *grandes écoles* in relation to the labour market, and Blöss and Frickey (1994: ch. 2) for a useful survey of women in the education system.
12 In fact, measures designed to help both parents deal with the dual demands of family and work in reality tend almost exclusively to concern only women (Aubin and Gisserot 1994: 65–6).
13 It is interesting to note that in seven cases out of ten, divorce proceedings are instigated by women.
14 It was a theme in Jacques Chirac's presidential campaign in May 1995.
15 The writers stretch the notion of a rosy picture to its limits when they give us an example of how positive, energetic and resilient 'ordinary French women' remain even in the face of adversity: 'For example, there is a battered wife in Le Mans, who, twice a week, finds the energy to help sort out jumble with the *Secours populaire.*' No irony was intended.

REFERENCES AND RECOMMENDED READING

Anon (1993) 'Attribuer l'allocation parentale dès le premier enfant?', *Le Monde*, 17 December 1993.
* Aubin, C. and Gisserot, H. (1994) *Les Femmes en France: 1985–1995. Rapport établi par la France en vue de la quatrième Conférence mondiale sur les femmes*, Paris: La Documentation française.
An interesting update on how women's place in French society has evolved since 1985, including analysis of recent statistical data and surveys of women's groups.
Badinter, E. (1994) 'Ici, en droit, nous avons tout obtenu', *Le Nouvel Observateur*, 25 mai: 40–3.
Betbeder, M-C. (1995) 'Egalité professionnelle: on ferme!', *Le Monde*, 5 juillet.
* Blöss, T. and Frickey, A. (1994) *La Femme dans la société française*, Paris: PUF.
An exellent historical overview of the changing status of women in French society.
Chirac, J. (1993) 'Pour l'allocation de "libre choix"', *Le Monde*, 2 décembre.
Coignard, S. and Guichard, M-T. (1994) 'Vive les françaises! Enquête sur le rôle des femmes dans la société et leurs relations avec les hommes', *Le Point*, no. 1119: 45–51.
Cresson, G. and Romito, P. (1993) 'Ces Mères qui ne font rien. La Dévalorisation du travail des femmes', *Nouvelles Questions Féministes*, 14, 3: 33–62.
Delphy C. (1993) 'Le Baquelache en France', *Nouvelles Questions Féministes*, 15, 2: 1–7.
Dirn, L. (1991) *La société française en tendances*, Paris: PUF.
Documentation française (La) (1982) *Rapport au ministre des Droits de la femme: Les Femmes en France dans une société d'inégalités*, Paris: La Documentation française.
* Duchen, C. (1990) *Feminism in France*, London: Routledge.
An accessible source in English evaluating the contribution of feminism to women's lives in France.
Francis, C. and Gontier, F. (1979) *Les Ecrits de Simone de Beauvoir*, Paris: Gallimard.
Hughes, A. (1993) 'Gender Issues', in M. Cook (ed.) *On y va! French Culture since 1945*, London: Longman.
INSEE (1991) *Contours et caractères: Les femmes*, Paris: INSEE.

INSEE–CNIDF (1986) *Femmes en chiffres*, Paris: INSEE.

Lebaube, A. (1995) 'Femmes', *Le Monde*, 5 juillet.

Manière, P. (1993) 'Non au salaire maternel!', *Le Point*, no. 1107: 43.

Marks, E. and de Courtivron, I. (eds) (1994) *New French Feminisms*, Brighton: Harvester Press.

Menanteau, J. (1995) 'Battantes et "plafond de verre"', *Le Monde*, 5 juillet.

Mermet, G. (1994) *Francoscopie 1995*, Paris: Larousse.

Normand, J-M. (1994) 'L'allocation parentale d'éducation', *Le Monde*, 19 février.

Remy, M. (1990) *De l'utopie à l'intégration. Histoire des mouvements de femmes*, Paris: L'Harmattan.

Roudy, Y. (1993) 'Femmes: renvoyées chez elles', *Le Monde* 11 décembre.

Roy, C. (1992) 'Vers un rapprochement des rôles masculin et féminin? Le travail domestique, une affaire de femmes', *Problèmes politiques et sociaux*, no. 685: 34–6.

Windebank, J. (1994) 'Comment expliquer le rapport des femmes au foyer et à la famille: les débats français autour du travail domestique', *Nouvelles Questions Féministes*, 15, 1: 9–34.

8

THE CHURCH

William Smith

On January 13 1995, the Vatican Information Service issued the following communiqué:

> The Holy Father has relieved Bishop Jacques Gaillot from the pastoral governing of the diocese of Evreux, France, transferring him to the titular see of Partenia. . . . Mgr Jacques Gaillot, bishop of Evreux since June 20, 1982, in the course of the last ten years, has never borne in mind the counsels and observations regarding his manner of undertaking the episcopal ministry on doctrinal and pastoral communion with the Church.
>
> . . . On the occasion of the *ad limina Apostolorum* visit, the Holy Father did not fail to issue him a strong admonition to no longer act outside of ecclesial communion.
>
> . . . In a joint declaration with Cardinal Decourtray, 15 February 1989, Mgr Gaillot committed himself on several points relative to the faith, the magisterium of the Holy Father and canonical discipline. Unfortunately, the prelate has not shown himself suitable to exercise the ministry of unity which is the first duty of a bishop.

How has it come about that Jacques Gaillot (whose new titular diocese is a deserted area of Mauretania), is the first bishop in France to be deposed since the liberation, when a few bishops, accused of collaboration with the Nazis by the provisional government, were deposed by Rome?

In 1983, shortly after his appointment, he went into the witness box to defend a conscientious objector from Evreux who was on trial and later that year voted against the French bishops' declaration justifying the nuclear deterrent. In 1984 during the controversy over state vs. religious education, he signed petitions in favour of the non-religious state system.

In 1988 he advocated the use of contraceptives as a precaution against Aids, quoting the commandment: 'Thou shalt not kill', and on Canal+ he declared: 'If people don't use condoms, they are guilty of failure to render assistance to a person in danger.' In 1993, he advocated the ordination to the priesthood of married men and women, declared himself against compulsory priestly celibacy, condemned 'regressive elements within the Church' and subsequently criticised the new *Catechism of the Catholic Church* for its defence of the death penalty.

Nor was he inactive in international affairs. He went to South Africa (before the change of government there) to demonstrate alongside a group of communists; he entertained in his home the PLO representative in Paris, Ibrahim Souss, and had talks with Yasser Arafat in Tunis in 1987, publicly supporting the latter's viewpoint. Just before his deposition in 1995, he visited President Aristide in Haiti, a suspended priest and *persona non grata* with the Vatican.

It was as much the manner as the content of his interventions which irritated both the state and church authorities. He never refused an interview or public appearance and, when accused of tarnishing the image of the Church, said that he reached in this way millions of people who never set foot in a church. In an interview with the homosexual weekly *Gai-Pied* in 1989 he declared 'homosexuals will get to heaven before us' (an allusion to Christ's concern for the marginalised of his own time). He was interviewed by the soft porn magazine *Lui* and, in 1994, appeared on the slightly risqué television magazine programme *Frou-Frou* where he denounced the Church's lukewarm support for the integration of immigrants. He subsequently published a pamphlet condemning the Pasqua immigration legislation.[1] As far as the Vatican was concerned, his debate in 1994 on the television channel Arte with the German theologian Eugen Drewermann (condemned by Rome as heretical) was probably the last straw.[2]

After his dismissal, Gaillot claimed that his provocative media appearances were not the real reasons for his dismissal. On 6 February 1995 he was interviewed on the primetime political programme *7 sur 7*, where he identified a number of Catholic movements whose pressure has been responsible for his forced resignation. He mentioned *Opus Dei*, the *Associations familiales catholiques*, the weekly magazine *Famille chrétienne* and the Benedictine monastery of Barroux. He also claimed that Charles Pasqua, the former minister of the interior, had complained to the Pope personally about Gaillot's book which had criticised his immigration legislation.

It is clear that the Vatican seriously underestimated the reaction in France to this anachronistic sanction against Gaillot, where no defence could be offered and against which there was no recourse. Cardinal Lustiger of Paris (who is widely perceived as the principal protagonist in the French hierarchy against Gaillot) was dismissive of him: 'Over the last 10 years we have watched Jacques Gaillot stick stubbornly to a sectarian course of action in spite of all the dialogue that his brother bishops have tried to have with him.' However, the public reaction was immediate and immense.

People demonstrated in their thousands in front of their local cathedrals and bishops' houses. Between 20,000 and 30,000 people went to Evreux for

Gaillot's last mass in his cathedral. The press and television followed his every action, whether occupying a social security office in Paris with a group of homeless or joining the Greenpeace ship *Rainbow Warrior II* at Papeete in Tahiti to demonstrate against the resumption of French nuclear tests in the Pacific by sailing into the exclusion zone. Far from inhibiting Gaillot, the Vatican's action has freed him to work even more wholeheartedly in favour of the marginalised and to continue his particular form of Christian witness.

MEETING THE CHALLENGE OF DE-CHRISTIANISATION

The Gaillot affair serves as a prism through which we can examine the issues and tensions which are present in the French Church in the second half of the 1990s: the declining numbers of those attending mass regularly and the problem of how to reach out into the secular world; the nature and extent of Christian pastoral commitment to the homeless, the unemployed, immigrants; the dilemma of the Catholic Church which seeks to be in the world but not part of it. The Gaillot affair also throws light on the extent of the influence of those who sought and achieved his dismissal: the traditionalist and integrist (here understood as meaning inflexible and dogmatic) lobbies, *Opus Dei*, the *Associations familiales catholiques* and the conservative elements of the French hierarchy.

The France to which Gaillot is trying to reach out through his appearances in the media is one in which, in 1994, 72 per cent of the adult population declared that they believed in God and 64 per cent declared themselves to be Catholics. Only 24 per cent were prepared to be described as 'convinced Catholics' and the number regularly practising was 9 per cent of the total population (Woodrow 1994: 643). It is a France far removed from the stereotype of Cartesian rationalism where people acknowledge their interest and belief in the paranormal and in superstition: reincarnation, telepathy, graphology, witchcraft, astrology and fortune telling are given widespread credence, not only among individuals but in the world of business. It is a France in which people are looking for an aim and purpose to their existence. Recent publications such as the *Catechism of the Catholic Church*, Pope John-Paul II's encyclical *Veritatis Splendor* and his book *Crossing the Threshold of Hope*, Jacques Duquesne's revisionist life of Christ, *Jésus*, have all been best-sellers in France and none of them can be said to be easy reading. Mother Theresa and the Abbé Pierre are seen as inspirational rôle models.[3] This search for a sense of purpose is carried on in the context of a decline in the influence and power of ideology. Marxism is no longer seen to be credible. In so far as Christianity, and in particular Catholicism are concerned, the overall impression is that the Church with its tightly ordered dogmas and rules is rapidly losing ground to a 'pick-and-mix' approach to religion. So, for example, a refusal to accept the dogma of the virgin birth will go hand in hand with a deep belief in the teachings and a very real interest in the life of Jesus the man. Belief survives, but it does not imply acceptance of the Church's teaching on faith or morals. People take little account of the Vatican's teaching on contraception and abortion. These are seen by many French Catholics as a matter for their own individual conscience rather than an absolute wrong. They no longer have a sense of objective sin; they no longer acknowledge moral absolutes defined by the Church. They have lost their sense of fear and of catholic guilt.

It is not just in the major urban centres that this phenomenon is apparent. The decline of the parish as a social centre in rural France, accelerated by the exodus from the countryside to the towns, by the increased mobility of the car-owning society and by exposure to the national mass medium of television, is graphically illustrated in Yves Lambert's book (1985) *Dieu change en Bretagne*. He takes as a case study the small town of Limerzel in the Morbihan which, until the end of the 1950s, had remained solidly Catholic. More than 90 per cent of the population went to mass every Sunday and on feast days, virtually all children attended Catholic schools, there were numerous religious vocations, social activities all centred around the parish where the clergy exercised considerable authority. This was a world in which Catholic Christianity was accepted as self-evident truth, penetrating every aspect of daily life, shaping and structuring the people's world view: it was an all-embracing system of religious, moral, social and political attitudes and certainties.

By the end of the 1970s, less than half of the population still attended mass. By the mid-1990s the figure was around one-third (which is, of course, still markedly higher than the national average). There is no single dramatic cause which explains this rate of lapsation. The first to leave were the younger men; military service often brought about a break in the habit of church attendance and simultaneously the social taboo on Sunday work was relaxing. May 1968 challenged virtually all the certainties of French social life, including the life of the Church. Division within the Church itself between supporters of the reforms of the Second Vatican council (1962–5) and the integrists who hankered after Tridentine[4] certainties and forms of worship alienated many people. Liturgical reform did not meet with unanimous approval, many thought the new vernacular mass (said in the language of the people rather than in Latin) too cerebral and resented the participation which it required; they looked back with nostalgia to the theatrical and ritualistic Latin ceremonials.

A succession of priests attempted to stem the flow by changing mass times to fit in with secular activities. People began to feel that they had a 'right' to leisure and wanted their Sundays free so Saturday evening vigil masses were instituted. Individual confession which had became unpopular was replaced by penitential services with general absolution of all present. Throughout this time, only the four great rites of passage – baptism, first communion, marriage and funeral – have come through unscathed and continue to attract almost universal adherence. Attendance at mass is no longer necessary for keeping up social appearances, but those who do attend have become more involved. This is partly out of necessity. The priest in Limerzel, like the great majority of his colleagues throughout France, now serves several parishes and the involvement of lay people and married deacons (of whom there are now more than 1,000 in France) is essential to ensure catechesis, baptisms, funerals and the conducting of Sunday services when there is no priest available.

THE 'INTEGRIST' RESPONSE

For a vocal and powerful minority of French Catholics, the reason for the decline in religious practice is that the Church is no longer Catholic enough, it needs to be more rigid and rigorous in its approach. The most visible proponent of this point of view was Monsignor Marcel Lefebvre (1905–91). He was born in the year of the separation of Church and State in France, into a middle-class family in Lille which was both Catholic and monarchist. In Catholic circles at that time, there was a strong sense of being besieged by what was termed 'the world', that is to say, everything which was not Church, by a society which was born of the Revolution, hence of sin, and which denied God. He studied in the French seminary in Rome where the ideas of Charles Maurras were held in great esteem until Pope Pius XI condemned *Action Française*[5] in 1926. Marcel Lefebvre was ordained priest as a member of the *Congrégation du Saint Esprit*[6] in 1929 and after a short period as a curate in Lille went as a missionary to Gabon and later Senegal. He became Archbishop of Dakar in 1955 where he drew attention to himself by protesting against the expansion of Islam in that country (a theme to which he would return in later years in the context of France). The Catholic President of Senegal, Leopold Senghor, requested and obtained from the Vatican Lefebvre's transfer from Dakar and in 1957 he became Bishop of Tulle (Corrèze). He was also elected Superior General of his religious congregation and attended the Second Vatican Council. He was one of a handful of bishops to vote against the decrees of the Council which he denounced publicly and repeatedly thereafter:

> In fact, all the reforms have contributed and are still contributing to the destruction of the Church, to the ruin of the priesthood, to the annihilation of the Holy Sacrifice and of the sacraments, to the disappearance of religious life, to a teaching based on naturalism and the ideas of Teilhard de Chardin being disseminated in universities, seminaries and catechism classes. This teaching, which stems from liberalism and protestantism, has been condemned time and time again by the magisterium of the Church.
>
> (Lefebvre 1975: 5–8)

He constantly invoked a static Tridentine tradition to counter the Vatican II reforms, three aspects of which he found totally unacceptable. The first was the declaration regarding freedom of conscience: 'Henceforth, by virtue of his human dignity, Man can adhere to any delusion.' The second concerned ecumenism, a movement given impetus after the Council and which sought to bring together the separated Christian families and to recognise the common values of the great world religions. When John-Paul II prayed with other religious leaders at Assisi in October 1986 shortly after having visited the Roman synagogue, Lefebvre described him as an apostate who had 'encouraged false religions to pray to their false gods'. The third unacceptable aspect of Vatican II was the abandonment of the Latin Tridentine mass and the substitution in its place of a vernacular eucharist.

To combat these reforms, Lefebvre founded the Fraternity of Saint Pius X at Ecône in Switzerland in 1969. This was to be a seminary in the traditionalist mould where the theology taught would be that which he himself had learnt, where priests would continue to wear the cassock as everyday dress and where the only mass celebrated would be the traditional one. Having started with nine seminarists in 1969, by 1977 he had 140 and in 1988, 280 spread among new houses which he had opened in Austria, Germany, Argentina, France, Australia and the USA. Emboldened by his success, his declarations with regard to the Vatican became even more intransigent and he was suspended *a divinis* (that is, forbidden to exercise his ministry by Rome) in 1975.

During this time, he was the object of considerable media attention, particularly in France, where he had no problem in making his views known to a wide audience. At Easter 1977, his followers under the leadership of Mgr Ducaud-Bourget, decided that they deserved a church in Paris where the traditional mass could be celebrated. They therefore took over by force St Nicolas-du-Chardonnet and evicted the parish priest. For such a change to be sanctioned, two permissions are needed, from the ecclesiastical authorities and from the civil authority (because church property in France belongs to the state). The Archdiocese of Paris (under cardinal Marty) adopted a 'softly softly' approach in the hope that this would minimise the alienation of traditional Catholics from the official church and the then Mayor of Paris, Jacques Chirac, closed his eyes to the problem lest he lose a part of his natural electorate to the increasingly vocal *Front national*, which was becoming an objective ally of Lefebvre. This takeover has now become permanent and the example followed elsewhere in France.

Whilst it would be an exaggeration to claim that all of Lefebvre's followers are from the extreme right wing, it is nevertheless true that they have in common certain attitudes: they are bitterly opposed to freemasonry, Marxism and Islam and their declarations are often tinged with anti-Semitism. When Jean-Marie Lustiger was appointed Archbishop of Paris in February 1981, Lefebvre declared that he was 'surprised that someone who was not of French origin was heading the biggest diocese in France' (*Le Point*, 27 June 1988: 44).

In spite of his ever more hostile and outrageous declarations with regard to the post-conciliar Church: 'the Church authorities and the clergy are suffering from AIDS, that condition characterised by a lack of immunity to disease' (ibid.: 43), Rome explored every possible avenue to keep him and his followers within the fold. (They were not and would not be anything like so conciliatory towards those who stepped out of line on the other edge of the ecclesiastical political spectrum.) John-Paul II went as far as to offer Lefebvre a personal prelature, that is to say, the Fraternity of St Pius X would be responsible not to individual dioceses and to national bishops' conferences, but directly to Rome (the status accorded to *Opus Dei*, as we shall see later). Lefebvre turned down the offer, demanding that the Vatican set up a commission to review the decrees of Vatican II. This demand was refused and on 30 June 1988 Lefebvre consecrated without permission four bishops from his integrist congregation and by so doing led his followers into schism with the Catholic Church because he was immediately excommunicated.

He carried out these episcopal ordinations in order to ensure the survival of his integrist group after his death, but the inherent contradiction of his position – the designation of the Pope as the enemy of Catholicism – has caused a number of his followers to return to the institutional church where they remain a powerful presence on the right wing.

Opus Dei[7] did not make Lefebvre's mistake of alienating the Vatican and enjoys the full support of John-Paul II who has visited their Rome headquarters on at least three occasions. They correspond to his vision of the Church (unlike the Jesuits, the previous papal 'shock troops' who are seen to be too independent-minded and contaminated with liberation theology in South and Central America). The priests of *Opus Dei* are obedient, wear priestly dress, avoid theological speculation and are totally supportive of papal attitudes with regard to sexual and other moral questions.

Opus Dei is a very secretive, if not secret, society for lay integrist Catholics. It is now a personal papal prelature. It was founded by a Spanish priest José Maria Escriva de Balaguer (1902–75) in the 1930s. Escriva was beatified[8] on 17 May 1992 with what many Catholics considered indecent haste, but which indicates the degree of support which exists at the highest level in Rome for his ideas. Escriva was both authoritarian and fascist. He identified totally with Franco, was a supporter of Hitler, whom he saw as a crusader against Marxism who had saved Spain. He was also an avid supporter of General Pinochet in Chile. The mission of his society is to infiltrate the highest spheres of political, economic and cultural power with lay people bound by a common adherence to the same integrist and puritanical values. For *Opus Dei* members, most diocesan Catholic priests are too liberal and too lax, and the Church needs the rigour and stiffening of resolve which they alone can provide. *Opus Dei* is also extremely rich, but its money and property are owned not by the society itself but by front organisations which are difficult to penetrate and which allow the society to claim that it has very little money.

Between 70 per cent and 75 per cent of its lay members are celibate. They are known as 'numeraries'. The remainder (known as 'supernumeraries') are married or are free to marry. About 60 per cent are male, 40 per cent female. About 2 per cent of the membership of *Opus Dei* is made up of priests. The society is intensely secretive about its practices, its finances, its organisation and its membership. Information about it tends to come only from those who have left. It recruits its male members among those who are or who are likely to become leaders in society and rejects accusations (brought by some parents who have seen their children join the society and lose their autonomy) of cult-like brainwashing of its younger members. *Opus Dei* requires unconditional obedience of its members, images of 'father', 'family' and 'army' constantly reinforce this. Life is lived according to an inflexible pattern of prayer and spiritual exercises; weekly confession to a priest of the society is obligatory; physical mortification (hairshirt or scourge) is encouraged. Obstacles are placed in the way of those who wish to leave, either psychological pressures based on guilt or threats of hell fire. All reading, newspapers, films and television are heavily censored, as is personal mail. In every *Opus Dei* centre there is total and rigorous separation of the sexes. The male numeraries tend to be highly qualified and occupy prestigious posts, the women mostly serve as auxiliaries dealing with domestic tasks. Not unlike the Pharisees at the time of Jesus, they see themselves as an élite charged with the preservation of doctrinal and moral purity.

François Gondrand, who has been a member of the society for thirty years and is one of its leaders, estimates that *Opus Dei* has about 1,400 members in France (Terras 1992: 158), to whom should be added a further 5,600 'associates or collaborators'. It has one official address in Paris but, according to *Golias*, there are dozens of other establishments scattered across France with names such as the *Association de culture Universitaire* or the *Société anonyme d'investissement pour le développement culturel* which are, in fact, front organisations. Its influence is immense and tentacular, although almost totally hidden. A parish priest from Alsace, Fernand Schmitt, summed up the nature, the power and the threat posed by *Opus Dei*:

> Escriva's *Opus Dei* must be unmasked. It contains too many distortions of christianity: a spirituality inspired by neo-platonism and jansenism, *kadavergehorsam*[9] inspired by fascism, dissimulation and lack of honesty in all its activities, even in its relations with the banks. Even christian newspapers are wary of them and don't dare publish anything about them. *Opus Dei* is pervasive, it concerns itself with everything which is profitable rather than with the unfortunate or the victimised, fostering priests in cassocks and roman collars rather than in overalls. . . .

If Catholics in the Western world don't get a grip on themselves and confront this power which is growing within the Roman Church, one day they will have to ask themselves the tragic question: where is the real Church of Christ?

(in ibid.: 155)

The same strategy of re-evangelisation using political, cultural and social élites has been adopted by militant lay organisations under the banner of the defence of the family. These organisations have, to some extent, become the preserve of the radical Catholic right wing and, both in their tactics and in their strategy, have come to resemble the American 'moral majority', seeking a return to what they see as the traditional moral order. They denounce modern society and the preoccupation with money, the corruption of political and business leaders and the dilution of moral values. The two largest federations − *Familles de France* (569 associations and 157,000 members) and the *Associations familiales catholiques* (AFC) (480 associations and 45,000 members) are active and energetic (figures quoted in Makarian 1995: 57). They organise *colonies de vacances*, babysitting groups and clothing exchange schemes. They lobby parliamentarians on family-related issues. They publish newspapers: *Familles de France* and *Famille chrétienne* and have the active support of Cardinal Lustiger and many French bishops.

They believe that modern society has rejected the values of good citizenship which were not exclusively Catholic values but which were inculcated through the French school system from Jules Ferry[10] onwards and through national service. These values included the stability of the family, hard work, thrift, self-reliance, neighbourliness and patriotism which contributed to personal integrity, altruism and a sense of solidarity within the community. Modern society has rejected the notion that any set of principles, any set of moral codes should animate society. Morality has become a private affair and any external authority is seen as a form of repression. No one is entitled to pass judgement on the behaviour of others. They are vigorously opposed to this moral relativism and point to what they see as a moral vacuum at the heart of French society which must lead inevitably to social disintegration.

To counter this situation, they seek to defend and consolidate the traditional family unit, perceived as the basic 'building brick' in any society, and to roll back the tide of moral relativism which seeks to undermine it. Opposition to abortion (legalised in France in 1975) is an issue which commands virtual unanimity among them, although the manner and scale of the opposition varies. The more moderate would condone abortion in some cases. The most militant want abortion under any circumstances to be made illegal and are targeting clinics. Violent demonstrators, including priests, have forced their way into clinics, shouting at patients and chaining themselves to operating tables. Some of these anti-abortion commandos are close to the *Front national* which also has 'family values' as one of the planks in its electoral platform.

The *Associations familiales* also uphold traditional Catholic teaching on contraception, now widely ignored by most Catholics in spite of repeated papal injunctions on the subject. For the right wing, this is part of another agenda, that of *natalisme*, a preoccupation with the falling birth rate in France, currently estimated at 1.65 per woman of child-bearing age when 2.1 would be necessary for the replacement of older generations. Here too, they are in tune with the political right wing, which considers that a rising French population (the population density of France is only half that of the UK) is necessary if France is to remain a great power and a Christian country and they constantly brandish the spectre of an exploding birth rate among the Maghrebin population of the country. *Figaro Magazine* had on its front page on 26 October 1985 a Marianne, symbol of the French Republic, with her face covered with an islamic veil with the caption: 'Will we still be French in 30 years time?'

They see tolerance of homosexuality and of sexual hedonism (leading inevitably in their view to single parent families) as very damaging to the traditional family structure, and hence to France, and as a moral pollution fostered by pornography. To this end they mounted a campaign against the '*minitel rose*' which they claimed was the principal vector of pornography in France:

> The minitel service must be discontinued. . . . Homosexuals are the main users of the pornographic message service. And their natural tendancy towards sexual vagrancy is given free rein thanks to the minitel. I'm just waiting for the next appalling scandal when the state will be accused of having spread AIDS by encouraging sexual vagrancy via the telecommunications and telephone systems. If France is the country most affected by the virus, it is because of the minitel which only France has.
>
> (Perier, in Brunnquell 1994: 80–1)

The *Associations familiales* and their political allies are therefore a significant pressure group, not only within France but in Rome also. According to *Le Point* (Makarian 1995: 58), the president of the AFC in Evreux, Jean-Marie Cordin, had been bitterly opposed to Mgr Gaillot for ten years and even led a delegation to Rome to seek his deposition.

The third adversary mentioned by Gaillot was the abbot of the autonomous Benedictine Abbey of Barroux, Dom Gérard Calvet, a follower of Mgr Lefebvre, who has managed to remain within the Catholic Church without abandoning any of his integrist positions. Calvet founded and built his abbey (which currently has more than sixty monks) to ensure that traditionalist theology and worship could continue within his order, which he saw as going down the laxist, modernist path. The abbey, built between 1982 and 1989, is said to have cost between 80 and 100 million f. (Terras 1991: 114–19), and was financed by rich sympathisers, including General Mobutu, President of Zaïre, who is a supporter of the Tridentine mass, a regular visitor to the monastery and a generous contributor. The Barroux pressure group belongs to the extreme right wing, both politically and in terms of the Church. In his *Letter to Friends of the Monastery*, Calvet makes his ideological position quite explicit:

> Providence has decreed that the consecration of our Church should coincide with the bicentenary of the 1789 Revolution: we cannot but see in this a call to make this ceremony an act of reparation. Reparation for the crimes and sacrileges of the Revolution most certainly. . . . Reparation especially for the work of the devil: the destruction of faith and religion, replaced by the dogma of the rights of godless Man, the baleful consequences of which we are still experiencing two hundred years later.
>
> (in Terras 1991: 116)

Calvet was a witness for the defence in 1988 in the case involving five young traditionalist Catholics who set fire to the Gaumont Saint Michel cinema in Paris to protest against the screening of the *Last Temptation of Christ*, an incident which resulted in thirteen people receiving serious injuries. He declared that their only intention was to defend 'civilisation against Scorcese, a homosexual and a bigamist'.

Dom Gérard Calvet sees himself as a guardian of the true Tridentine faith and does not hesitate to delate to Rome those whom he considers unworthy. When he and eleven of his monks were received by the Pope on 28 September 1990, he gave John-Paul II a letter denouncing a number of individuals and institutions:

> Ordinary catholics suffer especially from the actions of their bishops.
>
> . . . Mgr Gaillot, to quote but one example, alienates and scandalises the faithful by his remarks concerning faith and morals. In the guise of an act of charity, he contributes articles to erotic magazines and encourages homosexual 'unions'.
>
> Diocesan synods urge the ordination of women to the priesthood and that divorced and remarried people should be able to receive the sacraments. . . . May the Holy Father reaffirm that the church, founded by God, is not, in its essence, a democratic organisation . . ., that it is unchanging and may he dismiss the unworthy bishop of Evreux and show clemency towards the old prelate of Ecône [Lefebvre] whose life and doctrine have always inspired confidence in us.
>
> (in Terras 1991: 112–18)

Unlike the Church, the French State is 'in its essence, democratic' and the 1995 presidential election gave some indication of the support which these right-wing Catholic views currently enjoy in France. Le Pen won 15 per cent in the first ballot and Philippe de Villiers (whose *Combat pour les valeurs* follows this agenda much more closely) won 5 per cent. It would seem reasonable to assume, therefore, that this group, although active, vociferous and well-organised, is still a small minority within the nation and a minority, albeit larger and exercising disproportionate influence, within the Church.

AGGIORNAMENTO:[11] AN OPPORTUNITY LOST?

The Church in France is highly diverse and its members (including its bishops) are no longer perceived as having links with any single political tendency. The traditional association of Catholicism with the Right and atheism with the Left has gone and prominent Catholic lay people (such as Jacques Delors, for example) are to be found in considerable numbers on the left of the political spectrum. Many of them, like Delors, were shaped in their attitude to social affairs by their membership of different Catholic action groups (*Jeunesse étudiante chrétienne, Jeunesse agricole chrétienne, Jeunesse ouvrière chrétienne*, etc.) during their formative years. As was mentioned earlier in connection with Limerzel, the increasingly chronic shortage of priests has had, paradoxically, some positive effects on lay involvement and awareness. Parish lay groups abound, many of them concerned with the developing world or with social issues. This social conscience finds its outlet in such organisations as *Secours catholique*, which addresses problems in France such as homelessness (where the inspirational and emblematic figure is Abbé Pierre who has spent his entire life improving the lot of the homeless) and abroad where *Secours catholique* provides assistance in areas suffering from natural or man-made disasters.

The charismatic movement which originated in the United States became popular in France in the 1970s with the foundation of a number of communities, the most notable of which are *Lion de Juda, Chemin neuf, Fondations du monde nouveau* and *Emmanuel*. They combine new forms of spontaneous worship with high-profile, often controversial evangelising and a traditionalist stance on moral issues. They are 'slain in the spirit', they speak in tongues. The experience in prayer groups is ecstatic and emotional rather than intellectual and is based on unswerving certainty born of the intensity of personal experience. A characteristic aspect of the charismatic movement is its appeal to, among others, social misfits in search of a sense of community and a meaning to life. Their simplistic faith and their uncritical devotion to the Pope make them potential 'loose cannons' on the deck of the Church in France and it is to ensure a measure of control that the French bishops' conference has appointed a number of its members to channel the enthusiasm of the '*chachas*', as they are known.

Most prominent among these is the Cardinal Archbishop of Paris, Jean-Marie Lustiger, who is one of their enthusiastic protectors. The son of Polish Jewish immigrants, he was appointed archbishop in 1981, succeeding Cardinal François Marty who had led the post-conciliar Church in France with some distinction, empowering the French episcopal conference to produce statements on contemporary problems which made a real contribution to national life and to the life of the Church. Bishops were appointed who were used to the Catholic Action method of collaborative team work.

Lustiger set about reversing this trend towards collegiality almost immediately after his appointment.[12] He was able to influence and often determine nominations to vacant bishoprics because he was a member of all the relevant Vatican dicasteries (as the different departments are called): the Congregation for Bishops which keeps files on possible candidates, the Council for the Public Affairs of the Church, which deals with episcopal appointments in the case of France because the government has to give its assent, and the Congregation for Religious which can provide a reserve supply of candidates. Strictly speaking, Lustiger had no right to exercise this degree of influence. The Primate of the French Church is the *Primat des Gaules*, the Archbishop of Lyon who, until his death in 1995, was Albert Decourtray. Cardinal Decourtray was well known for his liberal stance on social issues, notably his appeals for the just treatment of ethnic minorities. In 1989 he threw open the diocesan archives to a commission of historians to investigate the rôle of various religious communities in hiding, between 1944 and 1989, the notorious French war criminal Paul Touvier, an extreme right-wing Catholic who became a member of the *milice* during the Occupation and participated in the persecution of Jews. Touvier was condemned to death after the war but escaped from custody and remained at large for forty-five years until his arrest and subsequent condemnation to life imprisonment for crimes against humanity. The historians' published report (Rémond 1992) received massive publicity and was a painful reminder of church collaboration with the Vichy regime during the German occupation, but paradoxically, the Cardinal's openness enhanced the Church's standing in the eye of the public, by showing it to be capable of self-appraisal and self-criticism.

The French episcopal conference elects its own president and has shown no inclination to accept Lustiger as its leader. It elected first Albert Decourtray and subsequently Joseph Duval, the Archbishop of Rouen. The status of the conference has, however, been considerably weakened by Lustiger's disregard for it and for any real collegiality. Over seventy bishops have been appointed by the Vatican since Lustiger became Archbishop of Paris in 1981 – some of them in Lustiger's own image (former colleagues or classmates); others, men who see their rôle more and more in local terms and are less likely to play a part in the national life of the Church, leaving that scene free for media favourites like Lustiger himself. In common with many other countries since the beginning of Jean-Paul II's pontificate, episcopal appointments in France have gone to men who are safe and conservative. The one exception to this rule was, of course, Mgr Gaillot, and this 'mistake' has now been remedied.

The dilemma faced by the French Church and examplified in the Gaillot affair was summed up by Christian Terras, editor of the left-wing Catholic publication *Golias*:

> Lay people play an adult role in society but within the Church they are treated as children. As a result of this, we find ourselves today with a community of believers who are immature, even illiterate as far as theology is concerned. Moreover, many Catholics have freed themselves from the moral tutelage of the priest and have begun to lead lives in contradiction with the gospel message, especially with regard to their private lives.
>
> (in *Le Point*, no. 1166, 21 January 1995: 55)

At one end of the spectrum, there is the desire articulated by Terras to pursue the course opened up by Vatican II, to explore with open-mindedness the Church's rôle in society, to deepen faith in the light of new theological scholarship and to come to terms with the fact that, for most people, free will has replaced unquestioning obedience to the teaching magisterium of the Church. At the other end, there are those who are either totally opposed to everything which Vatican II tried to achieve or are at best lukewarm, wanting a return to old certainties and old hierarchies. For many of the latter, the Golden Age of modern French Catholicism occurred during the period of the Vichy government when, rather like Salazar's Portugal, Church and State worked hand in hand and the social agenda of the Church was that of the State.

THE AMBIVALENT LEGACY OF VICHY

Fifty years after the end of the Second World War, the conventional attitude is to revile the Vichy government and its leader Philippe Pétain as archetypes of collaboration with Nazi oppression. The French have had a long period of collective amnesia about the Vichy years which has only recently been disturbed by the emergence of the Touvier affair and by revelations of former president François Mitterrand's activities during that time.

In fact, Pétain was extremely popular in France, especially during the early years of the Occupation. He was perceived as having saved France from the full brunt of German oppression and to have set the country on the road to recovery through his 'national revolution' which was in fact a nostalgic and rather backward-looking vision, evoking a paternalistic and rural civilisation and idealising a France which had never really existed, but the idea of which was very powerful and very seductive amid the confusion and panic of 1940.[13] This was a period of intense religious fervour – churches were packed and there were huge demonstrations of popular piety. People tried to make sense of the disaster which had overcome them and decided that it was due to the fact that the country had sinned – the Popular Front government had led the country to expect an easy life. Immorality and sexual promiscuity were rife, the Third Republic was corrupt and religion had been neglected (Duquesne 1966: 26ff). To expiate this national guilt, this sin, penance was necessary; the German occupation was therefore a necessary evil in order to purge France of her weaknesses and evils. Weygand, commander-in-Chief of the French army, explained in June 1940 that 'France deserved her defeat; she was beaten because, for half a century, her governments banned religious instruction in schools' (in ibid.: 27).

'Pétain is France and France today, is Pétain', declared Cardinal Gerlier. Pétain appeared as the head of state who incarnated Christian values, the father of the nation, the providential man who had saved the nation twice, the first time at Verdun in 1916 and now again in 1940. Pétain's portrait was hung in every church and school. The song *'Maréchal, nous voilà!'* virtually became the national anthem and a man who had no personal religious convictions and had been known for his libidinous behaviour became a national icon: 'Marshal Pétain, you are the way, the truth and the life of the country' said one cleric in a sermon (ibid.: 59).

The Catholic hierarchy rallied behind a government which, with its national revolution based on 'work, family, fatherland', its cult of youth and its rejection of the anti-clericalism of the Third Republic seemed ready to push back the tide of paganism which had been engulfing France since the turn of the century:

> Without there being any sense of subordination, we want people to be sincerely and totally loyal to the established government. We venerate the Head of State. . . . We encourage the faithful to stand beside him and work for the recovery of France which he has undertaken: Family, Work, Fatherland.
>
> (Gerlier, in ibid.: 51)

It was under the heading 'family' that the Catholic hierarchy found the propositions of Vichy most seductive and it is there that 'national revolution' and 'Christian revolution' became synonymous. Vichy gave considerable financial help to Catholic schools, abrogated much of the previous anti-clerical legislation and modified syllabuses to allow religious instruction in schools which was anathema to anti-clerical teachers. Schools were to develop a spirit of discipline, of respect for authority and of self-abnegation which was also fostered by the different Vichy youth movements. Intense propaganda in favour of large families was put out by the *secrétariat général à la Famille* so that France would never again have the low birth rates of the 1920s and 1930s which were seen as a major contributory factor to the débâcle of 1940.

167

Given this concordance of vision between Vichy and the Church, the hierarchy was loath to take issue with the government over its anti-Semitic legislation, which was in fact supported enthusiastically by the right-wing Maurrassien element, of whom Paul Touvier was one of the more infamous representatives. As the measures against the Jews became ever more draconian and inhuman, culminating in the *'rafle du Vel d'hiv'* in July 1942,[14] the bishops protested on humanitarian grounds to the government, which took no account of their unpublished remonstration. Their rather pusillanimous official ecclesiastical stance stood in stark contrast to the actions of hundreds of Catholics, lay, religious and clerics who helped thousands of Jews, especially children, to escape from the Nazis, whether to neighbouring neutral countries or by issuing them with false baptism certificates and hiding them in convents or monasteries. The clandestine Catholic newspaper *Témoignage Chrétien* made repeated and explicit attacks against racism and anti-Semitism –'France, take care not to lose your soul' – and three bishops were deported to Germany for having helped Jews to escape. But it was left to Jules-Géraud Saliège, Archbishop of Toulouse, to make the first, most direct, hard-hitting attack on the French govenment for permitting and organising these deportations:

> There is a Christian moral code, there is a human moral code, which imposes duties and recognises rights. These duties and these rights stem from the nature of man; they come from God. . . . It is not within the power of any human being to abolish them. It fell to our times to witness the sad sight of children, women, men, fathers and mothers being treated like worthless animals, of members of families being split up and loaded on to trains for unknown destinations.
>
> (in ibid.: 256–7)

In spite of all the efforts of the civil authorities to suppress the pastoral letter, it was duly read in all the churches of the archdiocese of Toulouse and a number of other bishops subsequently followed suit. The rather ineffectual initial reaction of the French episcopate as a whole may be explained by their unwillingness to compromise the 'national revolution' which they saw as vital to the recovery of France as a Catholic nation, and a number of them went out of their way to separate the person of Marshal Pétain from their condemnation of the anti-Semitic policies being enacted under his name.

When Vichy announced in February 1943 that a conscript labour force (*le Service du travail obligatoire*) was to be raised to work in Germany (the Germans were recruiting thousands of workers from the occupied countries to replace their own work-force which had been conscripted into the armed forces), the bishops expressed their 'sadness' and their 'sympathy' for those affected but did not suggest any other course of action than obedience to the state. This timorous reaction was not well received by people of the *Témoignage Chrétien* persuasion:

We are unable to convince the bishops that a government which has so little freedom of maneouvre cannot be considered as legitimate, that the order relating to the conscript labour force comes from the occupying forces and does not entail any obligation to obey. How can these men, who are generally very experienced in church affairs, be so ignorant of the basic realities of secular affairs. . . . With the exception of Mgr Saliège, the very brave Archbishop of Toulouse and a few others, almost all the bishops have given the order to obey the established government. Even seminarians are interrupting their studies to go and make shells in Germany.

(ibid.: 303–4)

For many members of the *Jeunesse ouvrière chrétienne* (*'jocistes'*), the problem was one of solidarity with fellow workers. As Paul Léon, who was subsequently deported to Dachau, expressed it: 'I didn't want to show a lack of solidarity with the suffering working classes. . . . An active member of the JOC has to go with his workmates out of working class solidarity and loyalty to his apostolic mission' (in ibid.: 282).

Some 3,200 seminarians and many more *jocistes* went to Germany as members of the STO, where they carried on a very courageous apostolate among their compatriots. They countered national socialist and LVF[15] propaganda at the risk of their lives and many were victims of the gas chambers. The Germans had forbidden the Church to send priests to look after the spiritual welfare of the conscripted workers but Cardinal Suhard decided to send priests clandestinely, dressed as workers rather than in their usual cassock. By the middle of 1943, 273 worker priests were working in Germany. For the first time in generations priests were reaching out to the de-Christianised working classes which they themselves were 'discovering', often for the first time, and realising how much the Church through its culture and attitudes had separated itself from ordinary working people. Their experience was the basis of Godin and Daniel's book (1943), *'La France, pays de mission?'*, which was to serve as a starting-point for the extension of this apostolate to France after the war. It caught the imagination of the people but frightened the Vatican, which was horrified to see priests who were real workers, demonstrating in the streets and holding positions of responsibility in trade unions. Pius XII put an end to the experiment in March 1954 (half of the worker priests refused his order) and it was not started again until October 1965 when Paul VI authorised the resumption of this apostolate.

The legacy of Vichy is ambiguous. On the one hand there was a conformism on the part of many members of the French hierarchy who were unwilling to prejudice the corporatist 'national revolution' which they saw as vital to the survival and growth of the Church. There were also the wholly reprehensible actions of those right-wing Catholics who totally misread the significance of this global conflict and participated in racial persecution in order to protect France from what they saw as a 'Judeo-Bolshevik revolution'. As we have seen, these attitudes are still present in France today, and if Paul Touvier was able to avoid French justice for forty-five years it was due to the connivance of sympathisers with this view. On the other hand, the circumstances of the Occupation released dynamic and innovative initiatives both on the pastoral and on the spiritual level which were to have far-reaching consequences. The clandestine liturgies of the prison and work camps required the active participation of lay people rather than merely a passive presence. The masses celebrated by worker priests were more often around a kitchen table than at a high altar.

CONCLUSION

When the Second Vatican Council opened in October 1962 it was the French contribution which was to be one of the most decisive. The thinkers of the French Church – Lubac, Chenu, Congar and Daniélou, who had been condemned by Pius XII in 1950 in *Humani Generis*, were now the driving force of a new vision – a vision of simplicity where the old triumphalism would have no place, of unity among Christians, of collegiality between the Pope and the bishops, of full lay participation in liturgy, where vernacular language would be used. As we have seen both in the context of Limerzel and in the reactions of the traditionalists to liturgical reform, the new mass has not been universally popular in France and has even proved to be a major factor in the divisions between French Catholics. The right-wing has remained rooted in Tridentine nostalgia and in a rejection of many aspects of the modern world. Those in favour of Vatican II reforms have sometimes insensitively imposed conciliar liturgies when a more gradualist approach might have been more successful. Sensitivity to pastoral issues – the homeless, the handicapped, the aged, people with AIDS, the Third World – has characterised French Catholicism over the last few decades and thus social action, together with the increasing empowerment of the laity, make mainstream French Catholics a dynamic force in today's society.

A dynamic force but a minority and one which increasingly takes its own decisions, particularly in the moral sphere, taking cognisance of but not necessarily adhering to the teachings of the Catholic magisterium. Gaillot's appeal is to a lot of these people and to those who never set foot in a church. He is anathema to the integrists because he challenges the traditional notion of revealed moral theology (which for them is not subject to discussion), by his insistence on freedom of conscience. He does so in contradiction to John-Paul II's view, expressed in *Veritatis Splendor*, which is a resounding rejection of moral subjectivism. Gaillot's actions follow the logic of the *aggiornamento* opened up by Vatican II; today's church leaders, particularly in Rome and followed by important elements of the French hierarchy, are publicly backing away from that model, retrenching in a much more authoritarian and rigid stance. For them, the unity of the Catholic Church requires uniformity rather than the pluriformity which has often been the norm since Vatican II. Gaillot attempts to be fully part of the world, to preach the Christian message by any means available, to confront his beliefs with those of the majority of the French who are, in effect, de-Christianised and among whom he gained respect. By sidelining him, the Catholic Church in France has simply avoided the problem of how to be part of the world today.

THE CHURCH: CHRONOLOGY

1939 (2 March) Election of Pius XII
   (3 September) Britain and France declare war on Germany
1940 *(10 July) Pétain made head of the Etat français;*
   (3 October) Premier Statut des Juifs
   (19 November) Gerlier: 'Pétain is France and France today is Pétain.'
1941 *(2 June) Second Statut des Juifs*
   (4 July) Creation of the LVF (Légion des volontaires français)
   (24 July) Declaration of Cardinals and Archbishops of Occupied zone: 'Without there being any sense of subordination, we want people to be sincerely and totally loyal.'
   First publication of *Témoignage Chrétien*
   (2 November) Law passed allowing subsidies to Catholic schools
1942 *(22 June) Laval: 'I hope for the victory of Germany'*
   (16/17 July) 'Rafle du Vel d'hiv'
   (23 August) Public protest by Saliège against deportation of Jews
   (11 November) Italians and Germans occupy southern France
   (End of December) Development of the *réseau Garel* to hide Jewish children in Catholic institutions
1943 (January) Departure for Germany of first clandestine worker priests
   (30 January) Creation of French milice
   (16 February) Institution of STO (Service du travail obligatoire)
   (9 May) *Témoignage Chrétien* condemns STO.
   Publication of J. Godin and Y. Daniel, *La France, pays de mission?*.
1944 (26 April) Cardinal Suhard welcomes Pétain in Notre Dame de Paris.
   (28 May) Arrest and deportation of Bishop Pinguet.
   (6 June) Allied invasion of Normandy.
   (9 June) Arrest and deportation of Bishops Théas and de Solange.
   (10 June) Massacre at Oradour-sur-Glane.
   (15 August) Allied invasion of Provence.
   (26 August) 'Te Deum' in Notre Dame de Paris to celebrate Liberation. Cardinal Suhard excluded.
   (25/6 November) First national congress of the MRP (Mouvement républicain populaire).
1945 *(8 May) Capitulation of Germany.*
   (27 July) Seven bishops resign because of collaboration with the Germans.
   (21 October) Constituent Assembly elections: 24 per cent for the MRP.
1946 *Fourth Republic*
   Foundation of *Secours Catholique*

1954 (1 March) Worker priest crisis
(1 November) Beginning of the Algerian War
(Winter) Appeals and campaign by Abbé Pierre in favour of homeless
1958 *(September) Fifth Republic constitution approved by referendum*
(9 October) Death of Pius XII
(28 October) Election of John XXIII
1962 Vatican II (1962–5)
(19 March) End of the Algerian War
1963 (3 June) Death of John XXIII
(21 June) Election of Paul VI
1965 (23 Oct) Resumption of worker priest apostolate
1968 *The Events of May 1968*
(25 July) Encyclical *Humanae Vitae* reiterating ban on artificial birth control
1969 Lefebvre founds Fraternity of St Pius X at Ecône
1971 Beginnings of charismatic movement
1975 Lefebvre suspended *'a divinis'*
Abortion legalised in France
1977 (Easter) Occupation of St Nicolas du Chardonnet by Lefebvrists
1978 (6 August) Death of Paul VI
(26 August) Election of John-Paul I (Died 28 September)
(16 October) Election of John-Paul II
1980 First visit of John-Paul II to France
1981 (February) J-M. Lustiger becomes Archbishop of Paris
(10 May) F. Mitterrand elected President of the Republic
1983 J. Gaillot becomes Bishop of Evreux
1984 *Mass demonstrations against Savary school reform proposals.*
1988 (30 June) Schism of Mgr Lefebvre
1989 Consecration of the integrist Abbey of Barroux
Collapse of communist régimes in Europe; Bicentennial of the French Revolution; Paul Touvier apprehended
1993 Encyclical *Veritatis Splendor*
1995 (13 January) Dismissal of Mgr Gaillot
(25 March) Encyclical *Evangelium Vitae* (against artificial birth control and abortion)
(7 May) Jacques Chirac elected President of the Republic

NOTES

1 See Chapter 9, section entitled 'Immigration and National Identity'.
2 These incidents and declarations were reported in: *Le Point*, 21 janvier 1995; *L'Express*, 26 janvier 1995; *The Tablet*, 11 February 1995.
3 Abbé Pierre was held in immense esteem by the French people because of his work for the homeless. He dramatically fell from grace in May 1996 after voicing support for a revisionist interpretation of the Holocaust by his historian friend Roger Garaudy. He has now left France to go and live in an Italian monastery, where he may spend the rest of his life.
4 The Council of Trent (1545–63) defined and reaffirmed many aspects of Catholic dogma in reaction to the Lutheran reforms. Notably, it established a normative version of the mass (in Latin) which was to be the only one used in the Western Church until the 1960s.

5 *Action française*: a daily newspaper which appeared from 1908 until 1944 under the direction of Charles Maurras and which advocated the restoration of the monarchy and support for the Catholic Church as the guarantor of order in society. Its adherents were essentially anti-democratic and became ardent supporters of the Vichy government.

6 A religious society (therefore existing independently of diocesan structures) devoted to missionary and teaching work.

7 Much of the information about *Opus Dei* reproduced here is taken from the left-wing Catholic publication, *Golias*: (see Terras 1992).

8 The step preceding canonisation (i.e., sainthood) whereby the Church declares the life of a deceased Catholic to have been exemplary and offers that person as a model to the faithful with the title: 'The Blessed . . .'.

9 That is, a blind obedience to orders.

10 Jules Ferry (1832–93): French statesman during the Third Republic best remembered for his educational reforms (1881–2) which ensured that education in France would be free, secular, universal and compulsory.

11 When Pope John XXIII summoned the bishops of the Catholic Church to the Second Vatican Council which opened in 1962, he urged them to read the signs of the times, to be open to the current needs and different cultures of the world and to prepare for the *aggiornamento* (updating) of the Christian message.

12 See 'His man in Paris', *The Tablet*, 5 October 1991: 1201–2.

13 It is interesting that an election poster used by François Mitterrand in 1981 showing him set against a hill top village crowned by a church is almost exactly the same as one used by Pétain fifty years earlier.

14 With the active participation of the Paris police, the Gestapo rounded up thousands of Parisian Jews and interned them in the covered cycling stadium (the *Vel d'hiv*) before transporting them to the death camps.

15 *La Légion des volontaires français*: French men who had been persuaded to join an anti-Bolshevik crusade, fighting alongside the Germans on the Russian front. They wore SS uniforms with a shoulder badge reading '*Légion Charlemagne*' and a tricolour badge. Many of them were recruited among right-wing Catholics by Cardinal Baudrillart. The LVF were among the last defenders of Hitler's bunker in Berlin in 1945.

REFERENCES AND RECOMMENDED READING

Brunnquell, F. (1994) *Les Associations familiales*, Paris: Dagorno.

* Duquesne, J. (1966) *Les Catholiques français sous l'occupation*, Paris: Grasset.
  Using previously unpublished material, Duquesne details the actions and standpoints of the French Church during the Occupation and shows how the divisions and compromises which arose then have given rise to current attitudes within the Church.

—— (1995) *Jésus*, Paris: Flammarion-Desclée de Brouwer.

Godin, H. and Daniel, Y. (1943) *La France, pays de mission?*, Paris: Cerf.

* Hervieu-Léger, D. (1985) *Vers un nouveau Christianisme?*, Paris: Cerf.
  In the context of a decline in religous practice and the rise of sects and renewal movements, Hervieu-Léger gives a detailed evaluation of the state of religion in France today.

Lambert, Y. (1985) *Dieu change en Bretagne*, Paris: Cerf.

Lefebvre, M. (1975) *Itinéraires*, January: 5–8.

Makarian, C. (1995) 'Catholiques contre catholiques', *Le Point*, no. 1166: 52–9.

Mongin, O. (ed.) (1992) 'Que faire de Vichy?' *Esprit*, no. 181, special edition (May).

Rémond, R. *et al.* (1992) *Paul Touvier et l'Eglise*, Paris: Fayard.
Terras, C. (ed.) (1991) 'Le Retour des croisés', *Golias*, nos 27–28, special edition Autumn.[1]
—— (ed.) (1992) 'Le Monde secret de l'Opus Dei', *Golias*, no. 30, special edition Summer.
Woodrow, A. (1994) 'The Beliefs of the French', *The Tablet*, 21 May: 643.

[1] *Golias* is available from: B.P. 4034, 69615 Villeurbanne Cedex, France.

9

LAÏCITÉ AND ISLAM

Inès Brulard

Free religious practice is an essential principle of all Western countries. However, the place of religion and the extent to which the church is kept separate from the state can vary; so as better to appreciate the specific character of *laïcité*[1] in France, comparisons with other countries have to be made. In the United States and in Switzerland, there is no official church and the state does not finance any religious groups; yet the Swiss constitution begins with 'In the name of God Almighty' and the American president publicly swears allegiance to the constitution and closes his oath with 'And so help me God'. England has an official church: the Queen is head of the Anglican Church and only an Anglican can be head of state; moreover representatives of the Church sit in the House of Lords. In Belgium, all 'mainstream' religious movements (including Islam) are financed by the state, and Catholicism permeates public affairs, for one of the three major political groups is the Christian Social Party. In France, the principle of *laïcité* is stricter: the law of 1905 imposed a strict separation between the public and the private spheres of activity. From being officially considered as one of the institutions structuring society, religious practice has become a purely private matter, confined to marginal associations.

In the minds of many French people, secularism has merely to do with educational problems, and secular milieux are equated with the teaching profession. This association goes back to the establishment under the Third Republic of a state education system which had to be free, compulsory and secular.[2] The secular principle still applies to the contemporary state education system: teachers are lay people and there is no religious teaching. State schools are not against religion, they are neutral. While it is true to say that the debates concerning education are the most visible or known aspect of secularism, the principle of *laïcité* is in fact at the heart of French identity. And it may be surprising to find that it is no longer popular with the general public: as Baubérot (1990: 7) has pointed out, public opinion was largely indifferent to the celebration, in February 1981, of the centenary of the republican education system set up by Jules Ferry. According to some analysts, this 'decline of the secular idea' is evidence of its success:

175

secularism is such an important part of French identity that it is no longer worth talking about it. According to others, it is a moribund idea which only resurfaces in (much publicised) moments of crisis. Examples of such crises are the condemnation by the Pope (together with some Jewish and Muslim personalities) of Martin Scorsese's film, *The Last Temptation of Christ*, the Pope's position against the use of condoms and the pill, and the so-called 'headscarf affair'.

In this chapter we will go back to the time of the French Revolution to show that the common point between all these controversies is that they address a question which is historically connected to *laïcité*: that of religious freedom and the freedom to criticise religions. We will then examine what was specific about the headscarf affair: why was it that on 4 October 1989, the head of the Gabriel-Havez college in Creil forbade three Muslim girls access to the school because they insisted on wearing the headscarf, or *hijeb*? Why was this news item to result in one of the most passionate debates in the post-war period? It will be shown that this controversy raised both the question of a certain conception of education and that of a 'Muslim problem'. It brought important sociological concerns to the fore: was the republican education system, this neutral ground in which religion has no place, under threat; and what place should be given to immigrants and to Islam in France?

LAÏCITÉ AND FREEDOM

The development of *laïcité* in France has often been described in conflictual terms; one speaks of the conflict between 'the two Frances' since the Revolution (Birnbaum 1993). In one camp, one finds those defending the notion of a homeland founded on the Catholic Church and the army, often being anti-Protestant, anti-Jew and anti-freemason; they are conservative, even reactionary, often monarchist. In the other camp, one finds defenders of the republican ideals of 1789 founded on Reason (not on Catholicism): freedom, religious tolerance, a strict separation between the public and the private domains. Article 10 of the Declaration of the Rights of Man and the Citizen states that: 'Nobody should be persecuted for their opinions or their religious beliefs, provided that they do not cause disturbance of public order under the law'. This difficult compromise still represents the constitutional foundation of religious freedom in France today.

Protestants often found themselves in the republican, secular camp, although as lay believers, they should be seen as situated on the frontier between the two Frances (Baubérot 1990: 14). In the beginnings of the Third Republic, they played an important part in elaborating the republican policy of secularism; they also contributed to stabilising the republican régime, under constant threats from a counter-revolutionary Catholicism. It may be surprising that religious-minded people contributed to shaping the idea of secularism; however, in general terms, for the French Protestants, the cause of *laïcité* was synonymous with that of freedom; their wish was to reconcile religion and freedom.

If there were conflicts, there were also conciliatory pacts which kept French society from disintegrating; hence the notion of 'secular pact', a pact which was often threatened, and which, according to some, is threatened nowadays by Islam. The first conciliatory act was the Concordat or *pacte des cultes reconnus* (1801). This meant that the state had to accept the presence of these recognised religious groups (of which the Catholics constituted the largest part).[3] The Concordat, i.e., the convention signed by Pope Pie VII and the French government, is still valid in three French *départements* (Bas-Rhin, Haut-Rhin and Moselle) in which the priests' salaries are paid by the state. However, this first pact did not completely settle the religious conflicts, which kept cropping up in the form of crises such as the Dreyfus affair[4] or the attacks against congregations, so that in the end, another pact was necessary: this secular pact took the form of the Separation law, voted in 1905.[5] It established a situation whereby the Republic guarantees the liberty of conscience and free religious practice but it does not acknowledge or subsidise any religious group, thereby refusing to recognise the social function of religion, which then becomes a purely private matter. Religious associations are not allowed to have any secular activities (social or economic, for instance). The 1905 law complemented the 1901 law which forbade secular associations from having any religious activities.[6] In 1946, after the trauma of war and occupation, the principle of *laïcité* was enshrined in the constitution, and is one of the major characteristics of the republican state: 'France is an indivisible, secular, democratic and social Republic' (Article 2 of the constitution).

LAÏCITÉ IN EDUCATION

The 1905 Separation law was seen as the solution to the legitimacy conflicts between the Catholic Church and the Republic which tore France apart during the nineteenth century. Catholic schools had been part of this conflict, since they were seen as the places where anti-republican, anti-democratic ideas were inculcated. The solution to that problem was the establishment of a dual education system in which private (essentially Catholic) schools coexisted with secular state schools. This dual system still exists and religious instruction is still not allowed in state schools, which are required by law to be secular. Until the middle of the twentieth century, only state schools were subsidised by the state. However, when the Debré law (1959) allowed many private schools to receive subsidies from the state, the issue of *laïcité* began to be identified with educational issues. The debate around the revision of the Falloux law[7] in 1993 is an example of this: it raised the issue whether private schools (which were already partly subsidised by the state) should benefit from the *same* amount of subsidy as state schools and led, in January 1994, to a demonstration in defence of *laïcité*. Another example of the equation between *laïcité* and educational issues was Mitterrand's project to put an end to the dual education system by creating 'a unified secular state education system' (Mitterrand's ninetieth proposition, in the '110 propositions'). Although this project had already been fairly diluted in the Savary law (named after Mitterrand's Minister of Education), it met with resounding defeat when, in 1984, a massive demonstration took place in Paris, this time to defend private schools.

Secularism is a fundamental aspect of state education: 'it is the state's duty to provide public, free and secular education' and the constitution of the Fifth Republic (1958) added that France 'has respect for all beliefs' (Article 2 of Section 1 of the constitution). When the head of the Gabriel-Havez college in Creil expelled the three Muslim girls, he justified his decision by resorting to the principle of *laïcité*: wearing a headscarf in a state school was in breach of the secular principle of neutrality. In contrast, the position of the then Minister of Education, Lionel Jospin, was an attempt to reconcile a tenet of *laïcité*, namely that religion has no place in state schools, and the obligation for the state to provide education and to respect the pupils' beliefs. His view was that pupils should be persuaded not to wear religious signs at school, but they could not be forced out of school if they kept on wearing them.

This was the beginning of a controversy opposing those who upheld a strict idea of *laïcité* and supported the head of the school, and those who supported Jospin's more tolerant view of *laïcité*. Interestingly, in each camp, one found people who were not usual defenders of secularism, but also people who were, thereby suggesting a split in the pro-secularism camp (Baubérot 1990: 181). In their manifesto published in the *Nouvel Observateur* (2 November 1989), five intellectuals (amongst whom Elisabeth Badinter,[8] Régis Debray and the philosopher Alain Finkielkraut) characterised Jospin's position as 'the Munich of the republican education system' (the reference to capitulation before the Nazis set the tone). For them, the republican state school is where universal values are proposed, a place of freedom which cannot tolerate religious particularisms. Other intellectuals (in *Le Monde*, 10 November 1989) defended a more open type of secularism which would place the secular school 'above particularisms' but 'show respect for these'.

The debate went on to take a legal character, as Lionel Jospin decided to ask the opinion of the *Conseil d'Etat*. On 27 November 1989, the *Conseil* reiterated the liberal interpretation of secularism which had been that of the Third Republic: it made it clear that the principle of *laïcité* applied to the teaching staff and the educational programmes but that the pupil's 'liberty of conscience' had to be respected.[9] Second, the acknowledgement of the pupil's freedom had to go together with 'respect for everyone's freedom': pupils' beliefs could be expressed, provided that the 'the teaching, the curriculum and attendance requirements' were not affected. It concluded that religious signs were not *per se* 'incompatible with the secular character of the state school' (in Perotti and Thépaut 1992: 18); however, the *Conseil* allowed schools to ban any religious signs which might be 'ostentatious', 'discriminatory', 'militant' or signs which might disturb classes.

Between 1989 and 1994, five other cases were brought to administrative tribunals: parents either contested the exclusion measures imposed on their daughters, or challenged the schools' internal regulations. In 1992 and again in 1994, the *Conseil d'Etat* was called in to resolve disagreements. It reiterated its 1989 principles but this time explicitly referred to the headscarf (as opposed to signs in general). In the 1992 ruling, it made it clear that forbidding the wearing of the headscarf on the grounds that it was a sign of women's subservience presupposed an interpretation of the religious sign which was not the prerogative of the administration or a judge. Kessler (1995: 33) points out that, as opposed to the swastika, which in itself, because of its historical references, represents incitement to racial hatred or to violence, the headscarf *in itself* does not represent anything. Seeing it as a sign of women's subordination requires an *interpretation* of the sign, on the basis of what one knows (or thinks one knows) about Islamic civilisations.[10] On the other hand, the *Conseil d'Etat* confirmed a decision taken in May 1994 to exclude two girls from Xavier-Bichat college (Nantua) because by refusing to take off their headscarves during a gymnastics class, they had 'seriously disturbed pedagogical activities' (in Bernard 1995: 31). While the *Conseil d'Etat* favoured a case-by-case approach, in September 1994, François Bayrou, Minister of Education, published a circular which, without referring explicitly to the headscarf, banned all 'ostentatious signs' from schools. Only 'discreet signs' should be allowed, as they merely express 'attachment to personal beliefs' (in *Le Monde*, 21 September 1994).

So first of all, the headscarf affair questioned the meaning of secularism: was the principle of *laïcité* as understood by the head of the school still appropriate for contemporary France or should it be reinterpreted? This question was connected to another: what place should Islam be given in France? The symbolic meaning of the headscarf was at the centre of a debate which illustrated the difficulty for France in going beyond simplistic dichotomies such as *laïcité* on the one hand and fundamentalism on the other; against the idea that one must be opposed to wearing the headscarf, in the name of *laïcité*, or in favour of it, in the name of militant Islam. Moreover, the headscarf was sometimes seen as a symbol of women's subservience, which neither French schools nor French society could tolerate.

IMMIGRATION AND NATIONAL IDENTITY

The debate on the headscarf affair also addressed the question of the place immigrants should be given in France: the fact that the girls in question were *beurs*[11] caused the issue of *laïcité* to get entangled with the much wider debate about immigration and the integration of immigrants' children into French society. Indeed, some of those who argued against the exclusion of the three girls insisted on the fact that the 'feeling of exclusion' was growing amongst the Maghrebin community and could 'feather the nest' of both the fundamentalists and the *Front national* (*Le Monde*, 10 November 1989). We will show that the common point between the immigration question and the debate on the headscarf affair is that they both focus on cultural differences associated with Islam.

Not all immigrants are Muslims, of course, and not all Muslims are immigrants or even foreigners. The notion of foreigner is based on the criterion of nationality: a foreigner is someone who does not have French nationality (but s/he can acquire it in some circumstances). The notion of immigrant is based on a fixed criterion: the place of birth. An immigrant is somebody who was born abroad but lives in France. An immigrant may become French or remain foreign, depending on what the French Code of Nationality allows. It follows that a foreigner is not necessarily an immigrant and that an immigrant is not necessarily a foreigner. In 1990, amongst the 4.2 million immigrants in France, 2.9 million were foreigners and the others had acquired French nationality (INSEE data, in Champsaur 1994: 5). In a total population of 56.7 million in 1990, France has 3.6 million foreigners (i.e., 6.3 per cent) (OECD data, ibid.: 9). The 1990 census figures indicate a decrease in European foreigners (40.7 per cent in 1990 against 93.7 per cent in 1921 and 72.3 per cent in 1968), and an increase in African foreigners, the majority of them being of Maghreb origin (45.4 per cent in 1990 against 2.5 per cent in 1921 and 24.8 per cent in 1968).

In contemporary France, the notions of citizenship and nationality are intimately connected and tend to be based on cultural criteria. However, this association was only firmly established in the nineteenth century. The Revolution made a far less clear-cut distinction between the particular and the universal, and between nationals and non-nationals: it introduced the concept of the universal Rights of Man, but this concept was situated in the particularist framework of the nation. Rousseau's idea of 'Universal Man' was then immediately contradicted by that of the citizen: the 1789 Declaration of the Rights of Man and the Citizen put limits on the universal character of citizenship by making it dependent on nationality. By 'citizen' is no longer meant simply the inhabitant of France, attached to France's interests; a citizen is a *member of the nation* (Lochak 1991: 181). As Silverman puts it:

> The republican ideal – founded on the liberal conception of the free individual inherited from the philosophers of the Enlightenment – was therefore hijacked by the nation and was quickly incorporated within a distinction between nationals (citizens) and non-nationals (non-citizens).
>
> (Silverman 1992: 27)

This tension between the particular and the universal is central to the history of the French nation.[12] However, the contemporary opposition between the national and the foreigner does not go back to the Revolution. At the time, the difference between nationals and foreigners was 'more conceptual than actual' (ibid.: 28) and the concept of foreigner was not defined in the same terms (i.e., by the ethnic origin, a common language, territory and history). Until the middle of the nineteenth century, access to citizenship for people of foreign origin was fairly easy; the term 'immigrant' hardly ever appeared in documents.

A clear distinction between nationals and non-nationals was only established with the development of the nation-state, in the second half of the nineteenth century, during the first decades of the Third Republic (1870–1940) (ibid.: 28–9). Rapid industrialisation and a deep demographic crisis resulted in increased state intervention (in the form of social measures). This institutionalisation of social relations (for instance, in the education system) caused foreigners to be defined not only as people who were born outside France's borders but as failing to belong to the body of the nation. Already at that time, different identities brought about inequalities. In other words, equality was not independent of nationality: in the 1880s taxes were imposed on foreigners to protect French employment; foreigners had to declare their place of residence at the town hall; the 1890 law relating to accidents in the workplace only protected nationals. Article 39 of the first French Code of Nationality (1889) stipulated that the government could use the concept of 'insufficient assimilation' to prevent nationalisation by marriage; Article 69 stated that naturalisation could be refused to those who could not prove a sufficient degree of integration in French society, for instance if they could not demonstrate sufficient knowledge of French (ibid.: 173). The term coined by the nationalist right-wing movement *Action française*, '*Français de papier*' (i.e., 'Frenchman on paper': in the context of the 1920s, this referred particularly to the Jews), reflected this essentialist vision of the nation.

Since, in France, the ideas of cultural identity, nationality and citizenship 'are superimposed and indissociable' (Etienne 1989: 170), it is no surprise that the contemporary debates about the reform of the Code of Nationality have established a link between the symbolic/cultural concept of the nation and nationality as juridical category (Silverman 1992: 142–3). The 1993 Pasqua laws have made the long-established principle of the *ius soli* (or *droit du sol*, i.e., the right to be French if one is born on French territory) conditional instead of automatic: the young person born in France from foreign parents still has the right to become French but s/he will have to declare his or her willingness to become French between the age of 16 and 21. This means that only '*les Français de souche*' ('French people of old stock', whatever this means, given that any country is a blend of races and cultures) belong 'naturally' to the nation. The parliamentary debates showed that blood and race continued to be taken as the foundations of national identity, hence the distrust of the 1993 law with regard to mixed marriages.[13]

If the immigration question is, to some extent, still conceived of in economic terms (e.g. the problem of illegal immigrants or *'clandestins'* working in France), it often tends to centre on differences in cultural identity. It is legitimate to wonder why Maghreb immigration has been perceived as *Muslim immigration*, since it is and has always been first and foremost a work-force immigration. Immigration has always been connected to the economic situation of France. In the second half of the nineteenth century, it was encouraged by the industrialisation process: in 1881, there were 1 million foreigners (2.7 per cent of the population); they only represented 1 per cent in 1851 (Champsaur 1994: 6). Again, in the twentieth century, the immigra-tion rate has varied according to the economic cycles France was going through: there was an increase in immigration after the First World War (due to the need to reconstruct the country), which was followed in the 1930s by a fall in immigration, due to an economic crisis. As early as 1932, measures were taken to slow down the immigration process and encourage immigrant workers to return to their country of origin. In the immediate post-war period, economists, demographers and politicians agreed that the reconstruction of France necessitated a large increase in foreign labour. Since the 1950s, there has been a marked increase in Maghreb immigration (and a decrease of European immigration). The oil crisis which hit the 1970s led again to restrictive policies on primary immigration (1974). On the other hand, the right for immigration on the grounds of family reunification became more important.

As the policies of family reunification intensified, it became clearer that the immigrant population was going to settle down and stay in France. Interestingly, at the same time, the debates came to centre on the permanent presence of immigrants rather than on the temporary nature of an immigrant workforce, and thus on *social* rather than economic questions. So, since the 1970s, immigration penetrated the public and political arena as a social problem of ethnic/cultural relations (Silverman 1992: 85–7). From 'guest-workers', 'factors of production', immigrants came to be perceived as objects of a political controversy defined in terms of citizenship and identity. Silverman argues that the euphemism used of 'social phenomenon' hid the 'real' problem: the question of assimilating immigrants who were culturally different from the earlier categories of immigrants.

Some historians have highlighted the unifying, assimilationist and uni-versalising force of the Republic; others, like Fernand Braudel, have stressed the plural and diverse character of France. The immigration questions centre precisely on questions of assimilation, universalism vs. difference and particularism. In the French approach, it is for individuals to adhere to the body of the nation: they have to adhere to the national values (*laïcité*, equality between citizens, etc.); this model is often referred to as assimilationist

182

because it does not admit of the other's difference, of cultural particularisms (see Solé 1989). In the 1970s, the concept of assimilation was challenged because it was felt that the state did not have the right to erase regional or ethnic differences. This was when the term *'integration'* came to be used to refer to an open process in which the fundamental values of French society have to be preserved but without incurring total renunciation of the immigrant's original culture. However, the efficiency of integration measures is somewhat doubtful, as politicians on the Left and on the Right keep advocating policies which are contradictory: integration on the one hand and control on the other. The 1993 Pasqua law is a case in point: its author argued that fighting illegal immigration and its economic consequences was necessary to further the integration of those immigrants who are legal residents in France (*Le Monde*, 2 June 1993). However, the repressive character of this policy has recently appeared in what is now being referred to as *l'affaire des sans-papiers*, which exposed the plight of many immigrants who, until 1996, were legal residents in France but suddenly found themselves 'illegal'.

Some French people and politicians believe that Muslims cannot be integrated in French society because they are culturally different and their religion prevents them from being assimilated. Towards the end of the 1960s, the term 'immigrant' already meant 'non-European', and particularly 'North African'; it was argued that, while the earlier immigrants were able to assimilate into the French nation, the new ones, because of their cultural difference, could not easily integrate, and threatened social cohesion (Silverman 1992: 75–6). The claim that in the past, immigrants integrated easily because of their cultural proximity, is clearly a case of reinterpretation of history: towards the end of the nineteenth century, the 'immigration problem' referred to the Belgians and then the Italians; between the wars, it referred to the Slavs and the Jews. Moreover, Etienne (1989: 143) points out that before the colonial period, France had been able to absorb fairly large numbers of Muslims. Given that Muslim immigrants have been entering France for thirteen centuries, it is strange that 'Islam is not yet perceived as a native religion' (Clément 1991: 98).

MUSLIM 'COMMUNITY'

The tendency of the media to present Islam as the second religion in France[14] reinforces the idea that Islam threatens French identity; a question like *'Peut-on être musulman et français?'* ('Is it possible to be both Muslim and French?') (Jacques Julliard, in *Le Nouvel Observateur*, October 1987) is very telling. In addition to the perception of Muslim immigrants as culturally different, one is faced with negative clichéd representations stemming partly from colonial times but also from an essentialist vision of Islam, perceived as a body of practices which are always and everywhere identical. In reality, the Islam of the Maghrebins in France is very different from that of the

183

Pakistani in Britain or that of the Surinamese in Holland. These differences have partly to do with the variety in the cultural systems existing in the countries from which Muslims originate. Moreover, the way Muslims experience their religion is dependent on the cultural and institutional traditions of the receiving country (Césari 1995: 4–5).

In *Les banlieues de l'Islam* (1991), Kepel points out that there is no homogeneous 'Muslim community' and no single way of being a Muslim in France: the desire to practise Islamic faith in France can take various forms. Cesari distinguishes three categories of Muslims (1995: 22–6): the first group (a majority) consists of those who have been living in France for more than ten years and who have gradually come to wish that their Islamic faith was no longer confined to the private sphere. Since 1980, they have been asking for more praying spaces, for *halal* meat to be available in schools, etc. This change of attitude towards French society is motivated by a desire to counteract a deculturation process. A second (minority) group tends to favour a secularised form of Islam: they are usually young and middle-class people. For them, Islam is merely a source of values giving a meaning to their lives. They establish a distinction between belief and practice and they do not necessarily conform to the religious practices. A third (even smaller) group consists of young people, particularly those living in the *banlieues*[15] and on the point of marginalisation. They are often people who were previously committed to political causes (civil rights, anti-racism, etc.). But they realised that their ideals had not come true and they were still facing failure, exclusion, discrimination. Their position is diametrically opposed to those who hold a secularised vision of Islam: they want to give a central position to Islam in their lives (they speak of a process of re-Islamisation and, in some cases, Islamisation), an approach which they see as the most appropriate answer to marginalisation. It is important to distinguish between two tendencies within that group: a 'pietistic' tendency,[16] to which belong those who want to apply all the religious rules so that their whole life is marked by Islam, and a political tendency to which belong those who use the Islamic message towards political ends. This distinction is important because the two groups are often amalgamated and presented as fundamentalists. There are Islamic militants in France, but they are far less numerous than is often thought.[17]

One of the major challenges for Islam at present is the adaptation of its message in an unprecedented situation, i.e., that of a minority religion. This is a situation for which Muslims were not prepared, since they come from countries where Islam is either the official religion or the religion of the majority. For them, the question is 'how can they have a Muslim identity in a secular France?' The minority status of Islam was not taken into account in Muslim law, elaborated between the seventh and ninth centuries, at a time when Islam was politically and culturally dominant. Connected to that minority status is the problem of the status of the *imams* and of their training. Most of them are of foreign origin, and trained outside France, whereas half the Muslim population is French, which raises the question of adapting the religious message for the younger generations (Césari 1995: 29).[18] It is unlikely that European Islam will ever break away from its Middle Eastern and Maghreb centres of influence where Muslim law is now elaborated, but what is at stake at present is 'how it will manage to become more autonomous and to build its own minority specificity without cutting itself off from its sources' (ibid.: 29).

IS ISLAM INCOMPATIBLE WITH *LAÏCITÉ*?

Islam appears to be threatening and incompatible with *laïcité* because it is often viewed through its radical, fundamentalist form. Misrepresentations of Islam in France were triggered by international events such as the Iranian Revolution or the growing radicalisation of Islam in Algeria. While Muslims in France perceive Islam as synonymous with 'justice' and 'democracy', non-Muslims view it as synonymous with 'fanaticism', 'violence' and 'subservience' (see IFOP poll, in *Le Monde*, 30 November 1989). However, it has to be recognised that Islam as well 'feels threatened by the crumbling of its traditional structures and by the adoption of cultural models imported from the West' (Baubérot 1990: 214). For instance, according to Göle (1994: 67), Muslim women in Turkey and Egypt wear the headscarf as a symbol of 're-Islamisation of society'. But it is not clear whether wearing the headscarf should be interpreted as a U-turn from modernisation back to traditionalism. These women are often educated and some of them have become active in the public domain (they are against the oppression by men in the family, at work); they have nothing in common with the traditional docile Muslim women who confined themselves to their homes. For them, Islam is not a tradition to follow slavishly according to old customs: they are looking for a 'return to the sources', a deeper knowledge of Islam. As Göle (ibid.: 72) suggests, the 'headscarf is both the "lever" of their identity quest and the symbol of their resistance to the modern world'; they question the equation between modernity and the West. Women then seem to be at the centre of the debate around tradition and modernity, Islam and *laïcité*. As the Kaltenbachs (1991: 142ff.) have shown, the young Maghreb woman will play an essential role in the reform of Islam in France and in the integration of Muslims.

In the nineteenth century, it was Catholicism which was viewed as incompatible with *laïcité*, and like Islam today, it was viewed through its intransigent form. In 1889, for instance, the Catholic paper *La Croix* made it clear that 'the two Frances were facing each other, ready for a decisive fight; one of them must disappear' (in Baubérot 1990: 215). As in 1905 with Catholicism, a compromise with the different varieties of Islam in France has to be found, so that they can evolve without compromising their core values. The separation which was established, in the nineteenth century, between 'a civil (secular) society' and a religious society, was seen as necessary 'in an age when the uniformity, universality and unitary nature of the state were being affirmed in reaction to the sectional interests of the Church' (Silverman 1990: 77). But in the contemporary context of a pluralist and multiracial society, the opposition between the terms 'secular' and 'religious' has to be reconsidered.

While the French conception of *laïcité* confines religion to the private domain, the headscarf affair raised the issue of the social dimension of religion and demonstrated that religion and the surrounding society are far more intricately interrelated. The fact that it was felt necessary, in 1989, for secular, freemason, academic and religious organisations to debate on 'secularism and contemporary issues' at a conference organised by *La Croix* is evidence of the changes which have occurred in the past few years. Also, as the five intellectuals' manifesto showed, a narrow understanding of *laïcité* can lead to intolerance: the universal principles of Reason, Liberty, Secularism were irreconcilable with cultural particularisms/pluralism and Jospin's position was attacked on the grounds that it proposed 'indiscriminate tolerance', open to all kinds of particular pressures. The question is whether a strict *laïcité* is still valid in contemporary French society.

While in the nineteenth century it was necessary for 'civil society' to free itself from 'religious society', it now looks like religions have to be reintegrated into civil society (Baubérot 1990: 205). This integration may be particularly difficult for the Catholic Church, given its historical and social importance, and perhaps also the way it sees itself. The Pope's interventions, in 1988–9, against Scorcese's film and against the pill show that the Catholic Church still wants to retain its moral authority on people's conscience.[19] The problem is to give a place to religions in the public domain without running the risk of any of them becoming hegemonic and recovering their institutional authority on the individual's conscience. Instead of viewing secularism as 'promoting and reinforcing uniformity (thereby discriminating against minorities), secularism should be founded on respect for individual rights and the principle of diversity' (Silverman 1990: 78). After all, the main tenets of *laïcité* are still appropriate to contemporary society: the defence of human rights, the poor, democracy, tolerance and justice.

While some defenders of a strict brand of secularism keep wishing that religion be kept within the private sphere, in 1985, the signatories of a common text defending the principle of tolerance towards foreign populations and cultural/religious minorities included masonic humanitarian organisations (*Grand Orient de France, Grande Loge de France*), antiracist organisations (*Mouvement contre le racisme et pour l'amitié entre les peuples* (MRAP), *Ligue internationale contre le racisme et l'antisémitisme* (LICRA)), the *Ligue des droits de l'Homme*, and religious organisations (*Episcopat catholique, Episcopat orthodoxe, Fédération protestante de France, Conseil supérieur rabbinique, Grande Mosquée de Paris*). It may well have been 'a first' (Baubérot 1990: 206) in France, but it has probably signalled a need for reintegrating religions in a secular society.

CONCLUSION

Since the 1905 pact, new minorities have appeared, the most important of them being Muslims. Therefore, rethinking *laïcité* seems necessary to resolve the current tensions with Islam. It might be possible to come to what Jeanne-Hélène Kaltenbach calls 'a moderate *chariah*'[20] on the one hand and, on the other, a type of secularism which has respect for new religious minorities.

It has been underlined earlier that Protestants in France represent the only group which has the following three traits: it is a religious *minority*, a *secular* but *Christian* religion. At the crossroads between the 'two Frances', it is the only movement which shares characteristics with both (Baubérot 1988: 233). Perhaps they can point the way to future developments with regard to Islam in France. French Protestants still initiate actions which make them close to the 'secular camp'. For instance, they have fought, together with the CNAL (*Comité national d'action laïque*) to secularise the legislation concerning family planning: they wanted to refute the idea that changes in the law relating to birth control should lead to 'immorality'. In the 1982–4 conflicts on educational matters, the *Fédération protestante de France* also held an original position which, unfortunately, did not find a large echo (the text was typed out and circulated but it was never printed): they insisted on the urgency of having an open type of secularism which should not be tainted by any clerical or anticlerical sectarianism. They proposed a global reform of the education system which would go beyond the present dichotomies and which would be founded on a 'global conception of human beings, taking their spiritual dimension into account'. At the same time as the text reasserted its firm attachment to a secular state, 'the fundamental guarantee of public life', it stressed the need for openness: schools 'should take into account the diversity of local traditions, situations and aspirations, and the cultural diversity of the nation' (in ibid.: 229).

As Silverman points out (1990: 78–9), rethinking secularism 'rejoins similar ideas on a redefined notion of citizenship'. In the case of secularism, 'the emphasis is upon dissociating the concepts of the secular and the religious from their traditional dualism'; in the case of citizenship, one will be concerned to dissociate 'the rights of citizenship from its traditional link with nationality. Both discussions meet on a fundamental point: that in a plural society the old republican rhetoric of nationality and secularism is frequently discriminatory and often racist'.

LAÏCITÉ AND ISLAM: CHRONOLOGY

1801   Concordat (or *pacte des cultes reconnus*, i.e., Catholicism, Protestantism and, later, Judaism).
1881–6 Parliamentary debates and elaboration of laws establishing secularism in state schools.
1882   Schools made free and compulsory.

1905   Separation of church and state: 'The Republic guarantees freedom of conscience and of religious practice' but it 'does not recognise or finance any religious groups'.

1959   Debré law giving private schools public funding.

1973   The extreme right-wing organisation *Ordre Nouveau* launches a campaign against 'uncontrolled' and illegal immigration.

1974   Ban on primary immigration and suspension of family reunification.

1975   The right to family reunification is restored.

1977   Repatriation scheme (*'aide au retour'*) introduced by Stoléru which offers 10,000 f. as an encouragement to immigrants to return to their country of origin. The measure proves to be a failure.

1981   François Mitterrand's electoral manifesto *'110 Propositions'*.

1983   Government adopts the Savary law on private schools.

1984   Over half a million people demonstrate in Paris to defend private schools. As a result, the Savary law is withdrawn.
Formation of the anti-racist organisation *SOS Racisme*.

1986   Pasqua law on immigration, extending the already severe conditions defining entry and residence rights.
Introduction of bill to reform the Code of Nationality: essentially, it aims to remove the long-established principle of the *ius soli* (i.e., the principle by which all children born of foreign parents are automatically French nationals at the age of 18). It causes an outcry, is put in limbo and, finally, it is postponed indefinitely but re-surfaces in 1993.

1989   Beginning of the headscarf affair.
Creation of the Council for Integration (*Haut Conseil à l'intégration*).
In an interview on Antenne 2 Mitterrand declares that the threshold for numbers of immigrants in France had been reached in the 1970s. This notion of 'threshold of tolerance' equates concentrations of certain immigrants with social problems.

1993   Pasqua laws on the reform of the Code of Nationality, identity controls, and control of immigration flows.
Demonstrations against the abrogation of the Falloux law.

1994   Bayrou circular banning all 'ostentatious signs' from schools.

1996   Beginning of the *affaire des sans-papiers*.

NOTES

1 Secularism, or the secular state. While the term 'secularisation' was used in the previous chapter to refer to a marked decrease in religious practice amongst Catholics, the term *'laïcité'* has specific structural connotations which this chapter will endeavour to elucidate.

2 See Introduction.

3 See Note 2.

4 See Introduction, Note 13.

5 See Note 2.

6 One century later, things have changed: it is now possible for a religious association to endow itself with a sister association created under the 1901 law of association in order to manage a hospital, a school or a social centre. This shows that French secularism has already become more flexible.

7 See Introduction.

8 See Chapter 7.

9 These principles were to be reasserted in the *arrêté du Conseil d'Etat*, in November 1992.

10 This *subjective* interpretative process is also quite distinct from an *objective* practice like that of excision: what is at stake in this practice is the mutilation of a person's body.

11 I.e., children born in France to immigrant parents. Various origins of the word have been given, including the idea that it comes from the adolescent slang known as *le verlan* which reverses the syllables in words (puts them *à l'envers – verlan*), and was, interestingly, originally the inverted slang for *Arabe* (with the emphasis on the last syllable). See Chapter 11 for details regarding *cinéma beur*.

12 On the tension between the universal and the particular in France, see the interview with Jean Daniel in *Le Monde* (21 May 1995).

13 This law was sometimes defended as an attempt to put greater emphasis on individual freedom; however, this may be illusory, given the difficult relationship between young immigrants and the French administration (a topic discussed in Bruschi and Bruschi 1984: 2019–30). See also Chapter 8.

14 Some give the figure of 3 million Muslims in France (Silverman 1990: 77, Césari 1995: 21). See also Kaltenbach (1991: 219–33) on the problems concerning statistics.

15 I.e., working-class estates on the outskirts of cities.

16 The *Jama'at al Tabligh* (Association for the Propagation of Islam) is active in most European countries, but is better known in France as *Foi et pratique*.

17 One of these militant groups is the *Fraternité algérienne en France* (FAF), created in 1990.

18 Efforts in that direction have been made: an Islamic university was created in the *départément* of Ain in 1991; the teaching staff and students are mostly foreigners. Another Islamic university was created in 1993 by a Frenchman converted to Islam. Moreover, an *Institut de formation d'imams* was inaugurated in October 1993.

19 See also, more recently (November 1995), his urging the people of the Irish Republic to vote against legalising divorce.

20 The term *'chariah'* refers to Islamic legislation which contains norms that are often perceived as incompatible with Western legal and political systems. In addition to religious dogmas and culture, the *chariah* also includes rules concerning ethics and the rights and duties of Muslims.

REFERENCES AND RECOMMENDED READING

Baubérot, J. (1988) *Le protestantisme doit-il mourir?*, Paris: Seuil.

* —— (1990) *Vers un nouveau pacte laïque?*, Paris: Seuil.
  Contains both a historical and a contemporary perspective on the development of *laïcité*.

Bernard, P. (1995) '"L'Affaire du foulard": la circulaire Bayrou . . .', *Problèmes politiques et sociaux*, 746: 30–2.

Birnbaum, P. (1993) *'La France aux Français'. Histoires des haeines nationalistes*, Paris: Seuil.

Bruschi, C. and Bruschi, M. (1984) 'Le Pouvoir des guichets', *Temps modernes. L'Immigration maghrébine en France. Les Faits et les mythes. Questions sur la citoyenneté*, 3/4: 2019–30.

* Césari, J. (1995) 'Une Représentation religieuse plus "visible", une représentation éclatée', *Problèmes politiques et sociaux*, 746: 21–30.
  The first 37 pages of this issue (*'L'Islam en Europe'*) offer valuable recent

information on Islam, the place of Islam in France, and the headscarf affair.

Champsaur, P. (ed.) (1994) *Les Etrangers en France*, Paris: INSEE (Contours et caractères).

Clément, J.-F. (1991) 'L'Islam en France', in B. Etienne (ed.) *L'Islam en France*, Paris: Editions du CNRS.

Etienne, B. (1989) *La France et l'Islam*, Paris: Hachette.

Göle, N. (1994) 'Urbaine, instruite, revendicative . . . et voilée', in L. Addi, B. Botiveau *et al.* (eds) *L'Islamisme*, Paris: La Découverte, 67–73.

Kaltenbach, J-H. and P-P. (1991) *La France, une chance pour l'Islam*, Paris: Editions du Félin.

Kepel, G. (1991) *Les Banlieues de l'Islam*, Paris: Seuil.

Kessler, D. (1995), 'Du Combat au droit', *Problèmes politiques et sociaux*, 746: 32–3.

Lochak, D. (1991) 'La Citoyenneté: un concept juridique flou', in D. Colas, C. Emeri and J. Zylberberg (eds) *Citoyenneté et nationalité. Perspectives en France et au Québec*, Paris: PUF.

Perotti, A. and Thépaut, F. (1992) 'L'Affaire du foulard islamique', *Problèmes politiques et sociaux*, 693, 15–20.

* Rémond, R. (1995), 'La Laïcité et ses contraires', in *Pouvoirs: la laïcité*, 75): 7–16. Highlights the ambiguities inherent in contemporary *laïcité* and situates the controversies surrounding the headscarf affair in that context. This volume contains a few other relevant contributions.

Silverman, M. (1990) 'Peut-on être musulman et français?', in M. Cornick (ed.) *Beliefs and Identity in Modern France*, Loughborough: European Research Centre, Loughborough University.

*—— (1992) *Deconstructing the Nation. Immigration, Racism and Citizenship in Modern France*, London and New York: Routledge. A clearly argued book with extensive coverage of the development of the immigration issue in France, including many quotations from politicians.

Solé, R. (1989) 'Un Modèle français d'intégration', *Le Monde*, 7 December.

10

LINGUISTIC POLICIES

Inès Brulard

Linguistic policies are instances of language planning, that is, government-authorised efforts to change a language or one of its varieties, or to change the way a language functions in society. Language policies may seek to standardise a language or increase its status. These two approaches can coexist, as has been the case in France, so that efforts to develop an orthography, new sources of vocabulary, new uses, dictionaries and a literature fulfil the aim of increasing the status of the language and of extending its use to all areas of society (Wardhaugh 1986: 335–6).

As Lodge (1993: 237) has noted, French interventionism in language matters 'is much derided by English-speaking observers'. However, France is certainly not the only country which has elaborated vigorous language policies; this is hardly surprising since in the modern world there is a trend 'to make language and nation synonymous' (Wardhaugh 1986: 335). According to a recent study, 120 countries in the world include linguistic measures in their constitutions (Gauthier, Leclerc and Maurais 1994). And even if the official character of English in the United Kingdom, for instance, is not enshrined constitutionally, a policy of linguistic assimilation is apparent in the case of Gaelic and Welsh:

> Gaelic was not allowed to be taught in Scottish schools until 1918, and then only as a subject of instruction. It took a further forty years for it to become used as a language of instruction. The Welsh gained the same right to use Welsh as a language of instruction only in 1953.
>
> (Wardhaugh 1986: 340)

Even in such a linguistically plural and liberal country as the United States, there has been constant pressure for the past fifteen years, due to the increasing use of Spanish, to make English the official language of the United States, and seventeen states (including California and Florida) have already made it their official language in their constitutions.

What is particular about the case of France is the much-reiterated claim that there is a deep-rooted link between language and national identity: the UDF deputy Francisque Perrut, for instance, claims that since Louis XI

(1423–83), the French language has been 'the precious vehicle of [France's] culture and identity' (in Durand 1996: 85). However, as will be shown later, the French nation, in its twentieth century sense, has not always been co-extensive with the French language; in fact, under Louis XI, French was the language of an elite and it remained so for a long time. Moreover, as Durand (ibid.: 85) points out, 'the identification of the French language with the French nation is all the more pernicious as French is not the native language of many immigrants who have become French nationals'.[1]

INSTITUTIONS AND STRUCTURES

The amount of legislation and the number of governmental bodies and private associations dealing with language matters is quite striking. This is not the place to list them all but a general outline of the functions of some of these governmental bodies is necessary in understanding the development and the importance of linguistic policies in France.

In 1966, The *Haut Comité de défense et d'expansion de la langue française* was created by decree by Charles de Gaulle and was placed directly under the prime minister's control. It was the founding body of the present committees which have evolved from it: the *Délégation générale à la langue française* (created in 1989), the *Conseil supérieur de la langue française* (1989) and the *Haut Conseil de la francophonie* (1984). In her outline of the development of these bodies, Anne Judge shows that 'there has been a move towards prescriptivism and a more aggressive policy of implantation of linguistic directives' (1993: 17). The role of the *Haut Comité* was to establish the purity of the French language but it concentrated on co-ordinating the work of the various terminology commissions (each ministry has its own *Commission ministérielle de terminologie*, whose task is to create French equivalents of foreign words). The *Délégation* is supposed to encourage all public and private bodies to take measures to help defend the good usage of the French language and to co-ordinate 'the linguistic decisions taken by various competent bodies both in France and in the various Francophone countries' (ibid.: 16–17). It is responsible, for example, for publishing the *Dictionnaire des termes officiels*, which contains the work done by the terminological commissions, and approved by ministerial decree. One has to bear in mind that decrees have the force of law: 'the terms they prescribe must be used in official documents and in all documents produced by those contracting with the state' (Ager 1990: 242). The role of the *Conseil supérieur* is to deal with linguistic problems and then advise the prime minister on measures to be taken; it is also responsible for the promotion of the French language abroad. The *Haut Conseil de la francophonie* cooperates closely with the other two governmental bodies; its aim is to define the role of the French language and promote co-operation between the French-speaking countries in the world.

In addition to these formal governmental organisations, there are many Francophone associations and pressure groups working for the French language and Francophonia (246 is the figure quoted in ibid.: 235). There is of course the *Académie française*, whose role from its inception has been to regulate the French language; they insist that since 1900, their role has simply been to record changes in usage as they occur, but in practice, they make decisions between conflicting usages and their authority is often 'used as an argument against change' (Catach 1993: 143). *Défense de la langue française* (founded in 1959) is a high profile organisation which reports the work of the *Académie française* in its journal and also 'pillories the media when their standards slip' (Rickard 1989: 156).[2] The *Association générale des usagers de la langue française* (AGULF) created in 1977, has been active in detecting breaches of linguistic laws and in initiating the prosecution of those responsible. The most important private association is the *Alliance française*, founded in 1883 'with the aim of maintaining and expanding the influence of France through her language' (ibid.: 158).

Broadly speaking, the aim of all these organisations is twofold: the promotion of French across the world and the defence of the position of French within France and in Europe. While there is no doubt that the French are proud of their language, there is also a feeling that the French language is threatened from within (poor spelling, syntax, etc.) and from without, notably by the English language. This pessimism about the way the language is used has also been expressed in many books whose titles speak for themselves: *Et si l'on parlait français* (Gilder 1993), *Lettre ouverte à ceux qui en perdent leur français* (de Saint-Robert 1986), *Le Français pour qu'il vive* (de Broglie 1986), *Hé! la France, ton français fout le camp* (Thévenot 1976). The best known, Etiemble's *Parlez-vous franglais* (1964)[3], marked the apogee of a violent campaign against what was seen as the main cause of the 'degradation' of French, namely the 'invasion' of the French language by English. In his book, Etiemble made a forceful appeal to the state to intervene efficiently (the *Académie* did not have the powers to change what he thought was an appalling state of affairs). It was in fact this campaign which led to the creation of the *Haut Comité de défense et d'expansion de la langue française*. However, according to many observers, these organisations are largely ineffectual. Ball's explanation for this is that unlike in Québec, for instance, there is no widespread feeling in France that French identity is under threat:

> If government measures for dealing with a language crisis are to be effective, there needs to be a consensus in society that a crisis is actually present, and this in turn presupposes a much more broadly-based sense of collective insecurity.
>
> (Ball 1988: 104)

Ball then concludes that 'Despite the eloquence with which it is expressed and the publicity it attracts, linguistic *angoisse* in modern France seems to be a luxury reserved mainly for *belles-lettristes*' (ibid.).

THE CONTENTIOUS CHARACTER OF LINGUISTIC POLICIES IN FRANCE

Although it is probably true that French cultural identity is not seriously threatened by popular Anglo-American culture, it has to be noted that the French public at large are concerned by matters pertaining to the French language: many people write to the press and to the various governmental bodies to express their concerns about the language; according to many commentators there are as many language books as there are cookery books (Ager 1990: 222); indeed, it is difficult to imagine that Bernard Pivot's televised spelling competition could be as popular anywhere other than in France!

Other (more serious) instances of the public's concerns about the French language are largely echoed in the press: one example is the furore unleashed in 1990 after the Rocard government decided to get a spelling reform underway. The *Conseil supérieur de la langue française* was commissioned to look at some anomalies in the spelling conventions and the syntax. As Goosse pointed out (1991: 123–4), the multi-faceted character of the *Conseil* reflected the concern for the use of French in diverse areas such as the arts, the media, science and business; it included specialists from various Franco-phone countries and from various walks of life (ministers, the permanent secretaries of the French Academy and the Academy of Sciences, linguists, managers of important companies, scientists, media people, literati, a song-writer and a historian). The prime minister approved the *Conseil*'s report, which was published in the *Journal officiel* in 1991. The proposed reform was moderate, and it was decided that, for the foreseeable future, both the old and new rules would co-exist. According to Catach, one of the linguists involved in the reform, the majority of the French people (a *Lire* poll gives the figure of 76 per cent) were in favour of a plan to reform the writing system; and yet, 'a strange mixture of writers and policians . . . got up in arms about crimes being committed against the French language' (Catach 1993: 143–4) and voiced their concern that this reform might threaten the French cultural heritage and the 'genius' of the language.[4]

A second example, which raises interesting issues to be investigated further, is the controversy surrounding the Toubon law, the most recent linguistic law, which was promulgated on 4 August 1994, on the basis of a bill introduced in 1993 by the Minister of Culture and Francophonia Jacques Toubon. The controversy reached its highest point when, on 1 July 1994, some senators and deputies called for the law to be amended on the grounds that, as the bill then stood, it was unconstitutional. Their appeal to the *Conseil constitutionnel* resulted in the law being divested of two of its most contentious clauses: first, the obligation on private individuals and the media to use the official terminology (i.e., the neologisms grouped in the *Dictionnaire des termes officiels*), and second, making the allocation of public funding for research subject to an explicit undertaking to publish the work in French.

The Toubon law replaces and broadens the scope of the 1975 language legislation known as the Bas-Lauriol law, which established the compulsory use of French in three areas: 'in commercial and advertising contexts, to protect the consumer; in work contracts, to protect the employee; and in the context of information given to consumers either by private firms or public bodies, usually in the form of leaflets' (Judge 1993: 21). The problems with that law lay first in its actual implementation and second in its limitations by Common Market laws (it appeared to clash for instance with Article 30 in the Treaty of Rome, which outlaws measures which would restrict, or have the effect of restricting, imports amongst the European member countries). As a result, few cases actually led to convictions, and when they did, the fines incurred were too small to act as a deterrent.

The Toubon law reasserts the right of the French-speaking consumer, employee, researcher and the public at large, to be informed and to express themselves in French. Put that way, of course, it is unclear what the controversy around the elaboration of this law may have been about. However, a certain amount of heat was generated by the debates in the National Assembly and the Senate centring on the justification for adopting a defensive attitude towards the use of English words in advertising and in the media. These debates raised the question of the freedom of the individual *vis-à-vis* the state: could the state impose on private individuals the official neologisms created and published by governmental organisations? The reactions of the public echoed in the press were varied and sometimes presented a caricature of the proposals (e.g., the idea that Mr Toubon wanted to outlaw well-established anglicisms like '*weekend*' and '*football*').

The Toubon law enables us to highlight key issues behind contemporary language policy in France. They are threefold: first, why should the state interfere in language matters nowadays? In connection with this, the question of the 'invasion' by English of the French language will be examined. Second, the bill also raised questions concerning the status of the regional languages in France: indeed, behind its apparent linguistic unity, France hides a very varied linguistic profile. This is why, during the debates at the National Assembly and Senate, several regionalists – notably Mr Henry Goetschy (centrist) – voiced their concern that the Toubon law might be another step towards 'linguistic Jacobinism' (a reference to the Jacobin motto 'one nation, one language') and might jeopardise the efforts made to preserve the regional languages. These fears can be seen as an echo to the debates around the 1992 constitutional amendment, which was passed as 'The language of the Republic is French', without the desired addition of 'allowance is made for

France's regional languages and cultures'. Third, the introduction to the law highlighted the fact that the language issue was not merely a national one: it includes a reminder that the French language 'is the privileged link between the states which make up the community of French-speaking countries' (*Journal officiel*, 1994). The Toubon law was also a response to the concern of some of the forty-seven heads of state of the Francophone community that France was not doing enough to promote French.

FRENCH AND THE OTHER LANGUAGES OF FRANCE

The statement that 'the language of the Republic is French' may seem to fly in the face of the fact that France is 'the most linguistically plural state in Western Europe' (Winchester 1993: 227). Four other languages (Basque, Breton, Catalan and Occitan) and three dialects of major languages are spoken in France: Alsatian (German dialect), Flemish (Dutch dialect) and Corsican (Italian dialect). The history of what Laroussi and Marcellesi (1993: 97) call a '*processus de minoration*' of these languages (a process by which they became minority languages) is connected to France's traditionally strong assimilationist tendency and its strong central control over education and culture. These languages became minority languages as a consequence of the increasing predominance of a particular dialect, *francien*, spoken in the Middle Ages in the area of Ile-de-France, which gradually became the official language of France. In order to achieve this, from the fifteenth century onwards, a series of royal edicts gradually eliminated Latin, but the first step towards the establishment of French as official language was taken by François I in the Villers-Cotterêts Ordinances (a series of edicts promulgated in 1539): the text ostensibly outlawed Latin from legal procedures in order to ensure better understanding, but it was in fact also aimed at the vernaculars[5] other than French:

> All legal decisions and all procedures pertaining either to the highest courts or to the lower or inferior ones, whether they concern records, inquests, contracts, commissions, wills [...] should be pronounced, registered and delivered to the litigants in the French vernacular language and in no other way.
>
> (quoted in Lodge 1993: 126)

This was the first time the restrictive expression 'French vernacular' was used; until then, expressions like 'French *or* the mother language', 'French *and* the vulgar tongue of the area' were used (Giacomo 1975: 13). Gradually the Villers-Cotterêts edict was taken to mean that French was the official language of the state, even if it was not the mother tongue of the litigants. In fact, French was to remain the language of the intellectual élite and one of prestige for a long time.

The second landmark in the eradication of the other languages, dialects and also *patois*[6] in France, was the work of the revolutionaries. A survey carried out in 1790 by the Abbé Grégoire on the linguistic situation of France, showed that a large proportion of people in France did not know French:

> Out of the 25 million population of France, 6 million (mainly in the South) had no knowledge of French at all, 6 million more barely understood it and were incapable of maintaining a conversation. Only 3 million (12% of the total population) were fully conversant with the language, and only a small proportion of these were capable of reading and writing.
>
> (Ager 1990: 220)

Given that situation, revolutionary ideas were at first spread orally in the various idioms, and revolutionary texts and laws were translated into the various existing languages and dialects. But in 1794, in a climate of fear of counter-revolution from within the country as well as from outside, more drastic steps were to be taken, leading to the second major linguistic law of *2 Thermidor an II* (20 July 1794),[7] stating that all public acts would have to be written in French; failure to comply with this law led to six months' imprisonment and destitution. The Jacobin rhetoric expressed the idea that the French language had become a symbol of Republican identity and unity: it followed that an association was made between the regional languages and dialects, and the counter-revolution. Linguistic particularisms were seen as a danger for the nation. Barère's speech to the Committee of Public Safety was quite clear:

> Federalism and superstition speak Breton; immigration and hatred of the Republic speak German [Alsatian]; the counter-revolution speaks Italian [Corsican] and fanaticism speaks Basque. Let us smash these faulty and harmful instruments ... Citizens, the language of a free country must be one and the same for all.
>
> (quoted in Lodge 1991: 107–8)

This law was followed up by a series of education policies which were designed to eradicate languages other than French. In the nineteenth century, French was the only language used in education and it became increasingly necessary to have a good command of the written language, of its grammar and orthography, in order to gain employment. The Third Republic accelerated the diffusion of French in all classes of society with the creation of the free, compulsory and secular schooling, which also spread the idea that the usage of local dialects was a sign of lack of education and that it hindered the acquisition of French.

The first important step towards the recognition that regional languages not only constituted no threat to national unity but were also of cultural value, was the Deixonne law (1951), which allowed the optional teaching of regional languages in schools in the regions where they were in use. However, *de facto*, there were important restrictions: the law did not apply to the dialects, the exams did not have equal weight with the other subjects, there was no training for teachers in these languages and, due to subsequent educational reforms, the teaching of the regional languages was reduced to semi-clandestinity (Hagège 1987: 198). This is why in the early 1960s, the associations for the defence of regional languages, grouped together as the *Conseil national de défense des langues et cultures régionales*, put pressure on the government to set up a committee which would look into the teaching of regional languages and cultures. However, the results of the Commission's work (1964–5) were never published or implemented. Of course, in the case of some regional associations, the language issue was also connected with the issue of 'local autonomy, ranging from federation to complete independence' (Lodge 1993: 219), as it was felt that some regions were in a situation of 'internal colonialism' (Winchester 1993: 230) and, in the case of Corsican, Breton and Basque, this led to recurrent violence in the mid-1970s and 1980s.

Despite some symbolic measures brought about by the decentralisation legislation introduced by the socialists in 1982, one cannot help feeling that there is a lack of interest on the part of the government: the *droit à la différence* (or 'right to be different') highlighted in Mitterrand's 1981 manifesto, has not really materialised in language matters. Although Henri Giordan's report to the Ministry of Culture (1982) sought to establish guidelines to promote 'cultural democracy and respect for linguistic and cultural diversity', nothing much has changed.

The need for the ratification, on 23 June 1992, of the proposed amendment to Article 2 of the French constitution to include the statement that 'the language of the Republic is French' is not immediately obvious, given what has been said above. Yet it is no surprise that it gave rise to strong protests on the part of regional language supporters, who feared that the status of the regional languages in France might be further endangered; after all, Mr Goetschy's apparently innocuous proposal (France's regional languages and cultures should be respected) had been rejected. The Breton autonomists expressed their fear that this rejection might make unconstitutional any bill designed to promote regional languages in France.

The justification for this constitutional amendment is only apparent when situated in its political context, namely, that of the ratification of the Maastricht Treaty (Wilcox 1994: 269–78). In the event, under pressure from the group *Avenir de la langue française*, the government showed its determination to ensure that French would continue to be one of the major working languages within the European Union, alongside English and German. Moreover, in the course of the debate in the National Assembly, Alain Lamassoure (UDF) made it clear that the concept of sovereignty was a key issue:

As France is about to sign a treaty which will make national currencies disappear in favour of a European currency, to express our attachment to our national language is a strong and necessary symbol.

(quoted in Wilcox 1994: 272–3)

The question of the status of French and the place of the regional languages within France has therefore to be read in the light of a broader political issue, namely, the place of France within the European Union. These debates highlighted a paradox: while it was felt that it was legitimate to protect the position of the French language in Europe and that linguistic pluralism was viewed as being in line with the European vision of a Community which contributes to 'the flowering of the cultures of the member states, while respecting their national and regional diversity' (Article 128 of the Maastricht Treaty), a reference to the regional languages of France was deemed undesirable.

In view of all this, one can understand the regionalists' renewed fear, in the context of the Toubon law, that the use of the *other* languages of France might be outlawed (see 'Breton hors la loi', in *Le Monde*, 19 March 1994). Their insistence that the law should express a reference to regional languages was taken into account: Article 11, making French the language of education, examinations, doctoral theses and dissertations, includes the explicit exception of the teaching of foreign and regional languages and cultures. In more general terms, Article 21 makes it clear that 'the law will be implemented without prejudice to the legislation concerning the regional languages of France, and that it does not go against their use' (in *Journal officiel de la République française* 1994: 1193–4).

THE DEFENCE OF FRENCH AGAINST ENGLISH

Because of the perspective adopted in this chapter, the role of the state in increasing the status of French has been emphasised. However, as Lodge points out (1993: 219–20), it was not only the state policies, followed up by the school system, which were responsible for making France a largely monolingual country: economic and social forces contributed to that process as well. Nowadays, especially over the past twenty years, government policies and associations have gradually given more emphasis to the defence of French against the influence of the English language. Although Etiemble's book marked the apogee of a movement in that direction, concern about the increasing use of anglicisms in French was already expressed in the second half of the nineteenth century and again in the mid-1940s. It is worth noting that this latter wave of English borrowings coincided first of all with the increased military, political and economic power of the United States, but also with the increased power of the media.

The reactions in the press to Mr Toubon's proposals focused on the issue of whether or not the state should intervene to defend the French language.

These views were to a large extent polarised: some people advocated the principle of *laissez-faire* and the supreme principle of the right of the individual above the state; others thought that strong governmental policies to defend the French language were necessary. The argument of the former centred on the fact that a language evolved naturally and borrowed from other languages, and there was nothing that the state could or should do about it; the argument of the latter expressed the view that a language had to retain its supposed purity and that it was incumbent on the state to prevent its national language from degeneration caused by the 'invasion' of English words and syntax. In order to assess these views, it is necessary to examine the following points: first of all, to what extent is it true that the French language has been 'invaded' by English? Second, is Ramus' sixteenth-century statement that 'the people are sovereign lords of their language' still true today? Finally, can government action on the language be equated with some form of authoritarianism?

The assessment of 'the reality of the invasion' of the French language by English has been made in detail by Hagège (1987: 24–74). The picture that emerges from his analysis can be summarised as follows: the hard core of the language (i.e., its grammar and pronunciation) has not been much affected by English: in many instances, the 'transgressions' attributed to the influence of English are in fact extensions of French uses; where the influence of English seems likely, it is restricted to particular contexts and does not affect the language on a large scale. For instance, the deletion of some prepositions as in *bureau informations* or *station service* is restricted to advertising or public notices; it is still impossible to say, for instance, *planche repasser* (ironing board) instead of *planche à repasser*. Moreover, these elliptical constructions follow the French word order (we do not say *informations bureau* or *service station*). Although French lexicon is more open to external influences, yet again it is a peripheral phenomenon, restricted to particular areas (especially technical vocabulary), some professional usages, or civilisation words (like *whisky, pub, music-hall*). A big cohort of anglicisms are words of Romance origin, whose meaning is now added to their French meaning (e.g., *attractif*, borrowed from the English *attractive*, and used instead of the French *séduisant*). Most of them are actually part of the French language now and it is a futile battle to try to eradicate them.[8]

This confirms the 'liberal' view concerning the evolution of a language. If borrowing is not a problem, as such, what has been the concern of the terminological commissions is the *best integration* of these borrowings into the French language, thereby contributing to its enrichment. It is a fact that the major challenge for the French language 'is that of developing a terminology adapted to the modern technological world' (Judge 1993: 17). This linguistic challenge is of course the concomitant of a scientific, economic, industrial and commercial challenge: the success of neologisms like *logiciel, matériel, planche à voile* (to replace *software, hardware* and *surfboard*) was probably helped by the fact that France started to produce the objects in question (Hagège 1987: 129). This is why the view that language should retain its (supposed) purity and thus reject any foreign borrowings is flawed: excluding borrowings and neologisms from a language can only contribute to its downfall. Therefore, deliberate interference in language matters need not be viewed in terms of authoritarianism. However, a linguistic law or a terminological decree, no matter how far-ranging its application is (in education, government bodies, organisations benefiting from state aid), ultimately needs to be accepted by the people; in this sense, it is true to say that the people are sovereign lords of their language. But this sovereignty is somewhat diminished by the prestige of the media and their power to promote and in effect impose particular types of usage.

The Toubon bill was an attempt to meet the challenge faced by the French language: it was targeting those areas which are more permeable to English influence (advertising, the media, scientific research).[9] However, the *Conseil constitutionnel* did not allow the law to jeopardise the freedom of the individual: following the appeal by some socialist deputies and senators, it partly censured Jacques Toubon's law on the use of the French language. Originally, the law explicitly forbade the use of a foreign expression whenever a French equivalent had been found by a ministerial terminology commission and approved by ministerial decree. The *Conseil constitutionnel* decided however that an official terminology could not be imposed on private individuals (including the media, whether public or private); it could only be imposed on corporate bodies and private individuals in public office. This decision showed the *Conseil constitutionnel*'s determination to reconcile two constitutional principles: one stating that 'the language of the Republic is French', and the other preserving the 'free communication of thoughts and opinions', as proclaimed in the 1789 Declaration of the Rights of Man. The latter principle was deemed to be violated since a state language was being imposed on private individuals; but in agreement with the first principle, the *Conseil constitutionnel* ratified the obligation for those who exercise a mission of public service, to use the terms elaborated by the ministerial commissions. On the other hand, the media's power of self-regulation was increased. The law as it has been amended preserves the necessary freedom of the media and, at the same time, highlights their pivotal role in the diffusion of new French usages. It also preserves freedom of communication in the academic sphere: the *Conseil constitutionnel* ruled out the proposal to grant public subsidy only to the researchers who would commit themselves to publishing their findings in French.

FRANCOPHONIA

Apart from the United Nations Organisation, the Francophone community is the only world-wide organisation which includes states from all continents, of different political inclinations (ranging from traditional monarchy to Marxist one-party systems) and of different economic development (for more details on individual member countries, many of whom are former French colonies, see Offord 1990: 195–225). The notion of Francophonia itself is multi-faceted: it relates to the use of the French language in particular geographical areas of the world; it also refers to a more idealistic vision of a cultural community, sharing common values; finally, Francophonia has an institutional meaning since it operates through a number of organisations and is represented at various Francophone summits, such as that held in Port-Louis (Mauritius) in 1993, and which thirty-three representatives (out of the forty-seven members) attended.[10]

The initial impetus given to this concept in 1962 is attributed to the writer and academician L.S. Senghor, who was at the time President of Senegal; French-speaking Belgians and Québecers were fast to jump on the band-wagon as well. The reasons why France, at first, dragged its feet are twofold: in contrast to Québec and Belgium, where the language issue was (and still is) a major political issue, the status of French in France is such that any interest in the periphery was bound to be minimal; more importantly, the French decolonisation process was still recent and France was anxious not to be accused of neo-colonialism in the guise of cultural links. In 1982, however, François Mitterrand was in a position to express his 'passion' for Franco-phonia (Hagège 1987: 212): by then many former colonies had *chosen* French as their official language or as the language used in education. The reason for adopting French may be economic but also ideological, as a rejection of any form of hegemony: as M.B. Boutros-Ghali, the Egyptian Minister for Foreign Affairs said in 1981, to justify the membership of his country in the Francophone community, 'French is interesting to us as a non-aligned language'. Similarly, for the Egyptian film-maker Y. Chahine, 'Francophonia has lost its colonial character because it has become an instrument, a link, a binder between the national identities of the various Mediterranean countries, faced with the American steamroller' (quoted in *Le Monde*, 12 December 1984). The first three Francophone summits organised in Paris and Versailles in 1986, in Quebec in 1987 and in Dakar in 1989, focused on the institutional organisation of the Francophone community, and on establishing its major aims. These were to centre on cultural development (e.g., more attention paid to the language industries, the expansion of Francophone media in the world, education) but also on economic development – they include projects concerning agriculture, energy, science and technology – and, though to a lesser extent, political development.

These objectives are served by French organisations (see above), but there is also a vast number of international organisations which can be inter-governmental, semi-official or private: for example, the intergovernmental *Agence de coopération culturelle et technique* (1970), whose task is 'to co-ordinate technical and cultural activities in member states, and to provide

202

assistance in the domains of education, medicine and science' (Offord 1990: 223), and which is now due to extend its role to economic development in general.

Despite the success of some initiatives to promote *la francophonie*, such as improvements to the Francophone television channel TV5, and its wider availability, and, since 1989, the organisation of Francophone games, there is a fear that the very plethora of Francophone organisations may hinder progress. One of the weaknesses of Francophonia (but also perhaps its richness) is that France is the only Francophone country in which French is both a mother tongue and a majority language: Belgium, Canada, Switzerland have French as a mother tongue but it is a minority language; in Africa, French is either the language used in education or in internal/external communication, but it is not a mother tongue. In addition to its heterogeneous character, Francophonia is further threatened in some countries by a return to national languages (e.g., Arabic in Mauritania) and illiteracy in African countries. Another problem is that the enthusiastic governmental rhetoric is far from being translated in the budget devoted to the promotion of French abroad (see de Saint-Robert 1986: 106ff. and *Le Monde*, 27 September 1994).

CONCLUSION

The status of French on a world-wide basis is the concern of government: because of the 'numerical superiority and widespread distribution of English-speakers ... the commercial, industrial, political, scientific and technical prestige of the United States and the United Kingdom' (Offord 1990: 232), it seems that French has secondary status as an international language. In demographic terms, the number of French speakers in the world (that is, including countries like the United States or Algeria, which are not members of the 'institutional' Francophone community), is relatively small: according to a study by Van Deth (in de Saint-Robert 1986: 100), there are roughly 120 million speakers of French in the world (the difficulty in finding reliable criteria to establish the number of speakers of French appears in figures ranging from 90 million to 230 million).[11] However, French is the official language or the language used in education of around 24 per cent of the states in the world and one-third of these states use French in international organisations (ibid.: 100).

However, even if the juridical status of French in many international organisations is undisputable, in practice, the use of the French language often gives way to English. At the United Nations, French is an official language (i.e., used in official documents) and a working language (i.e., used in everyday correspondance like internal memos, reports) alongside English; yet, only 20 per cent of the documents are written in French (Délégation générale à la langue française 1994: IV) and, as de Saint-Robert points out (1986: 101–3), the recruitment policy of international civil servants is paradoxical since in many cases, it allows the recruitment of people who have the command of only one language, namely, English (for more details see Haut Conseil de la francophonie 1991: 245–69). Interestingly, the use of French is more prominent in European institutions: 66 per cent of the documents from the Council of Europe and 46 per cent of the Commission documents are produced in French (Délégation générale à la langue française 1994: IV).

Present government rhetoric emphasises the idea that the promotion of French is a symbol of the promotion of cultural and linguistic diversity: in the context of Francophonia, it is expressed in the slogan for the 1993 summit, 'Unity in diversity'; similarly, the 1992 constitutional amendment was presented as a defence of linguistic pluralism in Europe. The Toubon law also aimed to promote multilingualism: Article 11 states that the command of the French language and of two foreign languages is an essential educational objective. More efforts in that direction are being made via organisations like the *Centre d'information et de recherche pour l'enseignement et l'emploi des langues* (CIREEL), which aims 'to create favourable conditions for learning and using languages in general and to promote international co-operation in this area, paying particular attention to the European dimension' (Offord 1990: 13).

Although France sees itself as the defender of the politics of diversity, its lack of linguistic policy with regard to its immigrant languages reflects a strong monolingual vision of the state, based on the old equation between language and a narrow notion of national identity. Also in stark contrast with the arguments in favour of cultural and linguistic diversity is, as we have seen, the government's lack of interest in France's minority languages. According to Jacob, militant violence in the 1970s and 1980s has damaged the survival of minority languages; as he says:

[language policy dating back to the Deixonne law] today vacillates between benign neglect and active repression, softened by periodic symbolic concessions rarely implemented in fact. The greatest political burden borne by France's linguistic minorities in 1985 may be the bittersweet realisation that ethnic violence was a fatal trap that played into the hands of the state. Thus, any future government concessions in the area of language policy might well reflect the French government's judgment that these languages have been elevated to the nostalgia of folklore, and so no longer pose a threat to the national unity of France.

(Jacob 1990: 61–2)

Also, the fact remains that, in the consciousness of many French people, regional languages and *patois* are socially stigmatised. The prestige of the standard, educated Parisian usage, promoted by vigorous official action, is such that many speakers of these languages and *patois* often do not think it desirable to pass them on to their children. They are also an expression of a traditional rural past which is equated with backwardness. Legislation is insufficient to overcome such barriers unless accompanied by social measures making the possession of such languages socially advantageous. As yet, French policy makers show no signs of doing either.

LINGUISTIC POLICIES: CHRONOLOGY

1539   François I's Villers-Cotterêts Ordinances.

1635   Founding of the *Académie française*.

1794   Abbé Grégoire submits his report on 'The necessity and the means of annihilating the use of the *patois* and of universalising the use of the French language'.
      Law of *Thermidor an II* requiring all public acts to be written in French in all parts of the French Republic.

1883   Creation of the *Alliance française*.

1951   Deixonne law which aimed to 'favour the study of regional languages and dialects in the areas where they are used'. In fact, it only applied to Occitan, Basque, Breton and Catalan. Subsequently, the measures were extended to German (in Alsace) and to Corsican.

1964   Publication of Etiemble's *Parlez-vous franglais?*

1966   *Haut Comité de défense et d'expansion de la langue française* created by decree by Charles de Gaulle.
      Creation of the *Conseil international de la langue française* which carries out detailed work on language-related questions.

1970   Creation of the *Agence de coopération culturelle et technique*.

1975   Bas-Lauriol law, imposing the use of French in commerce, advertising, work contracts and any information given to consumers.

1982   Henri Giordan's report (*'Démocratie culturelle et droit à la différence'*) to the Ministry of Culture.
      Defferre law giving new economic power to the regions and departments.

1984   Creation of the *Haut Conseil de la francophonie*.

1985   Creation of the *Conseil national des langues et cultures régionales*

1986   First Francophone summit in Paris and Versailles.

1989   Creation of the *Délégation générale à la langue française*.
      Creation of the *Conseil supérieur de la langue française*.

1991   Publication in the *Journal officiel* of the spelling reform proposed by the *Conseil supérieur de la langue française*.

1992   Constitutional amendment passed as 'the language of the Republic is French'.

1994   Toubon law on the use of the French language.

1995   Decree of application of the Toubon law.

NOTES

1 For a discussion of the importance of cultural criteria to define nationality, see Chapter 9 (section entitled 'Immigration and National identity').

2 This is also done by the *Conseil supérieur de l'audiovisuel* in its monthly newsletter; see Chapter 6.

3 Respectively: 'How about speaking French?', 'Letter to those who are losing their French', 'French: long may it live', 'Hey, France, your French is going down the plughole', 'Do you speak Frenglish?'.

4 For a discussion of linguistic conservatism, see Ball 1995: 61–78.

5 According to Petyt's definition, a vernacular is 'a form of speech transmitted from parent to child as a primary medium of communication' (in Wardhaugh 1986: 37).

6 A dialect is 'a regional variety of a language that has an associated literary tradition'; a *patois* is similar in that it is a dialectal usage of a particular area, but it lacks a literary tradition and therefore the term is often used pejoratively (Wardhaugh 1986: 25).

7 For details of the Republican calendar, see Introduction: France in the Making, Note 8.

8 Time seems to be an important factor here: most people probably cannot identify words like *paquebot*, or *gratte-ciel* as borrowings from the English *packet-boat* and *skyscraper*.

9 For more details see Brulard (1997 forthcoming).

10 One of the major themes of this summit, situated in the context of the GATT negotiations, was the *exception culturelle*, to be applied to all cultural productions (*Le Monde*, 19 October 1993; see also Chapter 11).

11 Leaving aside languages like Chinese or Russian which, despite a greater number of speakers, are not internationally diffused languages, there are 350 million English speakers and 200 million Spanish speakers (in de Saint Robert 1986: 100).

REFERENCES AND RECOMMENDED READING

* Ager, D. (1990) *Sociolinguistics and Contemporary French*, Cambridge: Cambridge University Press.
  In addition to an outline of contemporary language policies, Chapter 11 usefully confronts contemporary views about the French language.

Ball, R. (1988) 'Language insecurity and state language policy: the case of France', *Quinquereme*, 11, 1: 95–105.

—— (1995) 'Plus ça change . . .? The enduring tradition of linguistic conservatism', *French Cultural Studies*, 6, 1: 61–78.

Brulard, I. (forthcoming) 'The *loi Toubon*: Linguistic Interventionism and Human Rights', in M. Cross and S. Perry (eds) *Voices of France*, London: Pinter.

Catach, N. (1993) 'The reform of the writing system', in C. Sanders (ed.) *French Today*, Cambridge: CUP.

Délégation générale à la langue française (1994) *Les Brèves. Lettre du Conseil supérieur et de la délégation générale à la langue française.*

—— (1995) *Les Brèves. Lettre du Conseil supérieur et de la délégation générale à la langue française.*

Durand, J. (1996) 'Linguistic Purification, the French Nation-state and the Linguist', in C. Hoffman (ed.) *Language, Culture and Communication in Contemporary Europe*, London: Multilingual Matters.

Etiemble, R. (1964) *Parlez-vous Franglais?*, Paris: Gallimard.

Gauthier, F., Leclerc, J. and Maurais, F. (1994) *Recueil des clauses linguistiques des constitutions du monde*, Québec: Publications du Québec.

Giacomo, M. (1975) 'La Politique à propos des langues régionales: cadre historique', *Langue française*, 25: 12–36.

Gilder, A. (1993) *Et si l'on parlait Francais*, Paris: Le cherche midi éditeur.

Goosse, A. (1991) *Mélanges de grammaire et de lexicologie françaises*, Louvain-la-Neuve: Peeters.

Hagège, C. (1987) *Le Français et les siècles*, Paris: Odile Jacob.

Haut Conseil de la francophonie (1991) *Etat de la francophonie dans le monde*, Paris: La Documentation française.

Jacob, J.E. (1990) 'Language policy and political development in France', in B.

Weinstein (ed.) *Language Policy and Political Development*, Norwood: Ablex Publishing Corporation.

Journal officiel de la République française, 5 August 1994.

Judge, A. (1993) 'French: a planned language?', in C. Sanders (ed.) *French Today*, Cambridge: Cambridge University Press.

Laroussi, F. and Marcellesi, J-B. (1993) 'The other languages of France', in C. Sanders (ed.) *French Today*, Cambridge: Cambridge University Press.

—— (1993) 'La Révolution française et la politique d'unification linguistique', in C. Sanders (ed.) *French Today*, Cambridge: Cambridge University Press.

Lodge, A. (1991) 'Authority, prescriptivism and the French standard language', *Journal of French Language Studies*, 1, 1: 93–111.

* Lodge, A. (1993) *French: From Dialect to Standard*, London: Routledge.
  Useful historical and linguistic account of the development of standard French.

Offord, M. (1990) *Varieties of Contemporary French*, London: Macmillan.

Rickard, P. (1989) *A History of the French Language*, London: Unwin Hyman.

Saint Robert, P. (de) (1986) *Lettre ouverte à ceux qui en perdent leur français*, Paris: Albin Michel.

* Schiffman, H.F. (1996) *Linguistic Culture and Language Policy*, London and New York: Routledge.
  Chapter 4 ('Language policy and linguistic culture in France') and Chapter 5 ('French in the marginal areas') are especially interesting as detailed accounts of the marginalisation process of the regional languages in France, especially during the Revolution but also in contemporary France.

Thévenot, J. (1976) *Hé! La France, ton Français font le camp!*, Paris: Dueulot.

Wardhaugh, R. (1986) *An Introduction to Sociolinguistics*, Oxford: Basil Blackwell.

Wilcox, L. (1994) 'The amendment to Article 2 of the Constitution: an equivocal interpretation of linguistic pluralism?', *Modern and Contemporary France*, NS2, 3: 269–78.

Winchester, H.P.M. (1993) *Contemporary France*, London: Longman.

11

CINEMA

Ann Marie Condron

France was the birthplace of cinema, which may explain why the French see themselves as its guardians, leaders in the battle against 'Hollywood hegemony'. The Lumière brothers gave the first public projection using the *cinématographe* one hundred years ago in Paris. With hindsight Murat (1995: 3) claims that this invention was to revolutionise man's relationship with the world and open new horizons for the imagination and artistic creation. For historical, artistic and economic reasons cinema is an integral part of French cultural heritage, and by 1910 the French film industry was world leader on the international market (Billard 1994: 52).

The importance the French attribute to cinema was evident in the negotiations surrounding GATT (General Agreement on Tariffs and Trade) in 1993. The French felt that the GATT agreement constituted a real danger to the future of their cinema and, indeed, to French identity. In the agreement as originally conceived, cinema and television would be treated in the same way as all other commercial goods, meaning an end to all 'unfair' subsidies awarded to the film industry by the French state and an end to quotas on the number of foreign films screened in France. Wishing to avoid this, the French claimed that film is not just another product, but in fact a national art through which a country's culture and imagination are expressed; thus they argued that it should not be left to market forces to regulate this domain.[1] In the weeks leading up to the talks, François Mitterrand is reported to have said, 'What is at stake, and therefore at risk, in the current negotiations is every country's right to create its own images. ... A society which abandons the means of depicting itself would soon be an enslaved society' (in Goodell 1994: 135). These sentiments were echoed by Bertrand Tavernier, 'pictures have an enormous influence on people's lives' and Jean-Claude Carrière, 'A race which no longer creates its own images is certain to die out' (both in Murat 1995: 2).

However, it is important to realise that the discussions on free trade of audiovisual products as part of the GATT agreement were not an isolated incident, but part of an ongoing battle between the French and the Americans, now dubbed '*la guerre de cent ans*' (the hundred years' war) (Billard 1994:

56).[2] At various points over the last century the French have also had to compete with other film industries, not just that of the Americans. In the 1920s German cinema was the most innovative in Europe and *La Cinémato-graphie française* denounced the invasion of French cinema by the '*Boches*' (a pejorative term for Germans).

Since then various protectionist measures have been implemented. The first quota was introduced with the Herriot Decree in 1928, then in 1936 a ceiling of 150 dubbed American film imports was imposed, a limit which was lowered to 110 in 1952 (Hayward 1993b: 24). European screens had been starved of American films during the Second World War and as a result in post-war years masses flocked to see films like *Gone With the Wind* (dir. Fleming, 1939). During the war the French film industry had become used to a somewhat 'protected' market, therefore at the end of the war it seemed that French screens were being 'flooded' with American imports, representing 60 per cent of the market in early 1945 (Crisp 1993: 74).

On 28 May 1946 France and the USA concluded the Blum–Byrnes agreement, which stimulated discussion and provoked as much feeling as the GATT discussions in the 1990s. It stipulated that French films must be screened for at least four out of every thirteen weeks. Many were against this agreement and saw it as something from which the industry would never be able to recover its competitiveness. According to Colin Crisp:

> Raymond Bernard, for the Association of Directors, spoke of 'treach-ery'; Henry Jeanson, for screenwriters, spoke of the French government 'selling its soul'; Grémillon, for technicians, spoke of the agreement as suppressing French culture's right to freedom of expression; Jouvet evoked the cultural colonisation which must inevitably result; all were in favor of organising a Committee for the Defense of the French Cinema.
>
> (ibid.: 74)

A national movement from December 1947, in January 1948 this committee organised a demonstration in Paris by workers from the French film industry. Ten thousand actors, directors and technicians marched from la Madeleine to the Place de la République. Manifestos were published, public meetings were organised and well-known members of the profession toured cinemas speaking about the iniquitous effects of the agreement. Under its revised terms French films were now supposed to be screened for five weeks (instead of four) every three months. A quota for 121 visas per year for dubbed American films was reintroduced (ibid.: 75).

The French perceive American domination as a very real threat to the survival of their 100-year-old industry and indeed to their identity. Over the last fifteen years many feel that the situation has become particularly acute. Statistics seem to reinforce this view: in 1980 50 per cent of films shown in French cinemas were French, 31 per cent American. Ten years later the situation had been completely reversed: 31 per cent of films were French and 59 per cent American (Antoine 1995: 10).

American majors present awesome competitors: recent history shows that they have the power not only to flood the French market, but also to employ French talent (Louis Malle, Jean-Jacques Annaud). 'In the past decade Hollywood has come of age as a global economic powerhouse, with more than $18 billion in total revenues last year. Entertainment is now the country's second largest export business behind aerospace' (Goodell 1994: 132). European screens represent a major source of finance to the Americans. According to Goodell in 1994 they earned $4 billion from Europe alone.

In French eyes the American industry has a stranglehold on European screens: 80 per cent of all films screened in Europe are made in the USA. In France box-office sales for American films have rocketed over the last decade, rising from 36 per cent in 1984 to 57 per cent in 1994 (Antoine 1995: 10).[3] However, on the other side of the Atlantic the picture is quite different: 98 per cent of all films screened are American (French films accounted for a mere 0.7 per cent of the market in 1992) because, if we are to believe distributors, the indigenous public cannot tolerate dubbed films. Consequently, the only French films released in the US tend to be minority 'art' films shown in the original version or, if a film shows enough promise, an American remake is made.

Over the last decade a number of remakes have been very profitable for the Americans. Two of the most well-known are: *Sommersby* (dir. Amiel, 1993) based on *Le Retour de Martin Guerre* (dir. Vigne, 1982) and *True Lies* (dir. Cameron, 1994) based on *La Totale* (dir. Zidi, 1991). The success of *Nikita* (dir. Besson, 1990), the story of a young drug-addict 'tamed' and trained by the state in order to work as a 'hit-woman', inspired *The Assassin* (dir. Badham, 1993) starring Bridget Fonda. The success of *Trois hommes et un couffin* (dir. Serreau, 1985) in France and English-speaking countries took many by surprise and inspired the much bigger-budget Hollywood remake *Three Men and a Baby* (dir. Nimoy, 1987). The $2 million made by the subtitled version pales into insignificance when compared to the $168 million made by the remake (Guénée, 1995: 11). The figures speak for themselves: remakes are big business.

In the era of the 'talkies' French comedies were restricted in their appeal to French-speaking countries but French humour has evolved and their comedies now appeal to a wider, international audience. The first contemporary smash hit outside French borders was *La Cage aux Folles* (dir. Molinaro, 1978) which made over $40 million and has recently been remade under the title *The Birdcage* (dir. Nichols, 1996). *Les Visiteurs* (dir. Poiré, 1993) proved a huge box-office hit both in France (over 13 million box-office sales) and abroad. It was the biggest French language hit in over twenty years, reaching 1 million box office sales in Spain alone. It will be interesting to see what reception the dubbed version of *Les Visiteurs* has in the US (dir.

Mel Brooks and costing $500,000; Boudier 1995: 17). In true Hollywood style the French have made the sequel *Les Anges gardiens* (Poiré, 1995).

It was argued that French cinema must be given due recognition as an art form and granted the status of *'exception culturelle'*, thus allowing the French the freedom to set their own trade policies outside GATT. The French attitude to film as an art form is nowhere more apparent than in the words of Jack Lang (Minister of Culture 1981–6 and Minister of Culture and Communication 1988–93) 'It's not a victory of one country over another.... It's a victory for art and artists over the commercialisation of culture' (in Goodell 1994: 134). However, we should be wary of accepting this equation too easily, it would be wrong to dismiss all American films as 'commercial' products appealing to mass audiences.

Lang's words are not without a certain irony when we consider that the present Minister of Culture, Philippe Douste-Blazy, has made Sharon Stone a Knight of the Order of Arts and Letters, an award which is even more ironic when we consider that she is at present involved in making an American version of *Les Diaboliques* (dir. Clouzot, 1954). In the words of Kate Muir, 'French directors are desperately trying to create an anti-Hollywood trend, while behind their backs grand awards are being given to the enemy' (Muir 1995: 17).

However, there can be no doubt that the French are very proud of their film industry and refer to it in nationalistic terms. According to Bruno Gosset:

> The theory of *'l'exception culturelle'* is based on one assumption: that our films are outstanding; on one objective: maintaining our main wealth, which is the diversity of our films and on one belief: the conviction that the *'auteur'* can never be protected enough from realities such as finance and the public.
>
> (Gosset 1993: 10)

With the belated help of Germany, French negotiators eventually won the day, establishing their film industry's right to maintain its subsidies and quotas on imports of foreign (read American) films. The issue of subsidies is another bugbear for the Americans, as in France a tax of 11 per cent on all cinema tickets goes into a fund run by a government agency which uses the money to assist other French and European film-makers (Goodell 1994: 134).

It cannot be disputed, however, that public tastes have changed and over the last two decades of the twentieth century, for all their self-proclaimed individuality, the French have been very willing 'victims' of what some observers refer to as 'cocacolonisation'. This leads us to the question of whether the public will continue to demand American films because they prefer them and to prefer them because they are well promoted and generally perceived as products of mass entertainment. Since the mid-1980s the popularity of home-produced films has been in decline. In 1993 only 34 per cent of box-office sales were for French films, a figure which had fallen to

30 per cent by 1994 (Guénée 1995: 10). Only time will tell whether the GATT victory represents merely a 'temporary victory', as the CNC (Centre national de la cinématographie) declared in its annual report in 1994 (Jack 1995: 2). However, if they wish, the Americans could easily get around quotas by buying European studios in which to produce their films.

Ironically, films made during the *Nouvelle Vague* period are perhaps those with which the cinema-going public outside France is most familiar and hence perceive as representative of 'Frenchness', yet many of them were inspired by the work of American film-makers. Although *la Nouvelle Vague* never actually existed as a school or movement (the term was coined by Françoise Giroud, editor of *L'Express*) it is often looked back upon with nostalgia. Rejecting *le cinéma de papa*, the younger generation adopted film as their means of expression, they took control of the camera and began making films on subjects relevant to them, experimenting with different styles and techniques. Cinema was rejuvenated and advances in technology meant that lightweight, hand-held cameras could be used. The New Wave brought cameras out of the studios and on to the streets, in effect freeing film from the traditional constraints of studio production. Editing became easier, speeding up the production process and giving the impression that there was a surge of energy and creativity in film-making.

Truffaut, Chabrol, Godard, Rohmer and Rivette began their careers as film critics for *Cahiers du cinéma*. Americanisation was not an issue at the time and they admired Hitchcock, Hawks and Renoir because they produced distinctive films under conditions of financial constraint. Wishing to give the director as much freedom as possible, Truffaut advocated *'une politique d'auteur'*. Banned from the Cannes Film Festival in 1958 because his film criticism had become so aggressive, he went on to win the *Grand Prix de la Critique* in 1959 with *Les Quatre cents coups*. Many of his early films were semi-autobiographical and reveal his preoccupation with the feelings and problems associated with adolescence and childhood. Ironically, while his popularity declined in France, it grew in the States. His only Oscar-winner, *La Nuit américaine* (1972) (Best Foreign Film) is a classic example of the self-reflexivity said to be characteristic of film-making of the New Wave, despite the fact that it was produced somewhat later.

Of Swiss origin, Godard is probably the best-known 'French' director of the period. At present his films are experiencing a revival in interest due to fashionable directors like Quentin Tarantino, who is claiming him as a direct influence on his work. *A Bout de souffle* (1959) is often cited as the classic New Wave film, breaking with the conventions of commercial cinema. Jump-cuts alternating with long scenes of faltering conversation and characters speaking directly to the camera became hallmarks of Godard's films. Two of his most well-known films, *La Chinoise* and *Weekend* (both 1967) pre-figured the events of May 1968. To quote Reader (1993: 88): 'Godard's career-long interrogation of the relationships between image, sound and represented

reality is nothing if not political in its ceaseless problematizing o
of language and power.'

A cynical representation of French bourgeois society, its val
(customs) and duplicity characterise the early work of Claude Cɪɪᴀʋɪ
early films such as *Le beau Serge* (1959) and *Les Biches* (1968) are generally
agreed to be among his best. Like Truffaut he acknowledged the influence of
Orson Welles and Hitchcock upon his work, which may explain why some
of his other early films such as *La Femme infidèle* (1969) and *Violette Nozière*
(1978) have been 'social thrillers' or *polars*.

Eric Rohmer's early work can be divided into two main categories: *Six
contes moraux* and *Comédies et Proverbes*. The titles clearly indicate
Rohmer's literary and philosophical antecedents and highlight an important
cultural difference between the French and most other nations with regard to
philosophy. Lengthy shots and dialogues mean that, in the UK at least, his
films remain somewhat restricted in their appeal, appreciated mainly by 'art-
house' Francophiles.

PROMOTING FRENCH CINEMA

In spite of the New Wave legacy, over the last fifteen years French cinema
has witnessed a revival of what was dubbed *cinéma de qualité* (mainly studio-
based literary adaptations produced in the 1940s and 1950s), a trend much
reviled by François Truffaut at the beginning of the New Wave Period. There
are a number of reasons for this revival, economic factors being by no means
the least of these. French cinema remains Europe's most heavily subsidised
film industry and one cannot afford to ignore the financial aspect of film-
making. 'The French film market is estimated at roughly 500 billion francs
per year. A figure which is increasing but is still low when compared to the
4 billion dollars which the Americans earn from exports' (Guénée 1995: 7).

Jack Lang was convinced that the state should assist film-makers in the
double task of luring French audiences away from American movies and also
attracting audiences in the US and elsewhere to French films (Hayward
1993a: 384). He advocated a policy of investment in what has become known
as the 'heritage' film. Ironically, a number of directors involved in adapting
literary works were *auteurs* who had established their reputations during the
New Wave period. Doubtless Chabrol would have incurred the wrath of
Truffaut with his lavish adaptation of Flaubert's *Madame Bovary* (1990).

It would seem that the French considered the adaptation of literary classics
and costume dramas to be their ace card in the battle against Hollywood;
however, they may also be seen as part of the vogue for costume dramas and
literary adaptations prevailing at the time. Although Hollywood studios have
adapted literary works, the French have a much richer literary tradition on
which to draw:

213

Faced with an awesome American offensive the French film industry is not giving in without a fight, far from it. They intend to do battle with their finest weapons, their best directors and stars, with Depardieu on all fronts, but also making use of France's literature and history.

(Dronnikov 1993: 17)

Pagnol's life and work have been popularised by Claude Berri's adaptations of *Jean de Florette* (1985) and *Manon des Sources* (1986). Subsequently, in 1990, Yves Robert directed *La Gloire de mon père* and its sequel *Le Château de ma mère*. The image which these films present of rural, provincial life is often seen as representative of France and 'Frenchness'. To quote Susan Hayward (1993b: 284–5) their popularity coincides with a trend for nostalgic cultural stereotyping of the past and also of rural France.[4]

In economic terms the most popular French literary adaptation outside France is that of Edmond Rostand's play *Cyrano de Bergerac* (dir. Jean-Paul Rappeneau, 1990), which made more than 50 million f. ($9 million) in box-office sales abroad (Boudier 1995: 16). Anthony Burgess's excellent translation rendered in rhyming subtitles is probably one of the major reasons for the film's popularity in Great Britain (Reader 1993: 96). However, we should not overlook the importance of Depardieu, who unlike many of his counterparts has achieved international 'superstar' status and has featured in this and many other French heritage films. Ginette Vincendeau (1993: 360) has described him as 'the itinerant ambassador of French culture' and his current star status reflects his boundless energy and 'bulimia for rôles' (Murat 1995: 5). His international success as Cyrano perhaps led the French to believe that he would be their 'lethal weapon' in the battle against Hollywood. Despite his stature, he was unable to save *Le Colonel Chabert* (dir. Angelo, 1994) from box-office defeat.

The adaptation of Dumas' *La Reine Margot* (dir. Chéreau, 1994)[5] was well-received in France and abroad. Described as a 'juicy Renaissance bodice-ripper' (Romney 1995: 12), its success may at least in part be attributed to the combined talents of Isabelle Adjani and Daniel Auteuil who starred in the leading roles. It may be argued that the medieval gore of the St Bartholomew's Day Massacre satisfies today's audience expectations of, and desire for, on-screen violence and bloodshed.

However, investment in big budget literary adaptations has proved to be no guarantee of box-office success. One of the most expensive films ever produced in France, Claude Berri's adaptation of Zola's *Germinal* (1993) was not the great success anticipated, unable to lure audiences away from *Jurassic Park* (dir. Spielberg, 1993). Depicting a mining community at the end of the nineteenth century, *Germinal* signified a shift in focus from bourgeois society to that of the working classes, something quite uncharacteristic of late twentieth-century European costume dramas.

The swashbuckling adaptation of Dumas' *La Fille de D'Artagnan* (dir.

Tavernier, 1994) and *Jeanne la Pucelle* (dir. Rivette, 1994) form part of the same trend of epic, historical dramas along the lines of those being produced in Hollywood such as *Rob Roy* (dir. Jones, 1995), *First Knight* (dir. Zulker, 1995) and *Braveheart* (dir. Gibson, 1995). We should not underestimate the fact that such movies have provided French actresses such as Sophie Marceau, Isabelle Adjani and Sandrine Bonnaire with an opportunity to establish their careers on the international scene.

Over the last decade the enthusiasm for the adaptation of literary classics has been the subject of much debate. While several of these films have attracted mass audiences into cinemas in France and overseas, French critics have interpreted them as a sign of stagnation. In the words of Bruno Gosset (1993: 10) they represent 'the expression of a deep lack of belief in our ability to express our cultural vigour other than by the servile and academic glorification of the past'.

Although in future these films may be looked back upon as classics, investment in big budget epic costume dramas to the detriment of other more innovative projects has made it increasingly difficult for new directors to emerge. There has been a lack of investment in *films d'art et d'essai* and over-investment in big budget super-productions. Consequently, new directors have found it difficult to secure funding for their projects.

The revival of *cinéma de qualité* in the 1980s can be contrasted with what has been dubbed the *Forum des Halles* genre.[6] The main directors associated with this are Jean-Jacques Beineix, Luc Besson and Léos Carax. 'Their visual style . . . is determinedly contemporary, influenced above all by the video clip and the language of advertising' (Reader 1993: 96). This feature is not only particular to contemporary French cinema, but a reflection of the importance and influence of television and advertising in late twentieth-century society. Their films have been described as 'postmodern, anti-elitist and anti-intellectual' (Hayward 1993b: 35), which may partly explain their popularity with the younger generation.

Diva (dir. Beineix, 1981) is widely regarded as having inaugurated films of this genre: 'The end of the 1980s are marked by the "Diva syndrome", characterised by very slick photography and the striking use of special effects' (Passek 1991: 268). Beineix's films are distinctive for his inventive use of colour, a feature which is particularly striking in *37°2 le matin* (1986) (*Betty Blue*). Luc Besson has the reputation of having an extremely strict technical approach to film-making. His films are often instantly recognisable in the opening scenes, for instance the camera travelling forward over the sea (*Le Grand Bleu*, 1988), a dark street (*Nikita*, 1990) or Manhattan (*Léon*, 1995).

Many of these films reveal a preoccupation with marginal social groups and *exclusion*, often depicting a subculture, as in *Subway* (dir. Besson, 1985) or the 'marginal' world of those living outside or on the fringe of 'ordinary' society as in *Nikita* (1990). *Les Amants du Pont Neuf* (dir. Carax, 1991) incorporates the theme of 'marginal' society, albeit in a rather romantic way;

the 'new poor' of the 1980s make the Pont Neuf their home while it is closed for repair. Carax's depiction of the poor, dispossessed and homeless is in stark contrast to the extravagant firework displays celebrating the Bicentenary of the Revolution, which form the backdrop at several points in the film. This juxtaposition acts as a strong visual comment on French society of the 1980s.

Intertextuality is characteristic of Léos Carax's films and he has been described as more of a cinephile's director than either Beineix or Besson. Parallels have been made between *Les Amants du Pont Neuf* and the Orpheus tale and *La Belle et la Bête* (dir. Cocteau, 1946). However, the intrinsic importance of the elements in this film mean that Carax has been criticised for following trends set by Lucas and Spielberg and in so doing going against 'French' tradition:

> This type of cinema is new and clashes with French tradition because it abandons the exploration of complex feelings, the favourite topic of French *auteurs*, in favour of a very simplistic play on the elements (water, fire, earth etc.) which is aimed directly at the deepest parts of the psyche.
>
> (Gosset 1993: 10)

The preoccupation with the exploration of complex feelings associated with the French tradition is evident in many New Wave films and more recent films like *Un Coeur en hiver* (dir. Sautet, 1992) and *Ma Saison préférée* (dir. Téchiné, 1993). It is interesting to see the way in which the two genres are presented as characteristic of American or French tradition, as if they were in direct competition and the only choices open to contemporary directors. Over the last two decades the production of certain genres such as the detective story and *film noir* has declined in France, yet the psychological drama, which seems to be internationally perceived as characteristic of the work of the French *auteur*, is still popular, although by its very nature it cannot hope to appeal to as wide an audience as more escapist blockbusters.

The popularity and financial success of *The Assassin* eclipsing that of *Nikita* may have been one major reason behind Besson's decision to shoot *Léon* (1994) in English, rather than see a second-rate Hollywood remake of his film. It was also no doubt an attempt to secure a wider international audience for future films. Attracting one-third of all cinemagoers in its first week, *Léon* was described as 'a Gallic foray into everything the *véritable cinéaste* most loathes about Hollywood . . . hailed by some as proof that France can still beat the Americans at their own game' (Bremner 1994: 13). Whatever the reasoning behind Besson's decision, *Léon* (renamed *The Professional* in the US) attracted 3.5 million spectators, making $20 million in the US on 1,200 screens in only three weeks (Billard 1994: 61).

Jean-Jacques Annaud belongs to the same period if not the same 'school' as the '*Forum des Halles*' directors and established an international reputation for himself with *Le Nom de la Rose* (1986). According to Billard (ibid.:

6) he 'has two distinct qualities: he is not ashamed of taking public tastes into account, nor of telling stories which can be exported. Therefore he is one of the few French film-makers to be able to risk the Hollywood adventure.' However, like Beineix and Besson, he has been criticised for pandering to the tastes of the 'masses', using animals in his films and indulging in glossy images, occasionally to the detriment of narrative cohesiveness.

Unlike Besson, Annaud has no qualms about making films in English and does not seem to feel any particular attachment to France and the French language:

> I think it is wrong to identify film-making with language, as if film were literature. The art of cinema is the art of the image and language is really of secondary importance. When a French book is an international success it is because it is conveying the author's thoughts and not their language. The same applies to film-making.
>
> (Annaud, in Daniélou 1995: 11)

Due to the strength of American distribution networks, the French have lost many of their traditionally French-speaking markets, such as Belgium and Switzerland. This and the exodus of talented European film-makers is a source of alarm and despair to the French. In the media their departure is referred to in very negative terms and frequently presented as a betrayal. While the US represented a safe haven during both world wars and as such attracted many European artists and intellectuals, nowadays any move to Hollywood is equated with the pursuit of profit and putting economic interests before art. Nevertheless, Besson and Annaud are not the first foreign film-makers to shoot their films in English and one may safely assume that they will not be the last.

BREAKING INTO FRENCH CINEMA

So far we have referred to films deemed to represent a certain 'Frenchness', next we shall refer to trends which have tended to remain somewhat marginal-ised and are often overlooked in accounts of popular, mainstream French cinema. One example is the work of female film-makers, whose work according to Buet (in Vincendeau and Reynaud 1993: 11) in 1993 represented a mere 8 per cent of all films produced in France. Their work is traditionally perceived as 'arty', feminist and intellectual, yet ironically the majority of these film-makers reject the label 'feminist' and their work cannot be categorised so easily.[7] Although they tend to focus on themes like the family, adolescence, sexuality and women's role in society, some have not hesitated to film other more sensitive and controversial issues, such as rape and sado-masochism.

Agnès Varda is the most prolific and best-known female French film director outside France and one of the few to identify herself as feminist:

'I am a feminist, I am a filmmaker, I am a woman. That doesn't make me a feminist-woman-filmmaker. Film making is specific work. I do it. I try to do it well. But it includes the fact that my opinions as a woman, as a feminist, sometimes show up, sometimes are explicit, sometimes are implicit.'

(in Acker 1991: 305)

Georges Sadoul (1965: 196) has referred to Varda's *La Pointe-Courte* as 'genuinely the first film of the French *Nouvelle vague*'. Often associated with the *'Rive Gauche'* element of the New Wave, Varda's work is often cited as a direct influence on that of other film-makers, female and male. While one may argue that the choice of subject for *Cléo de 5 à 7* (1962) (a woman waiting for the results of a test for cancer) may be more likely to find empathy in a female audience, this does not necessarily apply to the choice of subject for her other films. Varda's work was original, as she subverted prevailing cinematic practice (that of women objectified by male directors) and the female character became the subject, rather than the object of vision. In *Cléo* a process of self-discovery and self-emancipation seems to take place and it is through Cléo's eyes that we see Parisians going about their daily life.

Conversely *Sans toit ni loi* (1985) begins with the death of Mona, the central character played by Sandrine Bonnaire. Varda uses flashbacks to recreate the last few months of Mona's life and documentary-style interviews with those who met her in what may seem an attempt at some kind of explanation. However, Varda makes no concessions, refusing to give any neat ending or reassuring explanations and Mona remains elusive. We do not find out who she is, where she came from, nor why she chose to live, and indeed die, in this way (Hayward 1993b: 257–8).

Diane Kurys began her career with *Diabolo Menthe* (1977), a bitter-sweet nostalgia tale of adolescence and first love set in the 1950s/60s, using contemporary music to situate it. However, she is best-known for what is widely agreed to be her best film, *Coup de foudre* (1982), which sensitively explores the story of a strong friendship/ love affair between two women played by Miou-Miou and Isabelle Huppert.

L'Amour violé (dir. Bellon, 1978) presents rape from a female perspective and explores the feelings associated with this violation and how it can affect a woman's perception of herself and her sexuality. This film caused a lot of debate and strong reactions from both feminist circles and the general public. Two films to portray sado-masochism from a female perspective are *Tapage nocturne* (dir. Breillat, 1980) and *Noir et Blanc* (dir. Claire Devers, 1986). Shot in black and white, the latter is extremely disturbing as Devers' unrelenting depiction of the escalation of violence and pain, forces us to acknowledge the aspect of voyeurism inherent in our position as spectators (ibid.: 259).

36 fillette (dir. Breillat, 1989), dealing with adolescent female sexuality, dispenses with any romantic notions associated with the loss of virginity. The film was quite daring for the time when it was, and probably still is, taboo to discuss the sexual desires of minors, perhaps even more so from a young girl's point of view. The story and the choice of female adolescent subject-ivity for this film are in direct contrast to other films being made by male directors at the time such as *37º2 le matin* (dir. Beineix, 1986) and *Nikita* (dir. Besson, 1990) in which a nubile young woman is presented as the object of desire (ibid.: 293).

Recently, more women such as Josiane Balasko have been attracted to a career behind the camera, achieving success in France with *Gazon maudit* (1995) (American title *Bushwhacked* and British title *French Twist*) with one million box-office sales in France only two weeks after its release. Balasko subverted the classic *menage-à-trois* theme usually presented from a male perspective, involving two men and a woman and humourously satirised popular anti-lesbian prejudice.

We shall now turn to *cinéma beur*[8] which, like the work of female film-makers, remains somewhat marginalised. According to Christian Bosséno (1992: 49), 'a *beur* film is one which was made by a young person of North African origin who was born or who spent his or her youth in France, and which features *beur* characters'. One could say that *cinéma beur* is to French cinema what Black cinema is to the American film industry. The term embraces both militant and more popular films. Unfortunately, this genre is not as yet very well-known outside France and it remains to be seen whether Black American cinema or *cinéma beur* will be able to sustain themselves or whether they will be forced to align themselves with mainstream, popular cinema. Paradoxically, while the French feel culturally threatened by Holly-wood domination and socially by Islamic fundamentalism, they have not sought to promote a minority cinema within their borders.[9]

According to Carrie Tarr (1993: 32) *Le Thé à la menthe* (dir. Bahloul, 1984) was the first film to have most clearly heralded the popular *beur* films. Bahloul went on to win a prize at the Chamrousse film festival in 1992 with his next film *Un Vampire au Paradis*, while Mehdi Charef won the *Prix Jean Vigo* in 1985 and a *César* for Best First Film with *Le Thé au harem d'Archimède*. The film got attendances of 100,000 in the greater Paris area alone, a good reception from the critics and to date it remains the only *beur* film to be distributed in the UK. With *Bâton rouge* (dir. Bouchareb, 1986) it is considered the first of two *beur* feature films to have known success at the box office in France.

Cinéma beur reflected part of the socio-political reality of 1980s France; representing the realities of racism, unemployment, drugs and poor housing in the suburbs. The images in these films are not all negative, however; they also present the hopes and desires of the younger generation with humour, challenging received images of 'the French' as opposed to 'others' (Hayward 1993b: 288). According to Bosséno, 'the key themes . . . are friendship, love and the need to escape' (1992: 50):

219

The chief interest of *beur* films is that by giving substance to a new component of French society and renewing the image of the immigrant in the French cinema they have galvanized the jaded imaginations of those responsible for mainstream productions: more and more movies – those of Jean-Jacques Beineix and Léos Carax, for example – have rediscovered the suburbs. *beur* cinema thus marks a return to realism and to real concerns.

(ibid.: 51)

As in mainstream French cinema, there is distinct lack of female *beur* or immigrant film-makers. Two exceptions, however, are Charlotte Silvera and Farida Belghoul. *Louise l'insoumise* (dir. Silvera, 1984) explores the problems of immigration, integration and identity as experienced by a young girl growing up in France feeling at odds with her Jewish Tunisian family. Belghoul, a militant activist in the *beur* movement of the early 1980s, has made two shorts, *C'est Madame la France que tu préfères?* (1981) and *Le Départ du Père* (1983). Like Silvera's film they explore the dilemma of a young *beur* woman trying to work out her own identity yet maintain good relations with her family.

Hexagone (dir. Chibane, 1994) was made outside the constraints of normal French cinema structures and despite its successful forerunners it was widely perceived as the first film to be made *for Beurs by Beurs*. Financed by the local community, friends of Chibane acted for free. Shown in more than eighty French towns, it enjoyed critical success.

Other innovative trends prevail in France today, and two younger directors to have become renowned outside France are Jean-Pierre Jeunet and Marc Caro, whose first film *Delicatessen* (1991) depicting a bizarre, futuristic, cannibalistic society, has become a cult film for many. While Jeunet and Caro acknowledge the influence of Beineix, Besson and Carax upon their work, they assert their eagerness to create *une nouvelle esthétique*. Their latest film *La Cité des enfants perdus* (1995) presented at the opening of the competition in Cannes, caused much controversy and has frequently been described as 'a fairy tale for all ages'. It draws widely on myths and fairy tales, but above all shows that the French can use special effects as skilfully as the Americans, who are still seen as leaders in this field.

Xavier Beauvois, Karim Dridi and Mathieu Kassovitz are being hailed as '*la nouvelle Nouvelle Vague*' partly because of their youth and partly because their films deal with topics such as AIDS, war, violence and *exclusion*, which are of relevance to us all but, one could argue, particularly to the younger generation at the end of the twentieth century. The subject-matter of their films stands in direct contrast to that of costume dramas and literary adaptations, and presents a refreshing change in style. There are clear parallels between *beur* cinema and the work of these new film-makers.

With *N'oublie pas que tu vas mourir* Xavier Beauvois won the *Prix Jean*

Vigo in Cannes in 1995. The story of a student who discovers by chance that he is HIV-positive, it has been described as 'a morbid and disturbing film which will cause either anger or rejection, but will certainly not leave the public indifferent' (Grassin and Médioni 1995: 55). All too aware of the demanding nature of the role, Beauvois took on the principal role himself and actually got himself arrested in order to get an 'inside' view of conditions in police custody. He also went to Mostar to experience war first-hand and the final scenes (apart from those with machine-gun shots) were filmed in Bosnia.

Karim Dridi's second film *Bye-Bye* (1995) received much acclaim in Cannes. The central theme is guilt, and we see Ismaël and Mouloud, two brothers of Algerian origin, at the centre of a tale of drug-trafficking, racism and violence in Marseilles. Like Kassovitz, Dridi acknowledges the influence of the British director Ken Loach, with whom he shares a preference for unknown actors and actresses. This preference is in direct contrast to the choice of famous actors and actresses to star in costume dramas or literary adaptations. Above all, Dridi did not want his work to be dismissed and 'ghettoised' along with that of *beur* film-makers.

Inspired by the death of Makome M'Bowole, a young Zairean killed in police custody in Paris, *La Haine* (dir. Kassovitz, 1995) is the tale of *bavures policières* and the violence which may erupt in their wake. In his representation of the *cité* Kassovitz wanted to avoid any hint of *misérabilisme*, a criticism often levelled at the first generation of *beur* film-makers. It is interesting to note his choice of characters, focusing not only on *Beurs* but on a Jew, a Black and a *Beur*. The use of black and white could be interpreted as an attempt to make the film seem like a documentary, but Kassovitz has claimed it was to reinforce 'the hard-hitting nature of the film' (Grassin and Médioni 1995: 53). For the same reason, all the major characters are male and Kassovitz deliberately chose not to include any love interest or sex scenes. There is a rich variety of accents and both music and humour are used to good effect. Only the future will tell whether these new directors will continue to produce distinctive films and deserve the title of '*la nouvelle Nouvelle Vague*'.

CONCLUSION

One hundred years after its birth, in terms of production the French film industry is the only one in Europe to have survived the Hollywood 'onslaught' and still retain 35 per cent of its own market. However, the French cannot afford to become complacent; survival is not merely a question of the quality and popularity of films produced. Future survival in the face of the arrival of 'information superhighway' technology on the eve of the twenty-first century will depend not only on maintaining quotas and subsidies but also on establishing strong distribution networks on both a European and global level. Producers have an extremely important rôle to play, yet in order to compete successfully, it seems that the French have little choice but to emulate American marketing and promotion practices.

The French have recently been financing and working on many co-productions, yet this concept is far from original as it was already introduced as a survival strategy in post-war years. As Crisp has pointed out:

> one central motive was the desire to counter the super-productions of the American cinema ... the solution was to think in terms of a transnational, and even European, film industry, able to call on the capital and on the technical and artistic personnel of several nations.
>
> (Crisp 1993: 79)

In 1992, 155 films were produced, or co-produced, with French backing (Andreu and Jordan 1993: 24). Successful co-productions include *High Heels* (dir. Almodovar, 1991), *The Piano* (dir. Campion, 1993), the trilogy *Bleu, Blanc, Rouge* (dir. Kieslowski, 1993) and *Les Silences du Palais* (dir. Tlatli, 1994) (British title *Silences of the Palace*).

Although often accused of protectionism, in recent years the French have none the less been energetically seeking to maintain the film industry in other countries.[10] Optimistic about the future, they can see signs of renaissance and renewal in their 100-year old industry, and behind the scenes they have been busy forging ties with other countries in Europe and beyond. Bertrand Tavernier was eager to point out that he and his peers are not engaged in a personal battle against the American industry, but are striving to allow the survival of an alternative type of cinema (Murat 1995: 2).

One should bear in mind that the French film industry has already survived the end of the Second World War and the subsequent 'invasion' of American films, which may partly explain why the French seem inclined to react more strongly than other nations in retaliation to what they see as an invasion of their cinema screens. In the words of the actor Daniel Auteuil, 'We're resistants. As long as we're not afraid of our difference, we'll get through' (quoted in Romney 1995: 12).

CINEMA: CHRONOLOGY

1895   (28 December) First public projection with *Cinématographe* by Louis and Auguste Lumière, 14 boulevard des Capucines, Paris.

1896   Alice Guy Blaché made her first film, *La Fée aux choux* – she is arguably the first female film director in history and arguably the first director to bring a narrative film to the screen.

        Georges Méliès builds film studio at Montreuil and makes *Escamotage d'une dame chez Robert Houdin*.

1902   Georges Méliès makes *Voyage dans la lune*.

1928   Invention of talking pictures.

        Herriott Decree: first quotas imposed on imported films.

1936   Henri Langlois founds *la Cinémathèque française*.

1945   *La Commission de contrôle des films* established to act as a censorship board.
1946   *Le Centre national de la cinématographie* established.
       Blum–Byrnes Agreement on Franco-American economic relations reached.
       French films to be screened at least four out of every thirteen weeks.
       Orson Welles's *Citizen Kane* released in France.
       First Cannes Film Festival.
1947   Committee for the Defence of French Cinema founded.
1948   (January) Committee for the Defence of French Cinema organises a demonstration in Paris by workers from the French film industry. They march from la Madeleine to the Place de la République. The Blum–Byrnes agreement revised: French films now supposed to be screened for five weeks every three months.
       First *Loi d'aide au cinéma* instituted, meaning a tax (*soutien automatique*) levied on all cinema ticket receipts automatically goes into the *Fonds de soutien*.
1954   François Truffaut writes *Une certaine tendance du cinéma français*.
1958–63 *La Nouvelle Vague*.
1960   The system of *avance sur recettes* instituted. This is a selective means of finance, benefiting 20 per cent of films made and representing 5 per cent of investment in production.
1969   Launch of *Cinéthique*.
1979   Opening of *Forum des Halles*.
1981   SOFICA (*Société pour le financement du cinéma et de l'audiovisuel*) established.
1982   Jack Lang sets up *L'Agence pour le développement régional du cinéma* to implement plans to build or refurbish cinema theatres in rural areas.
1984   Launch of Canal+ pay-TV channel; in return for more favourable film-showing rights than other television channels, Canal+ is committed to investing in film production.
       Le Fonds Sud founded to help film-makers in North Africa, Africa, Asia, South America and the Middle East.
1988   *Le Fonds Eurimages* established.
       La Vidéothèque de Paris founded.
1990   *Le Fonds ECO* founded to help film-making in Central and Eastern European countries.
1993   GATT discussions on free trade. Successful negotiations to leave cinema and audiovisual broadcasting out of agreement.

NOTES

1 A similar attitude has been adopted towards television. See Chapter 6.
2 See Introduction: France in the Making for details of the original Hundred Years' War.
3 Other countries fare even worse than France: around 60 per cent of all films screened in Italy are of American origin, 77 per cent in Spain, 82 per cent in Germany, 93 per cent in Great Britain and 95 per cent in Greece and Portugal (Antoine 1995: 10).
4 'These films point to the good/bad old days, rural revivalism and turn-of-the-century gentility – that is, all that we can no longer aspire to be or possess, or conversely, all that we are satisfied is no longer our lot in life. But these retro-discourses are precisely not about the past, but about our ideas or cultural stereotypes about the past' (Hayward 1993b: 284–5).

5 Based on the life of Marguerite de Valois and the future Henri IV; see Introduction: France in the Making.

6 '"Forum des Halles" after the modern or postmodern space in central Paris that is the focal point for endless youthful parades of style' (Reader 1993: 96).

7 Coline Serreau: 'I am not a woman who makes films'; Diane Kurys: 'It exasperates me when people talk about women's films'; Issermann: 'We resist any collective image or any attempt to make us into a school'; as quoted by Susan Hayward (1993b: 258). For a further discussion of the definition of feminist, see Chapter 7, Note 2.

8 For a definition of *beur*, see Chapter 9, Note 10.

9 A similar double-standard applies to language: see the concluding section of Chapter 10.

10 In Europe *le Fonds Eurimages* was set up in 1988 and it helped to fund 227 feature films between 1989 and 1993. Two organisations have been set up to help film-makers throughout the world: *le Fonds Sud* in 1984 to help those in North Africa, Africa, Asia, South America and the Middle East, and *le Fonds ECO* in 1990 to help *'la production cinématographique des pays d'Europe centrale et orientale'*. In France the role of the SOFICAs is to promote investment in the cinema and audiovisual industry. The film industry has also found an ally in the TV channel Canal+, whose contribution to French film production totalled more than 35 per cent, that is over 819 million f. or $149 million in 1993 (Luton 1995: 15).

REFERENCES AND RECOMMENDED READING

Acker, A. (1991) *Reel Women: Pioneers of the Cinema, 1896 to the Present*, New York: Continuum.

Andreu, A. and Jordan J. (1993) 'Le Gatt et le cinéma en quatre questions', *L'Evénement du Jeudi*, 4–10 novembre.

Antoine, C. (1995) 'Le Cinéma dans tous ses états', *Label France*, no. 19: 10.

* Audé F. (1981) *Ciné-modèles cinéma d'elles*, Lausanne: L'Age d'Homme.
  Very good on women in film and female film makers.

Billard, P. (1994) 'Cent ans de cinéma français,' *Le Point*, no. 1163: 52–63.

*—— (1995) *L'Age classique du cinéma français*, Paris: Flammarion.
  A good reference work on early French cinema.

Bosséno, C. (1992) 'Immigrant Cinema: National Cinema', trans. Peter Graham, in R. Dyer and G. Vincendeau (eds) *Popular European Cinema*, London: Routledge.

Boudier, C. (1995) 'Quand le cinéma français court le monde . . .' *Label France*, no. 19: 16–17.

Bremner, C.(1994) 'French film epics flounder', *The Times*, 29 March.

Crisp, C. (1993) *The Classic French Cinema, 1930–1960*, Bloomington, Ind: Indiana University Press.

Daniélou, L. (1995) 'Entretien: Jean-Jacques Annaud', *Label France*, no. 19: 11–12.

Dronnikov, A. (1993) 'Le Cinéma français avec panache dans l'an neuf', *Le Quotidien de Paris*, 31 décembre.

* Flitterman-Lewis, S. (1990) *To Desire Differently, Feminism and the French Cinema*, Illinois: Illini Books.
  Very good on female film-makers: Dulac, Epstein and particularly Varda.

* Frodon, J.-M. (1995) *L'Age moderne du cinéma français*, Paris: Flammarion.
  A good reference on modern French cinema from the New Wave (1959) to the present.

Goodell, J. (1994) 'Salut suckers!' in *Premiere*, April: 130–9.

Gosset, B. (1993) 'Le Cinéma français est-il au-dessus de tout soupçon?', *Le Quotidien de Paris*, 27 October.

Grassin, S. and Médioni G. (1995) 'Spécial Cannes', *L'Express*, 18 mai.

Guénée, P. (1995) 'Le Cinéma français sait-il s'exporter?', *Problèmes économiques*, no. 2: 435.

Hayward, S. (1993a) 'State, culture and the cinema: Jack Lang's strategies for the French film industry', *Screen*, 34, 4: 380–91.

*—— (1993b) *French National Cinema*, London: Routledge.
A useful general reference.

Jack, A. (1995) 'France defends cinematic legacy', *Financial Times*, 22 March.

Luton, M.C. (1995) 'La France terre d'accueil du cinéma étranger', *Label France*, no. 19: 14–15.

Muir, K. (1995) 'How Sharon and Kevin became chic', *The Times*, 26 October.

Murat, P. (1995) 'Cent ans de cinéma français', *Label France*, no. 19: 4–5.

Passek, J.-L. (1991) *Dictionnaire du cinéma français*, Paris: Larousse.

Reader, K. (1993) 'French cinema since 1945', in M. Cook (ed.), *On y va, French Culture since 1945*, London: Longman.

Romney, J. (1995) 'Versatile French master of the roles', *Guardian*, 11 August.

Sadoul, G. (1965) *Dictionnaire des films*, Paris: Editions du Seuil.

Tarr, C. (1993) 'Questions of identity in Beur cinéma: from *Tea in the Harem* to *Cheb*', *Screen*, 34, 4: 321–42.

Vincendeau, G. (1993) 'Gérard Depardieu: The axiom of contemporary French cinema', *Screen*, 34, 4: 343–61.

—— and Reynaud, B. (eds) (1993) *20 ans de théories féministes sur le cinéma*, Paris: Cinéma Action-Corlet.

12

A MARKET OF 58 MILLION CONSUMERS

Eve Gilliard-Russell

The introduction of the Single Market in January 1993 has intensified competition and the consumer should benefit from greater availability of goods and services from other countries. This major economic development in Europe has also coincided with a period of recession which has lasted longer than was first predicted and has had a detrimental effect on volumes of consumption. Thanks to the development of communications and transports, European consumers are beginning to form a more homogeneous market. Some sectors remain affected by national characteristics, as is the case with the food and drink industry, where national taste and habit still weigh heavily on consumer behaviour. However, some products are already targeted at the 'Euroconsumer' and many firms believe that there is little need to differentiate across national boundaries.

'France is the world's fourth largest market and its fourth largest importer of consumer goods' (BOTB 1990). As the UK's third main trading partner and its third-largest export market, France provides a potential market of 58 million consumers. This chapter, by examining the different characteristics of the French market, will establish whether it is possible to distinguish French consumers' preferences from those of their European counterparts. The evolution of socio-demographic trends will be outlined first as they constitute the major source of information available to identify and predict consumer preferences and needs. Those variables will then be complemented with the findings of lifestyle studies or 'sociocultural segmentation' (Lambin 1994), as the predictive value of the former tends to diminish with the standardisation of consumption patterns between social classes in all industrialised nations. Third, there will be a review of main trends in consumption patterns which have been affected by social, economic, demographic and cultural changes in France. These changes also have a bearing on the evolution of channels of distribution, which will be analysed last. Whenever possible, a comparison will be made with other European nations and in particular the UK.

SOCIO-DEMOGRAPHIC TRENDS

Socio-demographic parameters – such as age, social class, geographical location, gender – are traditionally used in marketing to identify and predict consumer preferences and needs. Socio-demographic changes have a direct bearing on consumption patterns. For example, with the increase of the over-65 segment of the population, there will be more demand for insurance schemes, leisure activities and health services and goods, and for domestic fuel. More women at work leads to an increase in convenience foods, in meals taken outside the home and in innovation in time-saving household durables. France is characterised by a geographically fragmented market, an ageing population, an increase in the number of households and an increasingly white-collar society struck by unemployment.

A geographically fragmented market

France, the largest country in Western Europe, is two and a half times bigger than the UK yet has roughly the same number of inhabitants. Population density is 105 inhabitants per square kilometre, as opposed to the UK's 240 (INSEE 1994). There is a split between large conurbations and small villages, between densely populated areas and sparsely populated regions.[1]

People continue to move towards the major conurbations as jobs disappear in rural parts. Seventy-five per cent of the French are now city-dwellers. Although most of the country's activity is still largely centralised around Paris, the market is geographically fragmented, a trait which is reflected in the importance of mail order and the resilience of small retailers in remote rural areas. France is a centralised nation which nevertheless displays marked regional differences. Regional differences are strongest in food preferences, with the diet of a Strasbourgeois, for example, resembling that of an inhabitant of Cologne more than that of a Bordelais.

Ageing of the population

The continuing fall of the birth rate (an average of 3 per cent per year) and the increase in life expectancy mean that France has an ageing population, as do other countries in the EU. In spite of considerable media attention to this problem in France, the phenomenon is not in fact as pronounced as it is in most European countries (see Table 12.1). The fall in the birth-rate is linked to a change in values similar to that in other industrialised countries and to the increase in the number of working women – 47.3 per cent of all women were working in 1992, a figure currently increasing at the rate of 1 per cent per year. The estimated fertility rate (1.65 in 1994) is falling, as in the rest of the EU, but is still one of the highest, although it is now closer to the European average.

Table 12.1 'Juniors' and 'seniors' in the EU, 1992 (as a percentage of the overall population)

Age	Germany*	UK	Italy	France	EU average
0–15	16.2	19.3	15.7	20.0	17.9
over 65	15.0	15.7	15.3	14.4	14.9

Note: *1991
Source: adapted from INSEE 1994

Life expectancy is close to the EU average for men (73.3) and the highest in the EU for women (81.5). The higher death rate of men at an earlier age is explained by a different lifestyle: more smoking, drinking, road accidents, teenage suicides, occupational hazards amongst men as well as fewer regular health checks. Infant mortality is low and continuing to decrease (6.8 per 1,000, the EU average).

The age imbalance resulting from the end of the baby boom[2] in the early 1970s will worsen over the next thirty years. The baby-boomers will start to retire around 2005, bringing an increasing dependence on an ever-decreasing working population. If the present system of pension funding is maintained, the dependency ratio (ratio of persons of working age to persons over 65) has to be 2.5: 1; it has been projected that by the year 2020, it will be 1.5: 1 (Delavennat, 1993). The system will have collapsed by then. This issue has been much debated in the 1980s and 1990s, raising both the awareness and the concern of the population, and resulting in considerable benefits for insurance companies. The market of private pension plans will flourish over the next few years.

Table 12.2 'Juniors' and 'seniors' in France as a percentage of the overall population

Age	1980	1994	2020*
under 20s	30.6	26.4	22.7
over 65s	14	15	25

Note *projections
Source: adapted from INSEE 1994

The over-65 market is the market of the future as it is expanding (see Table 12.2). At the same time, the under-20 age group has fallen both in numbers and as a proportion of the overall population. These two major demographic developments will have a profound effect on consumption and on channels of distribution in the next century. There will be an increased demand for health and leisure products and services, as well as a larger consumption of books, newspapers, personal care services such as hairdressing, and domestic fuel. Mail order and home delivery services will become more popular. The retiring baby-boomers will be in better health, more active and more technologically aware than their predecessors, which will have to be taken into consideration by firms both in terms of product offer and advertising strategy. At the same time, since children are becoming rarer, more is spent on them. Children also have an influence beyond the realm of products and services for which they are ordinarily targeted: food, parents' clothes, holidays and even the family car (an advert for the Peugeot 809 read recently 'the car recommended by your children'). Therefore the under-20 segment is also a promising one for the future, although not so much in terms of the size of the market.

Not only are people indulging their children more, they are also spending more on their pets. The market for pet food and accessories has a sizeable potential for the future. Gloria – a company specialising in baby milk – has, for example, compensated for the possible loss of revenue caused by the fall in the birth rate by diversifying into pet food.

Increase in the number of households

In the past thirty years, the number of households has increased by 47 per cent, with a corresponding decrease in size. This is due mainly to the growth in the numbers of both single and divorced people. Marriage is less popular and occurs at a later date in France, compared to other European countries. Single-member households are the fastest-growing phenomenon, accounting for 27 per cent of the total 21.5 million (INSEE 1994). Their presence is linked to the size of a city: the bigger the city, the higher their numbers, with the proportion in Paris reaching 50 per cent.

Single-member households – predominently young city-dwellers – have a much higher consumption of leisure activities than other households: they are, for example, twice as likely to go to restaurants and nine times as likely to go to the cinema than other households. The food industry has responded to this social phenomenon by launching food packaged as single portions. The idea was not very well received by people living on their own who do not want to be perceived as such, buying a product specifically labelled 'soup for one' – Campbell's most notorious failure on the one-person-household segment in France (Prod'homme 1992). However, the idea found unexpected popularity amongst families, because it meets the need for more personalised consumption, borne out of a growing feeling of individualism (to which reference will made later). The rise in the number of single-person households also has an influence on the increase in the demand for rented accommodation and should have a positive effect on sales of household durables in the future.

An increasingly white-collar society struck by unemployment

People are classed in *catégories socioprofessionnelles* (CSP) in France,

Table 12.3 Structure of French households according to social/occupational groups (%)

CSP	1982	1990
Farmers	5.4	3.3
Artisans, shopkeepers, small business owners	7.6	7.1
Managerial staff and professionals	8.9	10.7
Intermediary workers, foremen, technicians	14.2	14.5
White-collar workers	10.8	10.2
Blue-collar workers	31.4	28.2
Pensioners	16.6	20.9
People with no outside professional activity	5.2	5.1

Note: The first six categories comprise unemployed people who used to work; the last category includes the unemployed who have never worked.
Source: adapted from INSEE 1994

according to which social and occupational group they belong. There are eight such groups (see Table 12.3) in studies carried out by INSEE.

The increase in the number of managerial staff and professionals together with the decrease in the number of farmers and blue-collar workers is leading to the standardisation of consumption patterns between social classes, as is the case in all industrialised nations. As the nation becomes richer, the average consumer adopts spending behaviour which is that of the social class to which they aspire – in the case of France, the managerial and professional class. Hence, on average, people are spending a larger proportion of their budget on leisure and health than on food and clothes, for example.

The increase in the number of pensioners has consequences which are discussed elsewhere, as is the problem of rising unemployment (see under 'patterns of consumption'). There were 3.3 million unemployed in 1995, unemployment stood at 12.2 per cent, which is above the EU average of 10.6 per cent in 1993, above that of Germany and the UK (INSEE 1994).

The need for ethnic marketing

Despite a strong national identity, the French are a mix of peoples: Bretons, Provençaux, Basques, Corsicans, and so on, but also people of foreign extraction.[3] At least one-third of the nation has foreign forefathers, originating from Southern and Central Europe as well as Turkey, Yugoslavia, Africa and North Africa. France has the largest Jewish community in Europe outside Russia (700,000) and the largest Muslim community in Europe (between 3 and 5 million), making Islam the second religion in the country. The number of foreigners in France decreased in the 1980s. There were 3.5 million foreigners in 1990, representing 6.4 per cent of the total population (INSEE 1994), and originating mostly from Southern Europe and Northern Africa.[4]

The immigrant population is much younger – it has a higher fertility rate and fewer over-65s – and has more males than the rest of the population. Although, with time, its demographic behaviour is aligning itself with that of the rest of the country – it has been noted, for example, that the fertility rate of immigrants is also falling (ibid.) – nevertheless this population has needs which might be different and are not necessarily addressed by producers of goods or services. This could well be because recognising those needs would mean first recognising that there are cultural differences which could be equated with accepting them; an issue which still remains most sensitive.[5] Ethnic marketing does not exist in France as it does in the USA. The first industrialists to answer the needs of the various communities will reap the benefits.

SOCIO-CULTURAL TRENDS

Consumers belonging to the same socio-demographic segment have similar consumption patterns but still think of themselves as individuals and expect to be addressed as such. As they become standardised, consumption patterns also become more individualistic. In such a context, socio-demographic studies are no longer sufficient to predict trends, although for some sectors like clothes and cars they still remain adequate in France (Valette-Florence 1994).

Lifestyle studies are based on the assumption that individuals belonging to the same demographic segment behave differently, and also that individuals from different demographic segments behave in a similar fashion, according to the lifestyle segment to which they belong (Lambin 1994). Lifestyle studies are based on values, personality and motivation in relation to consumption. They offer a more personalised portrait of the consumer. They are useful as they offer complementary information to socio-demographic analysis, a point which is particularly pertinent at a time when boundaries between social class behaviour patterns are fading.

Centre de communication avancée (CCA) and *Compagnie française d'études de marchés et de conjonctures appliquées* (COFREMCA) are the two main bodies undertaking such studies in France. Although some doubts have been expressed about the validity of their findings and it is known that their predictive power is by far inferior to those using socio-demographic variables (Valette-Florence 1994), these studies are interesting as they identify characteristic values for the whole of the nation. According to lifestyle studies, society is mutating towards the cult of the self, a narcissistic rather than socially orientated approach to life. Individuals are becoming more isolated, withdrawn, they are worried about the future and, when faced with depersonalised consumption (because it is accessible to all), seek their own identity, adopting individualistic, multi-faceted behaviour. The expression '*La société mosaïque*' (CCA, ibid.) can be taken one step further and transformed into '*l'individu mosaïque*'.

Socio-cultural trends affect not only consumption but also the retail sector. For example, the rise of individualism is matched in the retail sector by specialised units within departments in department stores, specialised counters in hypermarkets and the growing popularity of mail order and home shopping, without forgetting the revival of small shops in the shape of specialised boutiques. Consumers are more sensitive to a more personal form rather than mass communication, which explains the success of direct marketing: France ranks second in Europe after Germany for expenditure in direct marketing (Lambin, 1994). The rejection of duty, of sacrifice, in order to seek pleasure for pleasure's sake, to feel good about oneself (hedonism), combined with the desire for novelty and social differentiation result in shopping becoming a leisure activity where impulse buying is paramount. The consumer feels no loyalty towards a particular outlet, shops around for bargains, frequents less traditional outlets (extremely specialised boutiques, flea markets, and so on). Rejection of authority can manifest itself in the emulation of younger generations, for example, or in the fact that major brands are not necessarily readily accepted. The minor importance of rules, of traditional habits is reflected for instance in the fact that meals are taken outside traditional hours, outside traditional places. The emulation of youth, the success of medicines both traditional and alternative, and the success of natural, health foodstuffs can also be attributed to the importance of personal appearance, of health. Elsewhere, the proliferation of religious sects or sports combining physical activity and mysticism illustrates an increasing desire for spirituality.

Similarly, there is a growing taste for food, clothing, and culture of different ethnic groups, not only on the part of ethnic minorities trying to maintain or revive their traditions, but also a general trend in the population as a whole. This trend stems from the search for authenticity, whether it is ethnicity or nature. People yearn for literally or symbolically natural products. Recent years have seen an increased demand for organic and natural foodstuffs (wheatgerm, freshly squeezed fruit juices, for example), promotional campaigns for natural fibres such as cotton and wool, the success of rustic furniture and household items from retailers such as Habitat (COFREMCA in Valette-Florence 1994) and Ikea. Green consumption is the consequence of an ideology rather than a phenomenon linked to socio-demographics. The ecological trend represents a lasting change in the consumer's attitude towards products. Products are no longer acquired solely as personal possessions or to satisfy personal needs, they must also contribute to the improvement or at least the non-degradation of the quality of life, that is to say, the environment.

State environmental expenditure is as high in France as it is in Germany and the UK (INSEE 1994). However, although there is increased concern over environmental issues, the French are still lagging behind the rest of Europe

(Ottman in Lambin 1994: 50). Nevertheless, environmentally friendly products and packaging as well as totally ill-founded environmental claims
('protects the ozone layer' on CFC-free products) have multiplied since the
late 1980s, with most firms jumping on the green bandwagon in order to
increase their profits. It has been noted though, that the French do tend to
support humanitarian and health issues more than environmental causes
(Dufour 1992). This is particularly highlighted in sponsorship campaigns
which favour sending rice to a famine-stricken African country or raising
funds for cancer or Aids research rather than saving whales or a forest.

In addition, the 'cocooning' syndrome, which results from individuals
wanting to 'withdraw' from society, can explain the growth in DIY and other
sectors linked to home improvement and decoration (CCA in Valette-
Florence 1994), expressing an ever-growing interest in the home and the
desire to personalise it. Finally, uncertainty in respect of the future, caused
by the fear of unemployment, war or Aids has dramatic consequences for
consumption growth as will be seen when trends in patterns of consumption
are examined later.

TRENDS IN CONSUMPTION PATTERNS

Under the influence of the demographic and socio-cultural trends that have
been examined so far and some aspects of the economic environment which
will be evoked in this section, the structure of household consumption has
been transformed (Fried 1994) during the past twenty years. Services occupy
a larger share of the budget, and goods, particularly foodstuffs, a smaller one.
Expenditure as a proportion of the household budget has decreased markedly
for foodstuffs, textiles and leather goods, and durables. It has increased
substantially for housing and energy, slightly for health, transport and
communications, leisure and other goods and services (see Table 12.4).

Table 12.4 Structure of household expenditure as percentage of total budget

| | France | | UK | Germany |
	1970	1995*	1995*	1995*
Foodstuffs	26.0	17.3	20.0	21.6
Clothing and footwear	9.6	6.7	6.0	9.2
Housing	15.3	19.1	13.6	19.9
Household durables	10.2	8.3	5.4	9.9
Health	7.1	9.4	1.2	5.2
Transport and communications	13.4	17.6	14.7	17.4
Leisure	6.9	7.6	8.7	11.7
Misc. goods and services	11.5	14.0	30.4	5.1

Sources: Adapted from INSEE 1994 and Euromonitor 1992
Note: * estimates

As seen in Table 12.4, domestic consumption is usually divided into eight sectors, which will be dealt with in turn, in order of importance as a percentage of total consumer spending.

In 1993 and for the first time in history, *housing* (rents, fuel and power, rates and water; not mortgages which belong to investments) became the category of spending with the largest share of total household expenditure, one-fifth of disposable income is now spent in this sector. Housing costs are higher in countries where renting is common (49 per cent of households in France). The increase in single-person households and one-parent families who tend to live in rented accommodation provides a first explanation of the phenomenon. Second, heating bills are higher because of the rising price of domestic fuels. A further explanation can be found in the fact that a growing number of people are staying at home – thereby increasing heating bills – because of unemployment or retirement. The phenomenon looks therefore set to continue and even accelerate in the future.

The French still spend a large part of their budget on *foodstuffs* compared to the rest of the EU, although it is not quite apparent in Table 12.4, which shows a lower level of expenditure than Germany and the UK. This is because the foodstuffs sector includes expenditure on *alcohol* and *tobacco*, both of which are still cheaper in France as excise duty is low, in spite of an attempt at harmonisation within the Single Market. Foodstuff consumption, although diminishing, is still the highest in the EU in volume terms, showing that food is of greater importance in France than in most other European countries, and corresponding to the image the French have of their country as the gastronomic centre of the world. Consumers have nevertheless become more diet-conscious: meat, oils and fats have declined in relative terms. Fruit, vegetables and dairy products are holding their share of spending. Processed food is still important though, as more women go out to work and there is little time to buy fresh food every day. The wider availability of freezers and microwave ovens makes it possible to combine natural, additive-free food and convenience.

A survey (MINTEL 1989) reveals that preference for national food is overwhelming, with Italian food in second position. Frozen recipe dishes are as popular as food low in fat and sugar, and foods with high fibre, except for the over-65s, who are more conservative. However, gourmet foods and delicatessen are high on the list, foods for microwave cooking very low, together with low-alcohol drinks, which seems to reinforce the idea that the consumer wishes to buy healthy, convenient products but not at the expense of the quality of the food and the pleasure derived from eating it, an aspect which does differentiate the French from other nations.

Furthermore, part of a general trend towards healthy living and eating is the fact that tobacco consumption is on the decline but remains nonetheless one of the highest in Europe. France is still the largest market for alcohol in the EU. However, as drink-driving legislation toughens and publicity campaigns and health awareness increase, there is a decline in consumption of alcoholic beverages.

Finally, a large proportion of the food budget is spent on meals taken outside the home. In the 1970s the trend was towards restaurants and canteens at the place of work or study; in the 1980s there has been a marked shift towards fast-food restaurants, a trend which is found elsewhere in Europe (INSEE 1994).

Costs of personal *transport* and running costs have increased dramatically but it is in *communications* that there has been a major increase in volume in the last ten years. The ageing of the population will reinforce this trend in the future since the use of the telephone increases with age, for instance.

Car ownership is one of the highest in Europe, with 76.8 per cent of households owning at least one car in 1991, as opposed to 66 per cent in the UK and 68 per cent in Germany (ibid. 1994). Multi-ownership of cars is on the increase. The increase in car ownership has transformed the retail sector with, for instance, the opening of hypermarkets on the outskirts of towns for weekly shopping (see Chronology). There is still a national preference for French-built cars. The growth of consumption of cars is not affected by inflation but is deeply affected by the level of income, which explains why, although inflation is low and purchasing power remains stable, since consumers are worried about the economic climate they postpone the renewal of their vehicle. As multi-ownership and renewals are more frequent in the case of cars than in that of other types of durables, car sales should resume at healthier levels when the economic outlook seems brighter to the consumer.

Consumption in the *miscellaneous goods and services* sector (hotels, cafés, restaurants, package holidays, personal care and effects, financial services) is affected by the level of income. In the uncertain climate of the early 1990s, growth of consumption in this category slowed down. However, this can only be temporary, as demographic trends (baby-boomers reaching the peak of consumption years, ageing of the population, fear concerning future pensions) and changes in values (hedonism, individualism) point towards a marked increase in this sector in future years.

Health expenditure, because of the differing extent of free national health service in the various countries is a poor indicator of consumption of health products. *Sécurité sociale* – the French National Insurance System – finances 74 per cent of medical expenses; this share is being eroded yearly. Patients contribute on average 19 per cent – a figure on the increase – and private insurance policies, the rest – 7 per cent, a figure which is remaining stable. Medical care and health expenses are rising in terms of expenditure and volume, with pharmaceuticals and the cost of physicians' services being the main contributing factors. As the ageing of the population becomes more acute, this trend is set to intensify. The French are amongst the biggest consumers of pharmaceuticals in the world. They are also more inclined to consult specialists directly, rather than their GPs, which contributes to the increase in medical expenses. Reforms put forward by Juppé's government

to curb the endemic deficit of *Sécurité sociale* provoked widespread demonstrations which brought the country to a standstill in December 1995.

Leisure expenditure (leisure, education, culture) is taking an increasing
share of household budgets: the share of entertainment, recreational and
cultural services outside the home has increased sharply because of rising
costs. Although consumers have reduced their leisure expenditure recently as
a result of the recession, socio-demographic and lifestyle indicators point
towards a substantial increase in such spending as a share of the household
budget in the next twenty years.

Nearly all households possess at least one refrigerator, one TV and one
telephone, and 89 per cent own a washing machine – which the French prefer
to be top-loading. The fact that most households are now equipped with these
durables explains the decline in expenditure on these items: effective market
saturation has been achieved. Increased ownership of freezers (44 per cent
of households) and microwave ovens is having an effect on the food industry
and the retail sector. Relative expenditure on furniture is in decline, and this
follows a European pattern. The growth in the number of households was the
main driving force behind the boom in sales of durables in recent years, but
falling population levels in the next twenty years will change all this.

Spending on *clothing and footwear* has declined in relative importance in
the past twenty years and will continue to do so as other sectors become more
important. Sports clothes are gaining ground as substitutes to more conventional clothing. The trend seems to be in favour of standardised outfits to
which personalisation is added by means of various accessories.

What do these trends show us about contemporary France? The growth of
consumption is closely linked to the wealth of the nation and is often used to
monitor its economic well-being. The economic climate, inflation and
purchasing power influence the growth of personal consumption. A high level
of unemployment, for example, is perceived as a major threat to consumer
confidence. In spite of good economic indicators (see Table 12.5), the average
annual growth of consumption in France has fallen to its lowest level in thirty
years (see Table 12.6).

One of the reasons why the growth of consumption has slowed down is
the uncertain economic environment in the whole of the EU since 1991. As
people are uncertain about the present (because of the high unemployment
rate) and the future (with pension funds on the decline), they restrain their

Table 12.5 Economic indicators for France in the 1990s

GDP	$18,590	1992	second-highest in EU
Inflation	1.6%	1994	EU average: 3.3% in 1993
Purchasing power	+ 2.2% per year	–	1990–95
Per capita consumption	$13,190	1993	Fourth highest in the EU

Source: Adapted from INSEE 1994

Table 12.6 Average annual growth of consumption in France, 1980–93

Years	Growth rate (%)
1980–90	2.6
1992	1.2
1993	0.4

Source: Adapted from INSEE 1994

expenditure and delay or cancel the purchasing of inessential goods (see Table 12.7). It might therefore be that the slump in consumption is due to the perceived state of economic prospects rather than an actual reduction in purchasing power. Other factors also need to be taken into consideration: tobacco sales, for example, could have dropped because of the anti-smoking legislation (higher taxation, ban on advertising, ban on smoking in public places) which was implemented in 1992, rather than as a result of the recession.

Table 12.7 Negative effect of recession on volume of sales in France, 1992–3 (%)

Sector	Sales
Clothing and footwear	– 2.2
Durables	– 1.4
Cars	– 15.1
Leisure goods and services	– 0.6
Hotels, cafés, restaurants	– 3.0
Tobacco	– 4.9

Source: Adapted from INSEE 1994

However, it must be stressed that per capita consumption is still high in France compared to the rest of the EU and in particular the UK. As for the future, even if the gloomy climate of the early 1990s persists, personal consumption in the second half of the 1990s will be boosted by the increased number of the 30–50 age group – the baby-boomers – who are the most prosperous consumers. Having established their families and reached the peak of their earning potential, towards 2000 they will consume more leisure goods and more health care goods and services.

A CHANGING RETAIL SECTOR FOR CHANGING CONSUMERS

Economic, demographic, social and cultural changes have affected the retail sector in the past twenty years. Legislative/economic changes have operated to ensure the protection of consumers with legislation on products, labelling and advertising. They have also ensured the protection of small retailers: the Royer law in 1973 to control the expansion of hypermarkets, the Doubin law in 1991 to enhance the rights of franchisees. Legislation such as the *NF-environnement* eco-labelling scheme in 1992 has been introduced to protect the environment. In the early 1990s the recession has led to the stagnation, if not the decline, of individual expenditure and the success of outlets offering cut prices.

Demographic changes such as smaller family units and increasing numbers of older people have contributed to the success of mail order and of changes in the packaging of goods.

Social changes such as the increase in the number of single-person households, of working women, in the level of education, the ownership of household and audiovisual equipment, and the high level of car ownership have all had an impact on the retail sector. For example, the availability of private transport has increased the range of shopping options, while the redevelopment of rural areas and city centres has led to the dynamic growth of shopping centres both out-of-town and in-town centres.

Finally, personal values have changed: quality wins over quantity; consumers yearn for novelty, a personalised service and a friendly atmosphere. Hence the importance of small boutiques, mail order, shopping centres. Buying has become an art, with very wise, well-informed, educated consumers who know exactly what they want and who will search for bargains. 'The French buyer is always conscious of design and style and this frequently takes priority over price. . . . The French are . . . sophisticated and discerning buyers' (DTI 1990: 12–13). Quality, design and price, if found superior in a foreign product, will sway the consumer away from their normally strong, national preference. *Le rapport qualité/prix* – whether a product is poor or good value for money – is a dominant consideration for French consumers. The importance of aesthetics is such that it applies not only to product design but also packaging and the decor of the distribution outlet.

There have also been structural changes. The development and rapid expansion of large retail outlets such as supermarkets, hypermarkets and large specialist stores, since the 1950s (see Chronology for definitions) has led to a large number of bankruptcies amongst small independent retailers, as has been the case in the rest of Europe. Independent retailing occupies 40 per cent of the market nowadays, a figure which is being constantly eroded but which is still strong both in relation to other forms of retailing in France (see Table 12.8) and in relation to its share in other countries. In a fragmented market such as France, the distribution level of retail outlets is one outlet for 84 inhabitants, whereas it is one for 167 in the UK (Mermet 1991: 239), showing how comprehensively served France is in comparison, and how healthy small retail outlets are, in relative terms, in France.

This decline is not as important as in other EU countries because independent retailers are responding to the changing needs of the consumer (consumers want to be treated as individuals; small retailers are more popular amongst the older generations) and are joining distribution chains (voluntary

Table 12.8 Retail sales by form of outlet in France (as percentage of total retail sales)

Form of outlet	Sales (1993)
Department stores	2
Variety stores	2
Mail order	3
Supermarkets	15
Hypermarkets	23
Small independent outlets	40
Miscellaneous	15
Total	100

Source: adapted from INSEE 1994 and Euromonitor 1995

chains, franchise networks) in order to compete with large outlets. Most small retailers are turning to specialist markets (niches) as more prosperous consumers require a more personal service, the success of franchises helping them to seize the opportunity. The future of small-scale retailing lies in affiliations such as franchises, as they offer the retailer the experience and competitiveness of such well-established companies as Yves Rocher, Benetton, Kickers, McDonald's or The Body Shop. France ranks second in the world after the USA for the number of franchise outlets – 30,000 in 1992 compared to 16,000 in the UK (Euromonitor 1995). The future of small retailers lies also in specialist shops both in the food and non-food sectors: butchers, bakers and fishmongers still have a large proportion of the market share; perfumeries, bookshops, jewellers are still thriving, whilst pharmacies, with an increasing share of retail sales, are proving to be the most successful small specialist retailers (Euromonitor 1992). France has twice as many pharmacies as the UK (Euromonitor 1995).

Furthermore, the market share of large-scale retailers is no longer increasing at the same velocity as in the past. After a period of increasing size and number of self-service shops, saturation point has been reached. Such outlets are entering the maturity phase of their life cycle. The price war, on the other hand, is on the increase, not only in the food sector but also for durables and textiles. The concentration of large-scale retailers – 42 per cent of market share to the five leading retailers, 65 per cent to the top ten (Nielsen, in Lambin 1994: 423) – is set to intensify, meaning a lesser differentiation of retail outlets. The same brands can be found everywhere. Credit facilities are offered by major chains, hence, together with the previous factor, there is less loyalty to a particular retailer. If retail outlets have a uniform image in the eyes of consumers, they have to differentiate themselves by other means, in order to have a comparative advantage. They can offer convenience, distinctive products, additional services (after sales, financial, technical advice, car parks, nursery, specialist corners, ease of access, ease of product identification, sufficient check-outs to avoid queues) and a congenial atmosphere, all of which are on the increase. However, this cannot be achieved alongside very low prices without running the risk of reducing profit margins even further. As a consequence, the market share of large-scale retailers is being eroded by alternative channels of distribution such as direct sales and hard discount stores. Mail order has always been popular in France, given the size of the country. The progression of direct sales (mail order, telephone sales and home shopping) in the area of both consumer goods and services in recent years has been made possible by technological advances such as Minitel, and the progress made in information technology. This type of distribution represents 3 per cent of retail sales (see Table 12.8) and its market share is increasing. Teleshopping, television programmes which sell directly to the consumer, took off in the late 1980s with the advent of private national channels[6] and the more recently created *Téléachat*, a twenty-four-hour cable channel entirely devoted to home shopping, with a wide variety of products ranging from food, jewellery, perfumes, to package holidays. The success of this particular channel mirrors changes in consumers' needs in the sense that it offers advice which is not available in large stores, and convenience (open twenty-four hours a day, facility of viewing and ordering from home with time to reflect). It also gives small retailers the opportunity to offer a complementary range of products which they could not normally stock for fear of non-viability, extremely rare records for example.

The first hard discount stores appeared in 1991 and within four years more than 600 were opened. Their growing importance as an alternative channel of distribution stems mainly from the recession. Customers find basic goods at lower prices in stores which achieve economies through stark surroundings, minimal packaging, minimal staff. If the popularity of such stores were solely driven by economics, it would be safe to assume that it will decrease once the recession is over. However, this popularity is also explained by more fundamental changes in consumer behaviour. A pleasure-seeking consumer will not hesitate to shop for basic food at a discount store, thereby saving some money which they can then spend on an extravagant meal from a *traiteur* or an expensive wine or a delicate cake from a refined *pâtisserie*, displaying once more what was called earlier 'multi-faceted behaviour'. Hard discount stores are more than a passing trend and everything points to the fact that they are here to stay. Another sign of their success is that many large-scale retailers such as Carrefour have either opened their own discount stores or launched *premiers-prix* products ('star buys') in hypermarkets in order to maintain their market share.

CONCLUSION

The changes in consumer behaviour outlined above show that there is undeniably a convergence throughout Europe of demographic trends (urbanisation, ageing of the population, increase in the number of working women, increase in the number of single-person households), values (rise of individualism, fear of the future, 'spiritualism', 'cocooning', hedonism), consumer behaviour (health, leisure and transport expenditure is increasing whereas relative spend on food and clothes is diminishing) and trends in the retail sector (increase of large scale retailers at the expense of small retailers, emergence of new channels of distribution). Nevertheless, in the midst of this apparent standardisation national differences still remain, particularly in eating habits and to a lesser extent in the choice of clothes and the characteristics of dwellings. Although these national differences are important, one can also perceive the impossibility of painting the portrait of the standard consumer for any nation. Indeed, it would be more accurate to talk of various, similar market segments throughout these nations.

The most homogeneous group of consumers in Europe are the young. They listen to the same music (largely of Anglo-Saxon origin), dress in a very similar way, have similar leisure activities and have all contributed to the popularity of McDonald's and Coca-Cola throughout Europe. They are the most threatened age group in terms of size, with ever-decreasing numbers. They are also and at the same time the most influential, as older people tend to emulate the young and youthful values are tending to become universally accepted. At the other end of the age spectrum, the 'seniors' are becoming more numerous, more affluent than in the past and have similar needs whether they live in Italy or Denmark, for instance. Patterns of consumer expenditure are the same within similar socio-economic groups, regardless of nationality: consumers in old, unemployment-stricken mining communities in the Nord-Pas de Calais have more in common with former miners in the north-east of England than with the executives who are thriving in the region's recently developed tertiary sector. Regional differences are more distinct than national ones because they will also be influenced by the climate or religion and therefore values. Someone living in Normandy will have more in common with someone in Kent than somebody from Provence. Does the typical French consumer exist?

Socio-demographic criteria already lead to a variety of consumer groupings: 'juniors', 'seniors', executives, employees, single-person households, single-parent families, urban or rural inhabitants, regional or ethnic origin, and so on. These criteria need to be complemented by lifestyle categorisation in order to incorporate the values of any given individual, to give a more accurate picture of the consumer. This profusion of categories points towards the fact that, although consumption patterns are becoming standardised, the typical European consumer does not exist any more than the typical French consumer. It would be more accurate to talk in terms of various and varied segments which can be defined using socio-demographic and lifestyle studies. However, with an increasing demand for personalised goods and services, and the advent of the individual over the collective, the challenge may well be how to appeal to 58 million 'Harlequin consumers' (Michel Serres in Le

Bris 1992) who all look uniform from a distance but at close quarters become very different.

A MARKET OF 58 MILLION CONSUMERS: CHRONOLOGY

Nineteenth century	Creation of **department stores** (*grands magasins*): large outlets with departments operating as a specialist stores; free access; offering extensive customer services; located in city centres; very limited car parking facilities – (*Bon Marché, Printemps, Galeries Lafayette, BHV*). **Mail order** (*vente par correspondance*) – *La Redoute, Les 3 Suisses, La CAMIF.* **Variety stores** (*magasins populaires*): Products of lower quality with rapid stock turnover, simpler décor than department stores with matching prices; located in town centres. At the beginning everything was at the same price, hence the names *Monoprix, Prisunic.*
1950s	**Supermarkets**: self-service with trolleys, low-cost, low profit margin food products and household goods. Located in town centres or outskirts with car parking facilities. Between 400 and 2,500 m^2 – *Carrefour, Leclerc, Auchan, Casino, Rallye.*
1963	Opening of first **hypermarket** by *Carrefour*: bigger version of supermarkets, over 2,500 sq. metres; located out of town with ample car parking facilities. Retailing chains own both supermarkets and hypermarkets.
1970s	**Large specialists** (*grandes surfaces spécialisées*): Self service, large retail outlet for non-foodstuffs; offering a wide choice within the same product range; located on the outskirts of towns generally but can be found in shopping centres located in town centres – *Fnac, Decathlon, Castorama, Monsieur Meuble, Darty, Habitat, Ikea.* **Shopping centres** (*centres commerciaux*): Concentration of various types of outlets both large and small under the same roof; located both in town centres and out-of-town, car parking facilities available.
1991	**Hard discount stores** (*hard discounters*): Mainly food outlets offering a limited range of choice for each product; low prices, stark surroundings, minimal staff. Originated in Germany – *Aldi, Ed (Carrefour), DIA.*

NOTES

1 See Chapter 4.
2 From 1945 to 1975, a period generally known as '*les Trente Glorieuses*', the bright economic prospects of the post-war period coincided with an unprecedented increase in the number of births. People born during those years are known as 'baby-boomers'.
3 See Introduction: France in the Making and Chapter 4.
4 For a discussion of how immigrant, foreign and Muslim can be defined, see Chapter 9.
5 See introduction: France in the Making, Chapter 9 and the end of Chapter 6.
6 See Chapter 6.

REFERENCES AND RECOMMENDED READING

* Anon. (1993) 'La France et sa population', *Cahiers français* 259: whole issue.
  A complete analysis of demographic trends.
BOTB (1990) *Marketing Consumer Goods: France*, London: BOTB.
Delavennat, C. (1993) 'Retraites: ce qui change pour vous', *Le Point*, no. 1094: 46–8.
DTI (1990) *Country Profile: France*, London: DTI.
Dufour, A. (1992) 'Les Français et l'environnement: de l'intention à l'action', *Economie et Statistique*, no. 258–9: 19–26.
Euromonitor (1990) *European Consumer Lifestyles to 1995*, London: Euromonitor.
Euromonitor (1992) 'France', *Retail Trade International*, Vol. 1, London: Euromonitor.
Euromonitor (1995) *European Marketing Data and Statistics*, London: Euromonitor.
Fried, M. (1994) 'Vingt ans de consommation des ménages', *Etudes Economiques*, no. 72: 13–20.
INSEE, (1994) *Tableaux de l'économie française 1994–95*, Paris: Hachette.
Lambin, J.J. (1994) *Le Marketing stratégique, une perspective européenne*, Paris: Ediscience International (3rd edn).
Le Bris, V. (1992) 'Vers un Euroconsommateur?', *Marketing Mix*, no. 67: 40–5.
* Mermet, G. (1991) *Euroscopie: les Européens: qui sont-ils? Comment vivent-ils?* Paris: Larousse.
  Detailed profiles of each European nation and its inhabitants to allow parallels to be drawn.
* —— (1996) *Tendances 1996: le nouveau consommateur*, Paris: Larousse.
  A detailed analysis of consumer behaviour and evolution of consumption patterns in France.
MINTEL (1989) *Special Report, European Lifestyles: France*, London: MINTEL.
Prod'Homme, G. (1992) 'Dix tendances pour comprendre l'an 2000', *Points de Vente*, 20 mai: 32–3.
* Vallette-Florence, P. (1994) *Les Styles de vie: bilan critique et perspectives*, Paris: Nathan.
  A critical review of main lifestyle studies in France.

INDEX